THE ENDANGERED SPECIES ACT

Published in cooperation with
the Center for American Places,
Santa Fe, New Mexico, and
Harrisonburg, Virginia

THE ENDANGERED SPECIES ACT

History, Conservation Biology, and Public Policy

BRIAN CZECH AND
PAUL R. KRAUSMAN

The Johns Hopkins University Press
BALTIMORE AND LONDON

© 2001 The Johns Hopkins University Press
All rights reserved. Published 2001
Printed in the United States of America on
acid-free paper
9 8 7 6 5 4 3 2 1

The Johns Hopkins University Press
2715 North Charles Street
Baltimore, Maryland 21218-4363
www.press.jhu.edu

LIBRARY OF CONGRESS
CATALOGING-IN-PUBLICATION DATA

Czech, Brian, 1960–
The Endangered Species Act: history, conservation
biology, and public policy/Brian Czech and Paul R.
Krausman.
p. cm.
"Published in cooperation with the Center for
American Places, Santa Fe, New Mexico, and
Harrisonburg, Virginia."
Includes bibliographical references and index.
ISBN 0-8018-6504-2 (pbk.: acid-free paper)
I. Endangered species — Law and legislation — United
States.   2. United States. Endangered Species Act of
1973.   I. Krausman, Paul R., 1946–   II. Center for
American Places.   III. Title.
KF5640.C99 2000
346.7304'69522 — dc21
00-008847

A catalog record for this book is available
from the British Library.

We dedicate this book to the brave and
selfless men and women who sacrificed
adventures in the wide open spaces to
wrestle for conservation in the policy arena.

Contents

Contents

Figures and Tables

Preface and Acknowledgments

Paul Krausman and I are steeped in the "old school" of wildlife ecology; we are certified wildlife biologists, active members of The Wildlife Society, and have focused much of our collective career on large mammals in the West. Paul has been in academia throughout, studying the ecology and management of bighorn sheep, pronghorn antelope, mule deer, and other species in the western United States. I have been in academia only for the purposes of graduate and postdoctoral research, having invested most of my career in federal and tribal government. Working in the early 1990s as recreation and wildlife director on the San Carlos Apache Reservation—nearly 2 million spectacular acres of desert, woodlands, and ponderosa pine forests embedded in eastern Arizona — I had been familiar with Paul's work for years.

By 1993, despite having many good friends among the San Carlos Apaches, tribal politics was taking its toll on me, and I was forced to think about what to do next. My perspective on wildlife conservation had changed dramatically. It seemed that the wildlife profession had reached a point of diminishing returns. We had theories to describe most phenomena and techniques to match most situations, and we were in demand, along with the resources we managed. During my last year with the San Carlos Apache Tribe, for example, I negotiated the sale of three elk tags for $43,000 each, and our department sold over a million dollars' worth of other permits. Nevertheless, wildlife habitat on the reservation was under constant threat from a variety of forestry, range, mineral, recreational, and other enterprises. And I'd seen the same throughout the country.

It occurred to me that the problem might be a function of federal policy. Although the vast majority of our recreation and wildlife budget consisted of tribal funds generated by the sale of hunting and fishing permits, land management decisions on the reservation were heavily influenced by federal policymakers in Washington, D.C. The Bureau of Indian Affairs (BIA) pumped vast resources into tribal forestry and range programs, both of which often worked to the detriment of wildlife habitat. Much of my time was spent fighting with BIA natural resources specialists, especially foresters, for wildlife interests. I was startled by the widespread failure to recognize that if the BIA shifted forestry money to the wildlife program, the economic returns would be higher *and* the reservation would retain more of its beautiful scenery and world-class wildlife. The tribe's recreation and wildlife department, I was sure, could do a better job of managing the forests and rangelands than the BIA foresters and range managers. And if the phenomenal wildlife ecology of the San Carlos Apache Reservation didn't get special recognition, how much more overlooked must wildlife conservation be on other landholdings around the country?

So I was driven toward federal policy. But how does one enter the policy arena with no political connections and a background entirely in wildlife? One way, at least, is the same way one enters the wildlife profession: by going to school.

The University of Arizona helped me lay the foundations for a comparative economics study of wildlife, timber, and cattle management on the San Carlos Apache Reservation. But the study was aborted by tribal politics — a development for which I was to become supremely grateful. Already, I had begun to notice that I would still not be covering the necessary ground with such a study. Comparative economics would constitute a constrained perspective and narrow approach to the policy arena, as would any study focused on the unique situation at San Carlos.

The next thing I did was look for Paul Krausman. If nothing else, our common interests in large mammals would put us on the same page while I searched for the appropriate research program. We built a broad-based graduate committee, complete with a range scientist and a forester from the natural sciences, and a public policy specialist and political historian from the social sciences. Paul was the committee chairman, and my major in renewable natural resources was designed precisely to bridge the gap between the natural and social sciences. My curriculum would be dominated by conservation biology and political science, and my research would integrate the two.

My first course in public policy was taught by the renowned political scientist Helen Ingram, who then served as director of the university's

Udall Center for Public Policy. I was fascinated by her brilliance, and as an older student, my intimidation was manageable, so I generally walked with her after class to pry more out of the lectures. Eventually, the topic turned to my research, and I expressed my interest in applying policy design theory — of which Helen was a founder — to wildlife policy. Could there be a wildlife policy, we wondered, that had done more to shape national affairs than the Endangered Species Act? My doctoral program came rapidly into focus, political science became my official minor, and Helen became my "major minor" committee member.

Toward the end of my policy design analysis of the Endangered Species Act (ESA), Paul and I decided to convert my dissertation into something more reader friendly and get it published as one among the many analyses of ESA. That conversion, as it turned out, was easier said than done. A great deal of statistical and biological jargon had to be eliminated, cross-referenced, or translated.

Two reviewers expressed doubts that the broad range of material presented could be synthesized. This presented one of the most challenging aspects of revision. On the one hand, synthesis was necessary to provide a holistic perspective of ESA. On the other, the book would be more useful in an encyclopedic sense if it consisted of individual chapters tending to their own respective specialties. The challenge was to make each chapter flow smoothly into a holistic common pool yet remain independently accessible for drawing upon. I am hopeful that Paul and I have succeeded to a reasonable extent — yet sure that we have fallen far short of perfection.

Most important, however, we came to view one more field of study as essential for a comprehensive analysis, ecological economics. We encountered the ecological economics literature relatively late in my doctoral studies but immediately recognized that it harbored the most potent conservation policy implications we had ever seen. Most notably, its theory of economic growth — so distinct from that of mainstream or neoclassical economics — seemed to explain so much about the real challenges facing wildlife conservation. As we contemplated the original portion of my analysis pertaining to the socioeconomic context of the Endangered Species Act, it became clear that the ecological economic theory of economic growth provided an explanation, and the manuscript evolved thusly.

During the publisher's peer review process, an anonymous reviewer insisted that we do a more thorough job of addressing the ESA/property rights controversy. We thank that anonymous soul, for although it entailed a tremendous amount of work, we think our account of the controversy (chapter 10) will help those with limited legal expertise to understand the critical issues. And our account of the bellwether *Good v. United States* is probably the most thorough available, short of the judge's opinion itself.

By the time we got this far along, it became clear that the book would have wide-ranging application. We decided that what we were after was *the* book on ESA. That is, if a person were to own only one account of ESA, this would be it. Thus, following an introductory commentary (chapter 1) and historical chapters on species endangerment (chapter 2) and the long-run evolution of ESA (chapter 3), we include a review of the other works on ESA (chapter 4). Chapter 4 is organized based upon the policy analysis perspectives of the various authors.

In chapter 5 we take the first step in policy design analysis by laying out the logical structure of ESA. Noting that many legal scholars have gone before us in this endeavor, however, we take a very different approach: we analyze the assumptions of the authors of ESA. Chapter 5, given its copious quotation of ESA chapter and verse, is perhaps the chapter most endearing to hard-core "policy wonks." The only part of the book with a similar style is the portion of chapter 11 that provides literal corrective language for ESA.

In chapter 6 we take on one of Helen Ingram's specialties: the social construction/political power dynamic suffusing a policy's design. Policy design theory entails a consideration of this dynamic, which at first we suspected of little application to the endangered species policy arena. The more we thought about it, however, the more it applied. After all, we had conducted a nationwide public opinion survey on the valuation of species for conservation, and data were readily available on the political power held in trust for species by conservation groups. Our resulting classification of endangered species as "advantaged," "contenders," "dependents," and "deviants" will strike an intuitive cord in many readers, but the resulting implications may not. And from there we proceed to broader issues of social construction theory as it affects environmentalism in a broad sense.

Policy design theory does not ignore the technical aspects of policy, and it will therefore attract an increasing number of other professions to the interdisciplinary study of political science and public policy in particular. Chapter 7, our most technical chapter, is where our true colors as wildlife biologists appear. Neither I nor Paul, with careers tied to the "charismatic megafauna," subscribed to the "equal rights for parasites" philosophy. And because one of the biggest ESA controversies had to do with the types of species that got listed, it was time to tackle this issue. Our synthesis of the implications of genome size, phylogenetic distinctiveness, and molecular clock speed, which we presented at the North American Wildlife and Natural Resources Conference in 1998, provides the antithesis of biocentrism and points to a "bio-logical" yet politically serendipitous way of prioritizing species for conservation. It also suggests that the time-tested species approach to conservation is alive and well, even when it is called "ecosystem management."

The coincidence of our prioritization proposal and its political feasibility by no means constitutes a win-win situation, however. No matter how species are prioritized, losing — that is, species and the values associated therewith — is literally what the biodiversity crisis is all about. In chapter 8 we provide a relatively exhaustive account of the socioeconomic context of species endangerment by considering each of the causes of species endangerment, least to most, relating them to each other and, ultimately, with the structure and scale of American economy.

In chapter 9 we get to perhaps the most distinctive aspect of policy design theory: the consideration of a policy's implications for democracy. According to policy design theory, all policies in America have the implicit goal of serving democracy. We scrutinize ESA with a five-part test, considering issues of equity, freedom of information, public participation, majority rule, and political representation. As it turns out, ESA is no threat to democracy, but the same cannot be said for a degenerative policy context replete with "brownwashing" propaganda. We describe why the particular version of technocracy spawned by ESA may actually serve democracy in such a context.

Chapter 10 includes our analysis of the property rights issue as it relates to ESA, with a focus on the potential of certain types of ESA implementation to qualify as an unconstitutional Fifth Amendment "taking" of property. *Good v. United States*, by which the Federal Court of Claims dealt a blow to developers' ability to hold the public liable for speculation gone sour, will probably go down as a major plank in the stage on which ESA is implemented. ("Probably" refers to Good's appeal to the Supreme Court, the results of which are pending.)

If chapters 1–4 are the roots and chapters 5–10 the stalk, chapter 11 bears the fruits of our labor. Here we provide recommendations on what to do about the ESA, its socioeconomic context, and policy design theory itself. In order to make all of our recommendations available in one unit of text, we also summarize our recommendations for prioritizing species for conservation, and we conclude with our appraisal of the relative merits of a national vs. global approach to species conservation. We have high hopes for all of our recommendations but emphasize the primacy of pursuing a steady state economy and the adoption of ecosystem health as an omnibus role for public policy.

We aimed our book at three major groups of readers. One includes those with practical and political interests in ESA, for example, policymakers, politicians, and a wide range of natural resources professionals involved in species conservation. A second includes academics — students and professors — with wide-ranging interests. Our application of policy design theory, related as it is to the other perspectives of policy analysis, may serve as a model for courses pertaining to public policy. Conservation biologists and ecologists at large, particularly those who struggle to understand the relationship of biological theory with the sociopolitical world of species conservation, will find common ground and, perhaps, new conceptual territory with us. Ecological economists will find one of the first explicit prescriptions for a steady-state economy based upon mainstream conservation concerns. Other academics we hope to serve include conservation historians, legal scholars, and that amorphous mass of interdisciplinary and transdisciplinary scholars that strike out in search of Edward O. Wilson's "consilience." A third audience includes that portion of the general public interested in the trials and tribulations of democracy in the United States, especially the ability of democracy to cope with environmental crises and conserve ecosystem health.

Paul and I thank Dave King, Bill Shaw, George Ruyle, Peter Ffolliott, the late Gene Maughan, Anne Schneider, and Hanna Cortner, all of whom provided valuable advice on various aspects of the research underlying this book. Jeanne Clarke provided expert review of the historical chapters. Bruce Walsh and Lucinda McDade critiqued our genetic arguments. Tanis Salant and Susan George provided information on local and state government initiatives. Michael Bean and Warren Flick provided information on ESA case law. Pat Devers and Rena Borkhataria assisted with data procurement and analysis. Pat Jones, Mark Borgstrum, and Bob Steidl provided statistical assistance. Jack Ward Thomas contributed valuable insights from deep in the trenches of conservation policy.

Funding was provided by the University of Arizona (School of Renewable Natural Resources and Agricultural Experiment Station) and the U.S. Forest Service. Pat Reid, director of the School of Renewable Natural Resources, was especially supportive. Terry Daniels (University of Arizona) and Tom Brown (U. S. Forest Service, Rocky Mountain Forest and

Range Experiment Station) brokered our agreement with the Forest Service. Survey Sampling, Inc. (Fairfield, Conn.) provided sampling assistance. The Center for American Places served as our liaison with the Johns Hopkins University Press. Mary Soltero, Marge O'Connell, Carol Yde, Tina Haag, Sue Klein, Carol Wakely, and Linda Lee (all with the University of Arizona) provided administrative support.

I thank the International Society for Ecological Economics and its ecologically informed theorists of economic growth for enlightening our analysis of the context of the Endangered Species Act. Posterity's big hope, I believe, lies in the wisdom and determination of the Society's practitioners.

I especially thank Helen Ingram, without whom this book would not have been conceived. She represents the rare political scientist — and an eminent one at that — willing to invest abundant time in the broader education of those previously trained exclusively in the natural sciences. To the extent that our efforts constitute a synthesis of natural and social science, the credit is hers.

BRIAN CZECH

Part 1

Setting the Stage

1

The Endangered:
Species, Acts, and Democracy

T he Endangered Species Act (ESA) was signed by President Richard M. Nixon on December 28, 1973. It has been called "the most far-reaching wildlife statute ever adopted by any nation" (Reffalt 1991:78), "one of the most sweeping pieces of prohibitive policy to be enacted" (Yaffee 1982:13), and "one of the most exciting measures ever to be passed by the U.S. Congress, perhaps to be passed by any nation" (Rolston 1991:43). The purposes of the act are to "provide a means whereby the ecosystems upon which endangered species and threatened species depend may be conserved, to provide a program for the conservation of such endangered species and threatened species, and to take such steps as may be appropriate to achieve the purposes of the treaties and conventions set forth in subsection (a) of this section" (Section 2[b]). Those treaties and conventions include migratory bird treaties with Canada, Mexico, and Japan, the International Convention for the Northwest Atlantic Fisheries, the International Convention for the High Seas Fisheries of the North Pacific Ocean, and the Convention on International Trade in Endangered Species of Wild Fauna and Flora (CITES).

The regulatory power created by ESA is wielded by the secretary of the interior through the Fish and Wildlife Service and the secretary of commerce through the National Marine Fisheries Service. With a history of strict interpretation by the courts, two ESA issues have become especially controversial: (1) the types of species that are listed and (2) the limitations that ESA imposes on economic growth, especially in the private sector. The accrual of political peril to ESA is reflected in its reauthorization and appropriations history. The ESA was originally authorized for five years, and reauthorization and/or authorization amendment occurred in

1976, 1978, 1979, 1982, and 1988, when ESA was again authorized appropriations for five years. A conventional reauthorization formulated during fiscal year 1992 would have authorized appropriations from October 1992 to October 1997. However, Congress has only authorized funds in one-year increments since fiscal year 1993, and bills to weaken ESA were introduced in both houses of the 104th and 105th Congresses. In fact, ESA was "at the top of the list of environmental statutes targeted by the 104th Congress to be weakened or outright eliminated" (Ehrlich and Ehrlich 1996:116).

Not only species and ESA are imperiled in the United States. Political institutions are faring poorly, too. American dissatisfaction with Congress revealed itself in the massive electoral turnover of 1994, and Americans are welcoming more outsiders to the presidential race. The party system is an exhausted façade of its earlier vigor (Greider 1992), and to some, the bureaucracy represents a "death of common sense" (Howard 1994). Reform suggestions abound, even from our own president and vice president (Clinton and Gore 1992; Gore 1995). Public cynicism with government has reached alarming proportions. While these developments have been so incremental as to be imperceptible to many individuals, American democracy itself faces a challenge to survive in the form it was conceived. As with species endangerment, concern about the endangerment of democracy became widespread in the 1970s. Buultjens (1978) even called democracy "an endangered political species."

The problems of ESA and American democracy are neither isolated nor independent. The Wise Use movement, for example, was mobilized largely in response to conservation laws, especially ESA (Echeverria and Eby 1995). A loose-knit but widespread campaign of defending property rights and the private use of public land, the Wise Use movement challenges democracy in several ways. Property rights are at the heart of a capitalist democracy but with the emphasis on *capitalist*, and the democratic principle of majority rule is challenged when the majority's interest in public lands is threatened by a vocal minority.

Another principle of democracy is freedom of information, where *freedom* refers not only to availability but to honesty and objectivity. Beginning with the very names of groups assembled under the Wise Use rubric, deceit is commonly employed. Names like National Wetlands Council, Alliance for Environment and Resources, and National Wilderness Institute belie the fact that these groups were organized in opposition to conservation laws and regulations (Deal 1993). Wise Use groups fight to reduce funding for endangered species research, knowing that a lack of information is a formidable obstacle to conservation policy (Ehrlich and Ehrlich 1996). In the absence of scientific information, the Wise Use movement is free to campaign against the Endangered Species Act by employing an us-versus-them mentality, as with the owls-versus-jobs controversy (Arnold 1998).

The Wise Use movement also poses a challenge to the federal system of constitutional democracy. In many areas, Wise Use activists object not only to federal but also to state authority. Wise Use activism has played a prominent role in states with strong county chartering movements, including Arizona, Montana, and Utah (Cowan and Salant 1999). While there is democratic value to be found in local organizing efforts, the *organizing* appears bent toward anarchy or secession in areas where antigovernment militia have formed. Militia have been especially volatile in states where counties are not granted home-rule authority, including Idaho, New Mexico, and Texas.

The Wise Use and militia movements share an antifederal, antiregulatory philosophy. In addition to the aforementioned states, these movements are mutually prevalent in Colorado, Michigan, and Washington. Although the convergence of Wise Use, home rule, and militia appears strongest in the West, there are many related organizations in the East. An especially troubling aspect of these developments is that while many see them as threats to constitutional democracy, others (often including the participants) see them as protectors thereof. The confusion is partly a function of the vast scope of interests assembled under the rubric of Wise Use, but if these interests have a common thread, it is a hatred of federal regulation, which to many is epitomized by ESA.

American public policy is supposed to serve democracy while solving important societal problems (Ingram and Smith 1993). In the case of ESA, the problem is biodiversity depletion. However, ESA controversies are primarily a function of cynicism over the way ESA is implemented. Partly due to the misinformation campaigns of antiregulatory interests but also due to the regulatory realities of ESA, many people are troubled by the technocratic power that the Fish and Wildlife Service has over species listings, and by the imposition of ESA on their legal capacity to develop private lands. These controversies have more to do with the democracy-serving function of ESA than with the technical aspects of conservation biology.

The Endangered Species Act has been analyzed by natural scientists, including researchers and managers. These analyses have focused on the technical and managerial challenges to saving species (usually a single species) from extinction. The Endangered Species Act has also been assessed by social scientists, especially legal scholars and economists, usually with more emphasis on political, constitutional, and economic implications. Books and book chapters by natural and social scientists have been published, and a committee comprising natural and social scientists coauthored a book, but it "was not asked to comment on the social and political decisions concerning the ESA's goals and tradeoffs, and it has not done so" (National Research Council 1995:4). The Endangered Species Act has also been analyzed by investigative journalists and critiqued by affected interests. Although there have been brief exceptions (e.g., Smith et al. 1993), nonintegrated policy analyses have been the rule — not only with ESA but throughout public policy.

Policy analyses have traditionally been performed from one of five perspectives. Pluralism focuses on the processes leading to the distribution of power and benefits, and sees the role of public policy as responding to the needs of interest groups and balancing power among them. The policy sciences view the role of policy as solving societal problems via institutional efficiency, with as little political interference as possible. Policy specialism focuses on the technical aspects particular to a policy and is undertaken by technical experts whose norms vary by profession. Public choice theory emphasizes the irrationality of collective choices that results from rational decision making by individuals, and typically prescribes privatization and a free market economy in response. Critical theory is an indictment of Western government whereby corruption and oppression are prominent features, while the democratic process is a disguise perpetrated by oppressors. Analyses of ESA via these traditional perspectives are reviewed in chapter 4.

Our analysis of ESA via policy design theory follows in part 2 (chapters 5–11). As described in the Preface, our analysis is an integration of natural and social sciences; particularly ecology and political science. Such integration is challenging because the standards and epistemological traditions of these disciplines are distinct. Ecological studies generally apply a hypothetico-deductive method of science — or at least have attempted to, especially since Romesburg's (1981) admonition. Political science, despite a much longer history than ecology (with Aristotelian roots), has struggled for scientific status. Ecological studies are characterized by attention to (if not consistent achievement of) tight experimental control, considerations of replication and inference scope, and statistical evaluation of data.

Political studies sometimes contain the same characteristics but usually include, and are often dominated by, logical deduction and induction, speculation, and philosophical elaboration. We have attempted to bridge the divergence between the epistemological traditions of ecology and political science by integrating methods and interpretations from both.

2

A History of Endangered Species in the United States

At a national level, the first signs of species imperilment in the United States surfaced during the frontier economy of the 1800s, as did the earliest public concern and the earliest political action. Bison were heavily hunted for the hide market, to clear the grasslands for a cattle economy and to starve warring Indian tribes into submission, especially after Custer was defeated at the Little Bighorn in 1876. They were extirpated from their haunts east of the Mississippi River by 1800, and from most of their former range by the 1880s. The destruction of the buffalo herds made wildlife protection a public issue (Dunlap 1988). In fact, Yellowstone National Park was created in 1872 partly for the purpose of preserving bison and other ungulates that had become rare elsewhere. As such, Yellowstone represents the first national political effort toward species preservation. By one estimate, only about twenty-five free ranging plains bison remained in the United States by the turn of the century — all at Yellowstone (McHugh 1972). (Simultaneously, an endangered population of wood bison persisted near Great Slave Lake in Canada.)

The plight of the bison made an impression on the public because bison were the largest mammals on the continent and had traveled in remarkably large herds. But all ungulate species were eliminated from large areas of their original ranges by the late 1800s. Especially in the East, populations that were never documented may have been extirpated. For populations that would have been classified as species under ESA, extirpation was equivalent to extinction. For example, the eastern subspecies of elk was so diminished in numbers that only marginal records were available by the 1900s, and it is probably extinct (Bryant and Maser 1982). From 1870 to 1900, whitetail deer were absent from most of their eastern range (Trefethen 1975). Given the amount of morphological and ecological variance of whitetails, and the fact that about thirty-eight subspecies are now recognized, it is reasonable to suspect that eastern subspecies went extinct in the late 1800s.

Extirpations and extinctions were not limited to the East. In the Southwest, where elk were hunted heavily for food and canine ivory, the barely (and questionably) documented Merriam subspecies was extinct by 1906 (Bryant and Maser 1982), which was about the same time as the Audubon bighorn went extinct in the Black Hills (Trefethen 1975).

In terms of local extirpations — which lead to species endangerment — large predators were doomed to mirror the ungulates in the East. Mountain lions and wolves are largely dependent on ungulates for food and therefore are threatened as ungulate populations decline. Although prey switching by large predators has been known to occur when ungulate populations have been reduced, it is doubtful that mountain lion and wolf populations can persist indefinitely in the absence of ungulate prey. And one kind of prey switching, from wild to domestic ungulates, became a detriment to the predators' survival because it motivated predator-control efforts.

The other megapredators, bears, are omnivorous but dangerous. Grizzlies were a serious human threat on the frontier, as *The Journals of Lewis and Clark* (DeVoto 1953) attest. In addition to the trophic vulnerability of lions and wolves, and the dangerous disposition of bears, all large predators were competitors to frontier man, whether hunter or agriculturist, and were actively destroyed with the westward progression of U.S. settlement. Appropriations to the U.S. Biological Survey for predator control began in 1915 (Trefethen 1975).

Other economically and aesthetically important species received widespread public concern in the 1800s. After becoming virtually extinct east of the Mississippi River, beaver became scarce nationwide by 1830 (Trefethen 1975); mountain men had been trapping in the Rockies even before Lewis and Clark passed through. The decline of salmonids in the Pacific Northwest was alarming enough to motivate the U.S. Fish Commission to send an ichthyologist to the Columbia River basin in the 1890s (Barker 1993). The heath hen, a heavily hunted eastern subspecies of prairie chicken, disappeared around the turn of the century (Mann and Plummer 1995).

Meanwhile, extinctions of economically important but tightly localized, coastal species had escaped the public's notice. Steller's sea cow, the only member of its genus and the largest of all sirenians, was slaughtered into extinction from 1741 to 1768 by Vitus Bering's stranded crew and subsequent visitors to Bering Island (Nowak 1991). The great auk was probably extinct in the wild by 1844 (DiSilvestro 1989), with the last survivors being killed by humans on an island near Iceland. The Labrador duck, once common on the meat market in New England, was not seen after 1875. The sea mink, inhabitant of rocky North Atlantic shores in America and largest of the seventeen species of *Mustela* in the world, was driven to extinction by pelt hunters around 1880 (Nowak 1991).

During the 1890s, after watching the bison disappear but largely ignorant of coastal extinctions, Americans suddenly became aware that numerous terrestrial species were endangered. The famed ornithologist James G. Cooper announced that the California condor was going extinct. Precipitous declines of migratory bird species became conspicuous. After the last clearly identified passenger pigeon was killed in the wild in 1900, it became an emblem of extinction when the last known specimen died at the Cincinnati Zoo in 1914. Four years later, the last Carolina parakeet died at the same zoo. Waterfowl of all varieties had plummeted by then, too, and an acting chief of the U.S. Biological Survey warned that "some species [of waterfowl] appear to be threatened with extinction in the near future" (Reeves 1984:87).

Although their work generally escaped public attention, botanists also began to document plant extinctions during the early twentieth century. The banded trinity (the only orchid of the genus *Thismia* ever found in North America) was discovered in a developing area of Chicago in 1912 and never again seen after 1914 (Mohlenbrock 1983). Some species were pronounced extinct but were rediscovered later in the century. Probably the most famous example was the Furbish lousewort, the "botanical Lazarus" that escaped numerous detection efforts from 1917 to 1976 (Ayensu and DeFilipps 1978:61). The lousewort's history inspired the singer Tad Johnson to release an album under the title *Furbish Lousewort*, in honor of survival (Hebert 1997). The Virginia round-leaf birch has a nearly identical sighting history, but such species rediscoveries have been exceptional. Of the 103 mainland species listed by Mohlenbrock (1983:230) as "presumed to be extinct," 39 had not been seen since the 1800s.

Much of the species endangerment of the 1800s was of a fundamentally different variety than that commonly observed throughout the twentieth century, especially for animal species. In the 1800s, animal species became endangered through blatant overharvest. After the transcontinental railroad was completed in 1869, and other lines and their feeder routes proliferated, a major logistical hurdle of wildlife marketing was overcome. Meanwhile, with the increased distribution of large-caliber, single-shot, breechloading rifles on the Plains, punt guns in the East and Midwest, and smaller repeating rifles and shotguns throughout the country, wildlife harvests grew from the impressive to the alarming. The need for public policy became clear and was gradually met. In many cases, strict hunting regulations solved the problem of species endangerment technically. They also served democracy, because there was public outcry against overexploitation, and preservationist interest groups, such as the Audubon Society, had mobilized to fight the market hunting interests. Groups interested in consumption of wildlife but realizing the need for conservation also formed in the late 1800s, including the Boone and Crockett Club and the National Rifle Association. These sportsmen groups, which tripled in number to more than three hundred in the 1870s, reflected the evolution of hunting in western culture from a frontier survival skill to a new concept of "sportsmanship" with character-building and recreational motives. The earliest groups with a scientific interest in species conservation also formed, including the American Fisheries Society in 1870.

Despite the proliferation of preservation and conservation groups, it is possible that the attitude of the public was quite different through the remainder of the 1800s. Manifest Destiny had become a domineering fervor that would not be easily suppressed, and its national security roots had branched into everyday social and economic life. Lund (1980:60) posited, "The spirit of the nineteenth century considered the potential extinction of these species a small matter. If one single incident expresses in a paradigm the public ethos of the period, it is that failed competition for the glory of killing the last surviving American buffalo."

Nevertheless, the challenge of overharvest was overcome in most cases, and the primary cause of species endangerment changed rapidly. Exponential growth of the American population was accompanied by increases in per capita consumption. The cash economy burgeoned as natural capital (e.g., minerals, fossil fuels, timber) was liquidated. The liquidation of natural capital, supplemented by agricultural and industrial pollution, entailed wholesale alterations of species' habitats. Early waterfowl biologists like Wells W. Cooke, in publications dating to 1906, commented often on this transition in the primary cause of endangerment as it occurred (Hawkins et al. 1984).

By the time ESA was passed in 1973, more than five hundred North American species had gone extinct since British colonization (Opler 1976). As with the eastern elk, many species surely went extinct prior to attaining clear — or any — taxonomic status. For example, the Atlantic gray whale, described by early whalers, probably went extinct early in the eighteenth century, with the scientific community doubting its existence at the time. Based on subfossil evidence, it is now considered an extinct population of *Eschrichtius robustus* (Nowak 1991), the gray whale that resides only in the Pacific today.

In some areas and with some taxa, extinction was probably even commonplace during the first ecological shock waves of American economy. For example, as the Southwest rapidly desertified in the late 1800s and streams dried up throughout the region, a number of native fishes, amphibians, and riparian plants may have gone extinct. The current situation — almost all the native fish species in the Southwest are endangered — may reflect only the remaining tip of a largely melted iceberg.

The salmon fisheries of Idaho serve to illustrate the accelerated and transitional nature of the extinction problem (Barker 1993). In the late 1800s, overharvest was widely recognized as the cause of salmonid declines. However, beginning in the 1860s, mining caused problems for salmon populations, too. Miners would occasionally divert or dredge long stretches of streams, thereby contributing to siltation that ruined spawning grounds. Then heavy cattle grazing denuded and eroded streambanks and adjacent uplands, causing more siltation. Irrigation caused stream beds to dry up, and salmon often were stranded in farmers' fields. Beginning with the construction of Bonneville Dam in 1937, hydroelectric dams blocked migrating salmon. Intensive timber harvesting, especially in the 1980s, added to the siltation load, and canopy removal near streams caused water temperatures to rise. The cumulative effects of mining, farming, ranching, logging, and hydroelectric power generation have overcome the benefits of the sound harvest regulation that finally did evolve. Now only about half of the original Idaho salmon stocks exist, and these exhibit very low production.

The history of plant endangerment is different because while the problem of animal overharvest reached its peak at the beginning of the twentieth-century, plant overharvest is a recent phenomenon. Furthermore, although abundance of game was a feature sought by market hunters that also gave conservationists time to operate, Ayensu and DeFilipps (1978:49) note a "current fad for rarity," whereby rarity is a major factor in determining demand for plant specimens. The classic examples are carnivorous species like Venus flytraps and pitcher plants, but most rare plants that are aesthetically pleasing or interesting are marketable. Many rare plants are not yet listed or otherwise protected, and the sale of protected species is accommodated through the black market.

Animals have some capacity to evade hunters, but plants are sessile and therefore more vulnerable. While varying levels of skill and technique are required to harvest animals, plant harvesting requires little more than knowledge of the plant's appearance and distribution. For example, illegal immigrants in Texas are paid minuscule amounts of money for "all the small globular cacti they can find" by dealers who mark up the price of rare specimens by one or two orders of magnitude (Ayensu and DeFilipps 1978:50). Entire populations of plants can readily be harvested. In Alabama, one dealer harvested one of the four last known stands of green pitcherplant from a state park. In Florida, the nursery trade threatens the last three stands of Chapman's rhododendron (Mohlenbrock 1983).

While the threat of overharvest remains more problematic for plants than animals, plants are like animals in that both are increasingly threatened by habitat destruction. The habitats of animals consist largely of food and cover plants, so the destruction of animal habitat is often equivalent to the destruction of plants and the correlated endangerment of plant species. But plants also have their own types of "habitats" based on climatic, edaphic, hydrologic, and topographic features. Endangered plants tend to occupy uncommon types of habitats that are particularly interesting to hikers, bikers, and climbers. Examples of unique habitats that host endangered plant species include sand dunes, shale barrens, talus slopes, cliff ledges, sphagnum bogs, hot springs, and vernal pools (Ayensu and DeFilipps 1978). And while animals have some capacity to disperse from degraded habitat, plants again have the problem of sessility. The proposed Dickey-Lincoln Dam in Maine, for example, would have eliminated more than half of the twenty-eight remaining colonies of Furbish lousewort (Mohlenbrock 1983).

Formerly expansive habitats that were commonly developed may also host numerous endangered and erstwhile species. The vast tallgrass and Palouse prairies, for example, have been put almost entirely into agricultural production. As with fish species in the Southwest, many plant species may have gone extinct on these prairies prior to identification. As Mohlenbrock described the endangerment of Mead's milkweed on the tallgrass prairie in the 19th century, "One of mid-America's great natural habitats was reduced overnight, and with it went the prairie grasses and the prairie wildflowers" (1983:95). Unlike the relatively well-known vertebrates, however, many plants species remain at the risk of habitat liquidation prior to their discovery, because parts of the West remain "certainly unbotanized" (43).

For plants and animals, loss of habitat quantity and habitat degradation have been important concerns, but to Noss and Csuti (1994) fragmentation has become the most glaring problem. For any species, a quantity of habitat may exist but may be so fragmented that it is far less capable of supporting the population of concern, due to the species-area relationship and other principles of island biogeography and metapopulation dynamics. Fragmentation was a common theme in the extinction of 90 plant species, subspecies, and varieties of plants on the continental United States, and an additional 270 in the Hawaiian Islands (Ayensu and DeFilipps 1978).

Since the market hunting of the late 1800s, then, species endangerment has become widespread and propelled at an exponential rate by habitat loss exacerbated by fragmentation and often supplemented by other local causes (chapter 8), including overharvest of plants. For hundreds of bird species that migrate to North America for the breeding season, habitat loss in the neotropics is another threat. Unlike the earlier stage of the extinction problem, when powerful interest groups successfully defeated the obvious transgressions of the market hunters, the insidious and overwhelming nature of the current habitat-based problem has prevented curative political action.

The best available evidence indicates that the worldwide extinction rate is of the same order of magnitude of the two most pronounced prehistoric extinction events; the Permian-Triassic (245 million years ago) and the Cretaceous-Tertiary (65 million years ago). This is despite a decline in background extinction rates since the Cambrian Period (550 million years ago) (Futuyma 1983). Although skeptics from outside the natural sciences exist (e.g., Simon and Wildavsky 1993), most scientists and many policymakers acknowledge the severity of the extinction problem. Edward O. Wilson has called it "the folly that our descendants are least likely to forgive us" (Meffe and Carroll 1994:110). Then chairman of the House Subcommittee on Fisheries, Wildlife Conservation and the Environment, Representative Gerry E. Studds, ranked it "among the highest-risk environmental problems facing the United States — even higher than oil spills, groundwater pollution, toxic wastes, and pesticides" (1991:602). As of August 31, 1999, there were 924 endangered and 263 threatened species in the United States (Bender 1999).

3

Statutory, Administrative, and Academic Evolution of the Endangered Species Act

Policy design theory recognizes the importance of considering the historical context of policy. In addition to the growing technical problem (species endangerment) and the social forces promulgating it (conquest of a frontier and subsequent economic growth), the historical context includes the legal and political institutions upon which the foundation of a policy is built. In the case of endangered species policy and ESA in particular, the most important institutions to consider are the body of federal wildlife law and its corresponding intellectual and administrative support. A thorough policy analysis, then, requires an understanding of the history of each.

FEDERAL WILDLIFE JURISDICTION AND ADMINISTRATION PRIOR TO ESA

Until the twentieth century, the protection of individual wildlife specimens and species in the United States was almost entirely the function of state governments. The doctrine of state jurisdiction over wildlife management — a natural progression from colonial law — is legally rooted in the 1842 case of *Martin v. Wadell,* in which the U.S. Supreme Court determined that the state of New Jersey had jurisdiction over oysters in a mudflat claimed as property by a landowner. State jurisdiction over wildlife was upheld and expanded by the Court in a series of cases, culminating in *Geer v. Connecticut* (1896). Addressing the defendant Geer's right to ship game birds out of Connecticut, contrary to the state's laws, the Court's opinion comprised a historical treatise of governmental control over wildlife that came to be regarded as "the bulwark of the state ownership doctrine" (Bean 1983:17).

State administrative structures for fish and wildlife affairs evolved rapidly from 1865 to 1900. There were signs, however, that the federal government had an interest in wildlife issues in the 1800s, including the formation of the U.S. Fish Commission in 1871, to effect a revival of the nation's fisheries. The Division of Economic Ornithology and Mammalogy was established in 1885. These two agencies, especially the latter, provided administrative roots for the future Fish and Wildlife Service (FWS).

Congress set a precedent for protecting habitat beginning no later than the creation of Yellowstone National Park in 1872, but states rightists made protection of individual bison difficult. Congress responded with the Yellowstone Park Protection Act of 1894, which established Yellowstone as a de facto national wildlife refuge, among other things.

Congress involved the federal government in direct, nationwide jurisdiction with the Lacey Act of 1900, which was constitutionally based on the commerce clause. Sponsored by Representative John F. Lacey, a member of the Boone and Crockett Club and a perpetual supporter of conservation measures, the act made it illegal for anyone to transport birds across state boundaries if such specimens had been taken in violation of any other law in the nation. Largely in response to the headlong plunge of the passenger pigeon and other migratory bird species toward extinction and the institutional inability of state jurisdiction to solve the problem, the Lacey Act has been called "the federal government's first attempt to deal with the problem of species extinctions" (Rohlf 1989:19), and in a broad taxonomic sense, it was. Although it faced stiff opposition from states rightists, the Lacey Act rode into the statutes on a great upsurge of public support for bird protection, organized in recently established groups like the League of American Sportsmen and northeastern chapters of the Audubon Society (Trefethen 1975).

President Theodore Roosevelt took an early and active executive approach to species protection. Standing philosophically between the utilitarian conservation of Gifford Pinchot and the preservation ethic of John Muir, he is generally credited with establishing the first de jure national wildlife refuge at Pelican Island, Florida, in 1903, although an 1892 proclamation of President Benjamin Harrison protected the fauna of Afognak Island, Alaska. While the motivation underlying the Afognak designation was to preserve salmon spawning grounds for commercial production, with the preservation of other species an incidental outcome, Roosevelt explicitly designated Pelican Island as a federal landholding to be devoted primarily to wildlife conservation and preservation. During his two terms as president, he established fifty-two other wildlife reserves. He also established sixteen national monuments and six national parks in addition to dozens of forest reserves, often with a wildlife conservation motive (Fox 1981).

Meanwhile, the legislative evolution toward ESA continued. Congress provided a statutory basis for Roosevelt's wildlife refuges with a little-known act of June 28, 1906 (Trefethen 1975:125). Waterfowl conservation provided a political platform for moving toward federal control on or off the refuges, because states were proving to the public their inadequacy for the task. It was a long-fought legislative battle. States rightists still stinging from the Lacey Act lost only after determined legislators invoked the treaty-making power to overcome constitutional challenges to federal management. After twelve years of legislative efforts to provide federal regulation, with new interest groups such as the American Game Protective and Propagation Association forming along the way, a treaty was signed with Great Britain (for Canada) in 1916 that provided protection for migratory birds. The Migratory Bird Treaty Act of 1918 ratified the treaty, and amendments ratified similar treaties with Mexico in 1936 and Japan in 1972 (and post-ESA with the U.S.S.R. in 1976). The constitutionality of the Migratory Bird Treaty Act was challenged by the state of Missouri but was upheld by the Supreme Court in *Missouri v. Holland* (1920). Thereafter, the federal government assumed unquestioned responsibility for a substantial portion of wildlife jurisdiction in the United States (Bean 1983).

The need for federal wildlife officials, especially in law enforcement, increased dramatically. A new democratic institution that was simultaneously sweeping the country was the Progressive reform movement, which advocated civil service regulations. The new wildlife conservation laws would probably have meant little in the field prior to the Progressive movement, when the spoils system often resulted in the appointment of corrupt political hacks, including "woods cops" who enforced wildlife law loosely (Trefethen 1975). The philosophy and success of Theodore Roosevelt's conservation policies were tied inextricably to his civil service reform measures, which emphasized the systematic and unbiased employment of professionally trained personnel in all fields. The first federal wildlife law enforcement officers were employed by the Biological Survey.

The next legislative landmark was the Migratory Bird Conservation Act of 1929, establishing the Migratory Bird Conservation Commission. As with the prior landmarks, the act had a champion interest group —

American Wild Fowlers — in this case, with a life span adapted entirely to passage of the act and oversight of its formative implementation (Trefethen 1975). The Migratory Bird Conservation Commission was charged with reviewing lands for purchase by the Department of the Interior to protect areas important to waterfowl production. This was the first acknowledgment of a federal responsibility to protect habitats on a national scale and may be viewed as the implicit creation of the National Wildlife Refuge System.

The Fish and Wildlife Coordination Act of 1934, though toothless, set the important symbolic precedent of requiring water development agencies to consider wildlife conservation in the planning process. The Federal Aid in Wildlife Restoration Act of 1937 (commonly called the Pittman-Robertson Act), which earmarked funding from excise taxes on arms and ammunition to state wildlife agencies, provided the fiscal foundation for much of the states' fish and game administration.

As politicians and policymakers began to attend to wildlife issues more frequently and required further expertise for decision making, the profession of wildlife management evolved from a hybridization of mammalogy, ornithology, and plant ecology. The 1930s was a banner decade, beginning with the pioneering research of Frederick Lincoln on waterfowl migration, research that gradually allowed the Migratory Bird Conservation Commission to operate with considerable confidence and some clout. At the University of Wisconsin, Aldo Leopold taught the first course in wildlife management, and his *Game Management* (1933) was the first wildlife management textbook. The new discipline distinguished itself with the formation of The Wildlife Society in 1937. The scientific aspect of wildlife management brought with it a concern for wildlife conservation and wildlife species of all varieties. Leopold (1966:190) himself provided an early and oft-quoted warning about the endangerment of species: "To keep every cog and wheel is the first precaution of intelligent tinkering."

Naturally, Leopold recognized the threat of overharvest. Although much of that problem had been solved by his later years, predator elimination remained a sanctioned state and federal activity. His observation of the Kaibab deer irruption caused him to reconsider — as valuable — the role of predators in the ecosystem. That well-documented reconsideration would gradually change the course of wildlife management. But Leopold was also one of the first to emphasize the transition from overharvest to habitat degradation as the primary threat to species' existence, as his recommendations as chairman of the American Game Policy Committee attest. In particular, the monoculture of "clean farming" that progressed from the agricultural colleges to the farms of the Midwest was anathema to the land ethic that Leopold prescribed.

In 1940 Congress passed the Bald Eagle Protection Act, which established another important precedent, being the first statutory law to prohibit the taking of an imperiled species. Whereas the Migratory Bird Treaty Act applied on a national level but sought to provide for a regulated harvest of migratory birds, and whereas wildlife refuges had been established in some areas to protect the specimens within those areas, the Bald Eagle Protection Act applied nationally and with a practically complete ban on the taking of bald and golden eagles.

As with most domestic affairs, there was a legislative lull in species conservation issues for about two decades following the passage of the Bald Eagle Protection Act. Congress was preoccupied with World War II, the postwar economic boom, and then the Korean War. However, the increased international communication resulting from World War II may have contributed to the International Convention for the Regulation of Whaling in 1946 in Washington, D.C., where the International Whaling Commission was born. Congress sanctioned U.S. participation in the commission with the Whaling Convention Act of 1949.

Despite the slowdown of domestic policymaking in the wildlife arena, expertise in ecology blossomed. That expertise would come to the policy forefront in coming decades. Large strides were made in plant ecology, while community ecology, ecosystem modeling, and what is now called "ecosystem management" were building upon their Leopoldian foundations (Czech 1995a; Czech and Krausman 1997a). In 1947, FWS adopted the flyway system in its waterfowl management plans, in recognition of the four major migratory ecosystems. The Society for Range Management was formed in 1948, when range managers "fully believed they were responsible for managing ecosystems" (Rumburg 1996:vi).

These mid-century scientific and professional developments contributed a conceptual framework from which to address the modern causes of endangerment in the policy arena, as well as the political motivation to do so. New scientific organizations of regional, national, and international scope proliferated during this period, among them the American Institute of Biological Sciences, the Conservation Foundation, and the International Union for Conservation of Nature and Natural Resources in the 1940s, the American Conservation Association, the American Institute of Fishery Research Biologists, and the Conservation and Research Foundation in the 1950s, and many others.

While most of these organizations were populated by scientists who revealed policy implications reluctantly, mid-century also spawned a new breed of "politico-scientists" for whom species endangerment was often a focal point (Fleming 1972:41). Prominent among these was Rachel Carson, a biologist and editor for the Bureau of Fisheries. While her earlier books were naturalistic endeavors about marine ecology, *Silent Spring* (1962) was a brilliantly calculated political effort to stem the widespread use of pesticides. The political influence of *Silent Spring* rested upon Carson's solid literary reputation, her scientifically documented basis for the ecological threat of pesticides, and her lucid connection between that ecological threat and the welfare of society. Barry Commoner, another biologist and perhaps the prototypical politico-scientist, was simultaneously warning the public about the effects of nuclear testing fallout. Concern about the prudence of man's subjection of nature was an increasingly tangible effect of World War II's nuclear conclusion.

The public was ready to seek, understand, and agree with *Silent Spring*, but the public's response was decidedly not silent. The publishing of *Silent Spring* is justly recognized as the dawn of the American environmental movement, from which species conservation is inextricable.

One trend readily apparent from the study of the endangered species issue is a gradual increase in taxonomic scope. Ahead of his time was the politico-bacteriologist René Dubos, who was uncannily to antibiotics what Carson was to pesticides. Research conducted and applied during World War II offered the hope of eradicating entire populations and even species of bacteria — a dream come true for social Darwinists. Dubos drew an ingenious parallel with Leopold's account of Kaibab wolves and lions. Fighting powerful and respected scientific health organizations with *Mirage of Health* (1959), he "was the first to extend the ecological hospitality to germs," and his adult life was a scientifically merited "tour de force on behalf of self-restraint toward nature" (Fleming 1972:37,39).

The profound eco-social debates of mid-century were accompanied by bureaucratic rumblings. The FWS had essentially been created by President Franklin D. Roosevelt in 1940 when he combined the Bureau of Fisheries and the Biological Survey. Rohlf (1989:20) viewed this New Deal reorganization of the Department of the Interior as an important stage in ESA policy, "fostering a broader view of wildlife as something other than simply a game resource." The causal relationship is unclear, however, because the New Deal was contemporary with the budding field of wildlife ecology. Indeed, one could argue that the roots of wildlife ecology, one of which would extend at least to Darwin (1859), lay deeper than the 1890s Progressive roots of the New Deal. It suffices to recognize that wildlife policy and wildlife science have fostered mutual concerns for the conservation of all species.

The subsequent history of FWS has had important jurisdictional implications for endangered species policy. President Roosevelt had brought the Bureau of Fisheries from the Department of Commerce and Labor together with the Biological Survey from the Department of Agriculture, to create FWS within the Department of the Interior. The Fish and Wildlife Act of 1956 split FWS back into counterparts of its formative components, a Bureau of Commercial Fisheries and a Bureau of Sport Fisheries and Wildlife. A 1970 reorganization under President Nixon sent the Bureau of Commercial Fisheries back to the Department of Commerce (where it became the National Marine Fisheries Service, or NMFS, and was merged with the National Oceanic and Atmospheric Administration), while the Bureau of Sport Fisheries and Wildlife became the modern-day FWS, which took on the administration of ESA only three years later.

ENDANGERED SPECIES ACTS, AMENDMENTS, AND RELATED ACTS

In 1964, during the early stages of the environmental movement engendered by *Silent Spring*, the Committee on Rare and Endangered Wildlife Species was established within the Bureau of Sport Fisheries and Wildlife. Comprising of nine biologists, the committee published the "Red book," the first official list of wildlife thought to be in danger of extinction. As such, the Redbook was the prototype of lists that would be developed pursuant to ESA, and it listed sixty-three endangered species. (There were no other categories of species in the original Redbook.)

In 1966, Congress passed the Endangered Species Preservation Act in an attempt to address species endangerment in a relatively comprehensive fashion. The act directed federal agencies to protect habitat for endangered vertebrate species but only to a "practicable" extent, and only when consistent with agency missions. The act's prohibition of taking endangered species applied only on national wildlife refuges, and it authorized the establishment of refuges for endangered species conservation. The act did not address the commerce in endangered species and parts. Rohlf aptly called it "a broad but toothless policy"(1989:21), but it added to a foundation for further legislation.

The 1969 Endangered Species Conservation Act extended to invertebrates the albeit weak protections of the 1966 act. Interstate commerce of illegally taken reptiles, amphibians, molluscs, and crustaceans was prohibited in expansion of the Lacey Act. These were the major domestic effects, although this act also called for the secretary of the interior to develop a list of globally endangered species and to prohibit the importation thereof. It directed the secretary to facilitate an international convention on the conservation of species. The resulting Convention on International Trade in Endangered Species of Wild Fauna and Flora (CITES) was held in Washington, D.C., during February and March of 1973, signed by the United States on March 3, 1973 (Ayensu and DeFillips 1978), and ratified by Congress on July 1, 1975. Instead of a broad program of species conservation, it amounted to an agreement to recognize endangered species and to ban international trade therein. However, it also set the precedent of recognizing varying degrees of endangerment, with the most vulnerable species being listed in Appendix 1 of CITES and species of lesser vulnerability being placed in Appendices 2 and 3.

The Fisherman's Protective Act of 1967 was designed primarily to protect fishermen from property seizure on the high seas by foreign nations, but the 1971 Pelly Amendment (Section 1978) authorized the president to ban fish and marine mammal product imports from nations violating the agreements of the International Whaling Commission. The Pelly Amendment paid off quickly when Japan and the Soviet Union set their whaling quotas higher than those proposed by the commission in 1974. Apparently, just the revelation of such legislation led to Japanese and Soviet agreement with commission quotas the following year, before any embargoes were instated (Bean 1983). In 1991, President George Bush successfully employed the Pelly Amendment to dissuade Japan from importing hawksbill turtles. Until the Pelly Amendment, the International Whaling Commission had been a relatively powerless meeting of the minds. The 1979 Packwood-Magnuson Amendment to the Fishery Conservation and Management Act of 1976 gave the commission additional teeth by requiring a reduction (by one half) of the fishing rights in American waters of any nation not conforming to commission quotas, rather than allowing for presidential discretion in applying sanctions.

Declining populations of most marine mammals and political pressure stemming from the unsportsmanlike harvest of harp seal pups in the North Atlantic prompted Congress to pass the Marine Mammal Protection Act of 1972, which banned the take and import of marine mammals and products thereof. The ban was intended to apply until NMFS could develop regulations and permitting programs. The act also authorized the secretary of commerce to transfer management authority of marine mammals to states.

With marine mammals covered, conservationists shifted their attention back to terrestrial fauna and flora. From the start, the 1969 Endangered Species Conservation Act had been insufficient to satisfy conservationists. They wanted a law that was not only strong and unambiguous like the Marine Mammal Protection Act but that also had taxonomic, geographic, and bureaucratic comprehensiveness. And by 1973, the political climate was much more favorable than in 1969, because environmental concerns had grown at an astonishing rate during the first few years of the 1970s (Yaffee 1982). Following Earth Day (April 22, 1970), as "the media embraced environmentalism as the all-inclusive cause of the day," issues like population growth, pollution, and species endangerment acquired a synergism of politically formidable momentum (Gottlieb 1993:113). The early 1970s saw a wave of environmental regulatory lawmaking, of which ESA represented the crest.

A few matters had to be overcome in the process, however. The prospect of a more regulatory law had reopened a debate about what types of species should be protected. Representative John Dingell (a Michigan Democrat), who introduced the bill that became ESA, noted that "some people in 1973 . . . belittled the goals of this great Act by belittling the species it seeks to protect. How easy it is to dismiss the protection of a fish, a mollusk, even a plant" (Dingell 1989:2). However, the 1966 and 1969 acts had done much to educate the public and Congress about the wealth of biodiversity in America, and the issue of taxonomic scope was resolved convincingly in the favor of conservation interests. In Section 29(a) of ESA, Congress declared that

(1) various species of fish, wildlife, and plants in the United States have been rendered extinct as a consequence of economic growth and development untempered by adequate concern and conservation; (2) other species of fish, wildlife, and plants have been so depleted in numbers that they are in danger of or threatened with extinction; (3) these species of fish, wildlife, and plants are of esthetic, ecological, educational, historical, recreational, and scientific value to the Nation and its people.

This language left no doubt that despite claims to the contrary made long after the fact (Heissenbuttel and Murray 1992; Simmons and Kay 1997), Congress fully intended the act to encompass far more than the large and popular mammals and birds. Section 3 defined fish or wildlife as any species in the animal kingdom, and plants were covered for the first time, with "plant" defined as any species in the plant kingdom. Furthermore, the definition of species included subspecies and even distinct populations, in the case of animals. (The ESA was amended in 1978 so that only vertebrates could be divided into distinct populations for listing purposes.) Species that even looked like an endangered species could be protected.

In addition to taxonomic comprehension, conservationists wanted an extension of the taking prohibition to all lands, not just the national wildlife refuges. This was an auspicious desire; federal regulation for the sake of environmental integrity was in vogue like never before. The Clean Air Act, Federal Water Pollution Control Act Amendments (Clean Water Act), Federal Environmental Pesticide Control Act, Noise Control Act, and Coastal Zone Management Act had all been passed from 1970 to 1972, each with an effect on the private sector. Supported by such precedent, Section 9 prohibited the taking of endangered species on all lands in the nation.

The public, meanwhile, had become aware of the plight of some extremely charismatic megafauna from overseas, including the giant panda, white rhinoceros, and African elephant. Species endangerment joined issues like population growth and atmospheric pollution on the list of global concerns. Under pressure to participate in a remedial program, Congress created Sections 8 and 8A. Section 8 called for international cooperation in general, and Section 8A mandated participation in CITES. Sections 8–9, then, embodied the geographic comprehension sought by conservationists.

Conservationists also viewed the federal presence in species conservation as inconsistent. They pointed out that while FWS might be protecting a species' habitat on one of its refuges, the Army Corps of Engineers might be endangering it next door. A valuable precedent was provided by the National Environmental Policy Act of 1970, with its bureau-wide charge to consider the environmental effects of all activities. Conservationists insisted that all agencies, not just FWS and NMFS, should take responsibility for species conservation on their lands or with their projects. Section 7 required the agencies to do precisely that.

With a taxonomically, geographically, and bureaucratically comprehensive bill, conservationists were yet concerned that protection might come too late for many species. They wanted a mechanism whereby species would be protected before they reached dire status. In a modification of the appendix approach of CITES, Congress responded with the concept of "threatened species," defined in Section 3 as "any species which is

TABLE 1. *General Contents of the Endangered Species Act*

Section	Content
2	Lists findings and declarations of Congress
3	Provides definitions
4	Outlines listing procedures
5	Authorizes land acquisition for habitat protection
6	Provides for FWS cooperation with states in endangered species programs
7	Requires federal agencies to pursue the preservation of species, and to consult with FWS before taking any action that could threaten the existence of a species or specimens thereof
8	Calls for international cooperation in general
8A	Provides guidelines for the implementation of the Convention on International Trade of Exotic Species of Fauna and Flora
9	Prohibits the taking of threatened and endangered species by any party, public or private
10	Provides exceptions to Section 9
11	Outlines enforcement mechanisms and specifies penalties
12	Directs the Smithsonian Institution to review the status of endangered plants and to develop methods for plant species conservation
13	Brings the act into conformance with other legislation
14	Repeals portions of the prior endangered species acts usurped by ESA
15	Authorizes appropriations in 5-year cycles
16	Specifies the effective date (as the date of enactment)
17	Prevents any interpretation of ESA that would weaken the provisions of the Marine Mammal Protection Act
18	Requires the secretary of the interior to submit an annual cost report on a species-specific basis

likely to become an endangered species within the foreseeable future throughout all or a significant portion of its range." Nuances distinguishing endangered and threatened species were elaborated in Section 4. The addition of the threatened category was welcomed by nearly all concerned (Yaffee 1982). While conservationists saw it as a way to protect more species, others saw it as a way to provide limited protection without having to resort to the highly regulatory provisions entailed by endangered status.

Most of these efforts encountered little opposition, but there was the perpetually controversial issue of states' rights to be dealt with before ESA could be passed. Many traditional conservationists, fearing that federal involvement in wildlife management could be extended to game species, wanted the primary regulatory authority for ESA to rest with the states (Yaffee 1982). The resulting compromise embodies much of Section 6, which directs the secretary of the interior to enter into cooperative agreements with states and provides states with considerable involvement in endangered species management. Nevertheless, ESA represents a wide inroad of the federal government into wildlife jurisdiction.

Viewed in historical context, ESA was a seemingly inevitable culmination of legislative evolution. It reflected continually expanding taxonomic, geographic, and federal concerns, and fit logically with the administrative structure for species conservation. It built heavily upon the prior endangered species acts, which it repealed (except for a portion of the 1966 act pertaining to the National Wildlife Refuge System). It was passed unanimously by the Senate, and there were only twelve dissenting votes in the House. Table 1 provides the general provisions of ESA. A policy design analysis follows in Part 2.

4

Traditional Analyses of the Endangered Species Act

Traditional theories of public policy include pluralism, policy sciences, public choice theory, and critical theory (Schneider and Ingram 1997). These theories provide foundations from which public policies are developed and analyzed. Czech defined another tradition of policy analysis: "policy specialism" (1997a:60). Policy specialism does not constitute a coherent policy theory, however, so we refer to the four theories and policy specialism as "policy perspectives." These five perspectives differ dramatically in epistemology, normative stance, and the role expected of public policy. The ESA has been analyzed from each of these perspectives. In this chapter, we review these perspectives and the ESA analyses performed pursuant thereto.

PLURALISM

Pluralism is the oldest theory of public policy. Dominating political science for much of the twentieth century, it serves as more than a model for policy studies. It is also one of the four dominant theories of American government, along with democracy, elitism, and hyperpluralism (Lineberry 1980). It incorporates four concepts: (1) limitation on the power of government, (2) responsiveness of government to public preferences, (3) multiple identities and overlapping memberships of citizens, and, (4) denial of the existence of a public interest (Schneider and Ingram 1997). It emphasizes the location of power in society and optimistically views the fragmentation of power in America as intentionally, constitutionally derived. It is supposed to be an empirically testable theory that documents how, and attempts to explain why, government behaves the way it does and why it remains stable. As such, its view of policy is process-oriented, focusing on power formation, agenda setting, and policy adoption. It usually gives less attention to the implementation and evaluation of policy content.

Given pluralism's seniority in public policy studies, it is appropriate that one of the first scholarly studies of ESA was conducted in classic pluralism terms. Yaffee (1982) portrayed ESA as a paragon of "prohibitive policy," a type of policy that defines societal goals, prescribes the means to achieve them, and restricts the behavior of citizens in the process. Yaffee's pluralistic perspective of ESA can readily be detected in the following statements: "The logic of the [legislative] process assumes that if there is a valid interest, then someone will rise up to advocate its position. In the pure model, the significance of an interest is measured by how effectively it can make itself heard" (43–44). "Implementation entails building support, mediating conflict, and negotiating compromise within agencies, between agencies, between branches of government, between agencies and interest groups, and between all of these parties and the media" (8). Most revealing of a pluralistic perspective "If there are ends that are well served by prohibitive policies, then perhaps inefficiency is tolerable. More important, if bargaining and negotiation do take place, then the outcomes cannot be considered to be inefficient unless the negotiations are inadequate" (15–16).

Yaffee addressed the pre-ESA evolution of wildlife law more thoroughly than would analysts from the other policy perspectives, but instead of focusing on the laws produced, he focused on the groups producing them. He identified the rapidly expanding wildlife profession of the mid-twentieth century as the most important party in determining the endangered species agenda, because wildlife ecologists were the first to define the problem, and did so as a technical one. Furthermore, wildlife professionals actively pursued species conservation legislation and federal land acquisition. They were supported, especially in the latter effort, by outdoor recreationists who had become increasingly powerful during the postwar economic boom.

While there were few detractors to endangered species legislation (chapter 3), Yaffee's investigation illuminated a fur industry mobilization against provisions of the 1969 act. This mobilization supported Yaffee's pluralistic vision of a group rising up to advocate its position. By the 1980s, however, pluralism had been much criticized, and pluralists were well aware of the weaknesses of a pure model. Yaffee noted, "In reality, however, some interests have limited resources to promote their case, others are ineffectual, and still others are unaware that their interests are at stake" (1982:44). The latter weakness of classical pluralism was exploited by interest groups, which later claimed that with ESA, Congress and many supportive interest groups had only intended to protect well-known, charismatic species.

Pluralism portrays the legislation of new agencies and programs as susceptible to sabotage through "political compromise," in which congressional opponents offer support only on the condition of including amendments subtly designed to cripple the program (Moe 1990). But such compromise is only necessary for highly contested, partisan issues — which ESA was not. Despite the relative paucity of political compromise manifesting ESA, with Section 6 the only noteworthy exception (chapter 3), Yaffee found ample compromise during implementation. For example, when ESA was passed, FWS recognized four subspecies of gray wolves: each were classified as endangered. The status of the eastern subspecies was controversial, because cattlemen in Minnesota wanted Section 9 flexibility in cases involving depredation. Responding to pressure from the cattlemen, FWS combined the four subspecies in 1978, making it easier to downlist the Minnesota population, which had suddenly become a subset of a much larger total population. Yaffee likewise found political motives behind listing decisions involving the Mexican duck, glacier bear, Furbish lousewort, and several sea turtle species.

Yaffee's pluralistic acumen was revealed in his interpretation of endangered species research. He saw the technical function of species research as secondary to the political function, at least in some cases. With empirical evidence from the Houston toad controversy, Yaffee noted, "One response to controversy is to study the issue further. A study gives added credibility, time to let things sort themselves out, and occasionally a better technical basis to make a decision" (1982:95).

Yaffee showed how the Progressive model of bureaucratic hierarchy is programmed to resolve interagency conflict. In Progressive bureaucracy, technical experts report to professional administrators, who in turn report to political appointees. With ESA, the model works well, at least in terms of resolving conflict. The biologists, who work directly with the species and would find it difficult to be flexible in negotiations, are largely information providers for higher-level officials, who then do the negotiating. The FWS officials in Washington, being far removed from the field and the species they protect, and closely connected with the secretary of the interior, president, and Congress, have considerable incentives for creative resolution of problems. Yaffee attributed a relative lack of conflicts between ESA and economic development projects to these incentives.

The preponderance of political pacification by FWS was a disappointment to early supporters of ESA, who thought that the clear objectives of ESA would result in quick, effective action. Yaffee ascribed their surprise to two errant assumptions. The first was that the endangerment of a species could be clearly and technically defined. The second was that prohibitive policy limits agency discretion and thus limits compromise. Yaffee noted that the two assumptions fall together, because technical uncertainty is what opens the door for agency discretion. Biodiversity issues are rife with uncertainty in the best of administrative situations, but combined with the classic underfunding faced by FWS (Clarke and McCool 1996), ESA implementation has inherited an inordinate amount. In such an environment, bureaucratic discretion thrives.

Yaffee's interpretation of ESA, then, stressed the balancing of power in endangered species controversies, the effective limitation of FWS power despite the prohibitive clout of Sections 7 and 9, the responsiveness of FWS to public preferences, and the importance of interest groups in ESA adoption and implementation. These are typical emphases of pluralism, but they are an incomplete set of criteria with which to analyze policy or government (Schneider and Ingram 1997; McCool 1995). There is an inadequate normative stance from which to judge policy outcomes as right or wrong, no standard of citizenship entailed, and no prescription for better policy. For the most part, Yaffee's account fits this criticism. However, he did relate a summary of the arguments for preserving species, including potential moral and ethical obligations.

Other accounts of ESA that generally fit the model of pluralism include those of Mann and Plummer (1995), Yaffee (1994a), Barker (1993), and Raven (1990). In addition, legal analyses that examine ESA's language, associated regulations, and resulting case law contain many pluralistic observations (Cheever 1996; Lin 1996; Houck 1995; Patlis 1994; Smith et al. 1993; Littell 1992; Yagerman 1990; Rohlf 1989; Bean 1983).

POLICY SCIENCES

The policy sciences are an attempt to apply scientific methods to the policy process, but they project no illusion of a "value-free" science. In contrast with the detachment of pluralist analyses, the policy sciences are intended to provide information that enables public policy to solve problems and achieve goals. As Brewer and deLeon described it, "Then and now the term defined an approach concerned with knowledge of the decision or policy process and knowledge in that process. The policy sciences join and integrate theory (knowledge of) and practice (knowledge in) to improve them both for human benefit" (1983:9). Policy scientists would replace the irrationality of politics and bureaucracy with the instrumental rationality of science and technocracy in the formulation and implementation of policy. The rational policy process would proceed as follows: (1) identification of goals; (2) formulation of policy alternatives; (3) assessment of the effects of alternatives; (4) adoption of the optimal policy; (5) implementation; and (6) evaluation of results.

An influential predecessor of the policy sciences was institutionalism, a prominent approach to policy studies until about 1960. The focus of institutionalism was the structure of government branches and agencies involved in policymaking and implementation. After being gradually superseded by behavioralist political science during mid-century, institutionalism has made somewhat of a comeback in the form of "new institutionalism," in which rules of behavior, norms, roles, and agency cultures are defined as institutions along with the basic structures of government that influence policy (McCool 1995:106).

Clark et. alia (1994) provided a policy sciences perspective of the endangered species issue. They presented nine case studies, which they followed with six theoretical perspectives. Indicative of the new institutionalism permeating the case studies, Reading and Miller found that, for the black-footed ferret, "Endangered species recovery programs could be greatly improved by addressing their professional and organizational weaknesses" (1994:73). Mattson and Craighead thought that a key to grizzly bear recovery" lies in changing the agencies and creating systemic risks and benefits such that managers are naturally led to pursue fulfillment of the ESA" (1994:121). Jackson said, "The major problem facing recovery [for the red-cockaded woodpecker] is the insistence by government agencies that management must fall within the constraints of "desired" management practices imposed by the forest industry" (1994: 202). Snyder remarked of the California condor recovery program, "The same mistakes in organization and implementation seem to recur endlessly, despite considerable discussion of these mistakes" (1994:222). After analyzing the Florida panther recovery program, Alvarez summarized, "the nation has not made the proper arrangements to carry out the mandate of the ESA. The government agencies in charge were not formed for that specific purpose" (1994:222). These authors tended to acknowledge but de-emphasize the specialized role of wildlife science in achieving endangered species recovery. Reading and Miller for example, thought that "these technical aspects, however, may be much simpler and less problematic than the professional and organizational issues facing ferret recovery" (1994:76).

Cumulatively, Clark et alia argued that "poor implementation of the ESA is itself a major cause of the continuing decline of species, and professionals and organizations are significantly responsible for the quality of implementation" (1994:4). Their major recommendation to those professionals and organizations was to learn more about policy sciences and to use that education in their management activities. In particular, they recommended the study of valuation, scientific management, innovation, psychology, small-group theory, organization theory, communications theory, and cybernetics. Their analysis revealed no flaws with the logic of ESA itself.

Following this illustrative effort, Clark (1997) more thoroughly employed the policy sciences to critique black-footed ferret recovery efforts and discussed the implications to endangered species recovery at large. Both studies constitute the major efforts to analyze ESA via the policy sciences. Meanwhile, some legal analyses have bordered on the policy sciences to the extent that they have provided abundant, systematic observations of the policy implementation process and the institutions devoted thereto (e.g., Lin 1996; Patlis 1994; Yagerman 1990). The same can be said for some pluralistic analyses, including those of Yaffee (1982, 1994a) and, most notably, Yaffee's (1994b) lead-in to the case studies of Clark et alia (1994).

The policy sciences are criticized for a lack of normative content (Schneider and Ingram 1997). Although the policy sciences acknowledge the existence of a public interest and were developed to serve the human prospect, a focus on material efficiency as typified by valuation studies has weighed heavily upon the reputation of the policy sciences. The lack of a consistent focus outside of cost-benefit analysis also reflects the difficulty of applying scientific methods to much of the policy process. Perhaps the policy sciences have not come far since Brewer and deLeon observed, "Policy research, analysis, and training were professional fads, and everybody wanted to get with it. The results are now in, and their sober appraisal directs us back to the intellectual drawing board if we are to prepare policy analysts and practitioners for their exceptionally difficult trade" (1983:9).

POLICY SPECIALISM

While the policy sciences apply scientific principles to the policy process, policy specialism applies the scientific method to the policy subject. In energy policy, for example, policy scientists focus on the efficiency of the nuclear bureaucracy, but physicists and engineers (policy specialists) determine what policy alternatives will work best from a technical perspective. In wildlife issues, the policy specialists are wildlife biologists. In the endangered species policy arena, they are often specialized further as conservation biologists, evolutionary ecologists, population geneticists, and landscape ecologists.

Providing a consummate example of policy specialism, the National Research Council (NRC) (1995) limited its analysis of ESA to biological and ecological considerations to determine if ESA had a sound basis in natural science. The NRC showed a penchant for defining the terms of the issue by introducing the "evolutionary unit . . . a group of organisms that represents a segment of biological diversity that shares evolutionary lineage and contains the potential for a unique evolutionary future." Adopting the term would subtly improve upon the problematic application of traditional species concepts — including the biological, cladistic, cohesion, evolutionary, phylogenetic, and recognition concepts (Cracraft 1989) — to ESA regulations.

In its consideration of habitat, NRC recommended the designation of "survival habitat," which would be designated for a species at the time of listing, and would be "that habitat necessary to support either current populations of a species or populations that are necessary to ensure short term (25–50 years) survival, whichever is larger" (1995:77). The number of years constituting "short-term" is left to adjustment by species experts, based upon generation time and other species-specific biological traits. The purpose of designating survival habitat would be to provide immediate, emergency habitat protection for a species until the "critical habitat" designation mandated by ESA can be developed by biologists. Policy specialism, more than policy sciences and far more than pluralism, would substitute political maneuvering and bureaucratic discretion with scientific knowledge.

For recovery planning, NRC (1995) found no scientific reason for the lesser protection of plant (versus animal) species afforded by ESA, or for different standards of protection on public and private lands. It recommended further quantification of recovery goals, which would be expressed in terms of survival probability per unit time, rather than the typically employed population size goals. For example, a recovery goal might be to achieve the conditions required for 95 percent probability of species survival for the next 200-year period. With the unrelenting emphasis on quantification that characterizes scientific endeavor, NRC proposed, "Although it will often be difficult to make these estimates, even the attempt to make them will have value by requiring an objective analysis and by requiring assumptions to be specified" (1995:10).

As no other policy framework would, the NRC's policy specialism identified a subtle weakness of scientific convention as applied to endangered species recovery. Studies designed to determine the impact of an activity on a population usually test a null hypothesis of the generic form: there is no effect of the activity on the population. Meanwhile, scientists traditionally emphasize the avoidance of Type I error (rejection of a true null hypothesis) at the increased risk of Type II error, in which one fails to reject a false null hypothesis. In testing for harmful effects of an activity on an endangered species, however, the consequences of Type II error are much more grave. The NRC cautioned researchers and research interpreters to take heed.

Overall, NRC provided a rational, specialized analysis of ESA from an eco-evolutionary and probabilistic perspective. The NRC focused its recommendations on the elimination of technically arbitrary ESA clauses, the development of quantifiable norms for implementation, and the continual refinement of ESA procedures by scientific experts.

There are practically innumerable critiques of ESA clauses and procedures that fall under the rubric of policy specialism (e.g., Waples 1998; Pennock and Dimmick 1997; Easter-Pilcher 1996; Tear et al. 1995), especially if one includes portions of articles that are primarily about other topics. The ESA as a whole has been addressed via policy specialism, too (e.g., Carroll et al. 1996; Miller 1996; Eisner et al. 1995). None of these analyses have the breadth or depth contained in the NRC report, however.

While the policy sciences are criticized for a lack of normative content, policy specialism is characterized by a lack of normative coherence. Each policy specialist tends to promote the values and goals of his or her profession, leaving the public and policymakers confused about widely divergent policy prescriptions. Policy specialists are hard to debate on technical grounds, and policy scholars concerned with the health of American democracy criticize the technocratic hegemony that policy specialism wittingly or unwittingly encourages (Schneider and Ingram 1997; Fischer 1990).

PUBLIC CHOICE THEORY

Public choice theory is characterized by a rather strict application of neo-classical economics to policy. Public choice theorists analyze policy under the assumption that human beings are self-interested utility maximizers and that maximization may be measured economically. Populated primarily by political economists, public choice theory supports the free market as the dominant form of social organization, while government is relegated to the role of policing the marketplace and providing goods and services not provided by the market. Privatization is the natural prescription.

Public choice theory developed in the 1950s and generated interest quickly. Green and Shapiro (1994) found that public choice articles first appeared in *American Political Science Review* in 1952 and, by 1992, nearly 40 percent of that journal comprised such articles. Public choice theory has greatly influenced American government, especially during the administrations of Presidents Ronald Reagan and George Bush, when public choice theory complemented presidential ideology (Schneider and Ingram 1997).

Some authors have recently employed a wide range of economic principles to analyze certain aspects of ESA (e.g., Bourland and Stroup 1996; Kennedy et al. 1996; Montgomery and Pollock 1996; Heinen 1995; and Heissenbuttel and Murray 1992). Although these authors have applied methods and concerns associated with public choice theory, they have varied in the degree to which they subscribed to the larger public choice philosophy (especially privatization). Conversely, at least one primarily pluralistic account exhibited a public choice philosophy (Mann and Plummer 1995). O'Toole (1996) edited a special journal issue that applied public choice theory to ESA, but Simmons and Kay (1997) were the first to write a book-length manuscript on the topic. (The 1997 manuscript has apparently evolved into a forthcoming book, *Political Ecology: Politics, Economics and the Endangered Species Act.*)

In their critique of ESA, Simmons and Kay focused on how property values may have been impacted by the listing of species. They referenced data presented at a Texas water law conference that property values in Travis County, Texas, declined $359 million after the golden cheeked warbler and black-capped vireo were listed. They also asserted that a landowner in North Carolina had effectively paid $73,914 apiece for twenty-nine red-cockaded woodpeckers that resided on his property. (Both of these accounts have been contested by the United States Fish and Wildlife Service [1995]). Simmons and Kay also noted that inaccurate data on population sizes can lead to erroneous listings and unjust economic hardships — a weakness of policy specialism.

Simmons and Kay took issue with the Supreme Court's 1978 opinion in *Tennessee Valley Authority v. Hill*, in which ESA was interpreted to define "the value of endangered species as incalculable." To Simmons and Kay, "It is, in fact an absurd statement. Few people can believe that preserving one of the thousands of varieties of beetles is more valuable than solving the economic and social crises in our central cities" (1997:93). (Simmons and Kay may have misinterpreted the word "incalculable," which literally means impossible to calculate, usually due to volume.)

Regarding species recovery, Simmons and Kay said nothing about the pluralistic process and focused on results. They noted that twenty species have been delisted, eight because they went extinct and eight because data supporting the original listings were inaccurate. They noted that ESA's contribution even to the other four delistings is controversial. After quoting praise for ESA delivered by Bruce Babbitt (secretary of the interior under President Clinton), Simmons and Kay said, "In our opinion, four contested delistings hardly qualify the ESA for such accolades" (1997:103).

In contrast to the pluralist Yaffee (1982), Simmons and Kay (1997:52) attacked the institution of Progressive bureaucracy: "Because public agencies are creatures of the polity in general and politicians in particular, they are political agencies, not the omnicompetent, impartial organizations envisioned by the designers of the civil service system. Because budgets are determined by political processes, the bureau must choose fiscal strategies of survival and growth that make political, if not economic sense." Not only is the political management of the bureaucracy inefficient, it discourages innovation and provides an incentive for bureaucrats to distort information about program activities and success, especially during the budgeting process. Once the distortion is perpetrated, it must be perennially perpetuated lest the bureaucrat responsible is discovered. Furthermore, policy implementation tends to the short term because top-level bureaucrats are tied to the election cycle.

Simmons and Kay presented case studies of the gray wolf, grizzly bear, and African elephant. The case studies highlight the skepticism of Simmons and Kay toward ESA, policy specialism, and Progressive bureaucracy. About the gray wolf, Simmons and Kay (1997:118) said, "All the government's recent wolf recovery reports, wolf population models, and studies regarding possible impact on big-game hunting are arbitrary and capricious. They represent not science but a masterful job of deception." Simmons and Kay supposed that the motive for deception was to get wolves into the Rocky Mountain ecosystem so that larger populations could be produced under ESA protection. They posited that wolves were never common in Yellowstone, as commonly believed, but that they would quickly repopulate other parts of the West once reintroduced and cause major economic hardship. Simmons and Kay concluded, "Wolf recovery is a bad idea whose time has apparently come, unless, of course, the Endangered Species Act can be changed" (1997:153).

Simmons and Kay used the elephant, a species with proven-in-detail market characteristics, to invoke public choice theory. They recommended a smaller role for government and a larger role for market processes, and discussed the pillars of the market: prices and property rights. Hearkening back to the classical economics of Adam Smith, they related that prices move like a hidden hand to prevent over-consumption, encourage efficiency, and distribute information about supply and demand. Meanwhile, property rights make owners responsible for their decisions, leading them to maintain their property in good condition. Government regulation is anathema to the market, because the resulting price regime is artificial and misleading, and property rights tend to diminish.

Simmons and Kay reviewed Hardin's (1968) tragedy of the commons and observed, "*Any action on a commons is intrinsically irresponsible because costs are socialized and benefits are privatized*" (1997:228, emphasis theirs). They classified species as common pool resources and cited the bison as a classic example of tragedy of the commons. They implied that treating species as private or toll goods would be a better conservation strategy.

A frequent criticism of public choice theory is the implications of its normative stance for democracy (Schneider and Ingram 1997). The degree of property rights championed by Simmons and Kay fits with the philosophy of the "rights revolution" discussed by Landy (1993), whereby ideals of citizenship and social responsibility have been neglected while the rights of individuals have proliferated. For example, Simmons and Kay claimed, "In the case of biodiversity, the landowners are producing a *benefit* and if members of society value the biodiversity the landowners produce, ways should be found to encourage the landowners to continue to produce the positive externality" (1997:275, emphasis theirs). This is an extreme view to nonpublic choice theorists because wildlife species were part of the environment pre-ownership and are perennially produced naturally. (It would be incomprehensible to credit a landowner residing along a stream, for example, with producing the water that runs past; likewise with wildlife that literally and evolutionarily runs through.)

Critics also view the application of neoclassical economics to endangered species conservation as overwhelmed by complexity and detracting from responsible citizenship (Erickson 2000). Economic efficiency would only be an adequate standard for endangered species policy were it to account for the needs of all humans, present and future — even more complex issues of biocentrism aside. As such, it would require the calculation of the incalculable (e.g., the worth of species), the knowledge of innumerable and unknowable economic and ecological variables, and a crystal ball. Minus an omniscient public choice theorist, public choice theory renders a highly constrained contribution to the evaluation and prescription of endangered species policy.

CRITICAL THEORY

Critical theory hearkens back to Karl Marx as the progenitor of the perspective. Critical theory is concerned primarily with oppression and domination, and engenders a commitment to participatory, nonhierarchical forms of political, economic, and social interaction (Schneider and Ingram 1997). With its overriding concern on oppression, the applicability of critical theory to endangered species policy is suspect at first glance. The only straightforward way that species endangerment could be considered an issue of oppression is to consider rare species as the oppressed — a truly biocentric and radical concept. As for human subjects, future generations denied a full endowment of species could also be classified as oppressed. Devall and Sessions, perhaps not critical theorists per se, nevertheless embraced both concepts explicitly in *Deep Ecology* (1985).

Critical theory rejects the benign view of government and policy processes held by pluralists and the economically derived priorities of public choice theory, but its most vitriolic critique is saved for the instrumental rationality of policy sciences and policy specialism. Instrumental rationality is viewed as the source of oppression in capitalist and socialist societies alike, and is cited as a root of species endangerment because it justifies the dominance of other species and the earth itself. One of the most consistent and intensive themes in critical theory, therefore, is the replacement of instrumental rationality with "communicative rationality" (Hayward 1994). In contrast to the abstruse jargon, distorted data, and "value-free" decision making that typifies instrumental rationality in the context of pluralist politics, communicative rationality occurs when policy discourse is technically accurate, attendant to human freedom and equality, and comprehensible to a participating general public.

As critical theorists are prone, Devall and Sessions addressed a much broader concern than could be contained in a statutory policy arena. Their ultimate goal was to evangelize the citizenry to an ecological consciousness whereby humans exist not as independent entities but as parts of a living, spirited "Nature," along with all other species: "We believe that humans have a vital need to cultivate ecological consciousness and that this need is related to the needs of the planet. . . . Deep ecology is a process of ever-deeper questioning of ourselves, the assumptions of the dominant worldview in our culture, and the meaning and truth of our reality" (Devall and Sessions 1985:8).

As for the lesser yet important concern of public policy, Devall and Sessions focused on endangered species and wilderness preservation. They identified a dominant worldview based in Judeo-Christian spirituality, instrumental rationality, capitalism, and patriarchal family structures. The characteristic of this worldview that leads directly to species endangerment and loss of wilderness is dominance: dominance of humans over other humans (including posterity) and over nature.

Devall and Sessions outlined the "reformist responses" to the ecological problems caused by the dominant worldview and found them wanting. In their view, the prominent philosophical reform has been the resource conservation and development philosophy, born during the Progressive forestry of Gifford Pinchot and subscribed to by the natural resources bureaucracy. This perspective is usually associated with utilitarianism but is more precisely defined by the application of instrumental rationality to natural resource management. Another philosophical response is humanism, which would replace God or gods with *Homo sapiens* at the rudder of existence, armed with the knowledge of nature's laws. The other philosophical responses include the animal liberation movement and the "limits to growth" response. Each of the philosophical reforms, however, are ultimately anthropocentric and therefore anathema to deep ecology.

Devall and Sessions did not deem the reformist responses as totally useless. They acknowledged the value of some resulting policies, especially ESA and the creation of the wilderness preservation system. What they deemed more important, however, was that "many people have sensed that something is missing. They are asking deeper questions. They understand that the environmental/ecology movement needs an articulate philosophical approach grounded upon assumptions which are different from those of the dominant worldview. They realize that a perspective is needed that will place the best of the reformist response into a coherent philosophical perspective — a philosophy based on biocentric rather than anthropocentric assumptions" (1985:61). Thus, they proposed deep ecology.

Critical theories supplement hypothetico-deduction and formal logic with what may arguably be classified as other forms of knowledge, including intuition, self-reflection, and normative valuation (Schneider and Ingram 1997). The norms valued by deep ecology are self-realization and biocentric equality. There is no firm line between self-realization and the understanding of nature, because humans and nature are one. The norm of biocentric equality assigns an equal worth to all species. Self-realization and biocentric equality are inextricable; when one endangers a species, one endangers nature and therefore oneself.

Aided by redundancy, Devall and Sessions were impressively clear, considering the metaphysical nature of their subject. Nevertheless, they had difficulty in analyzing ESA. They posited,

> The biocentric intuition that species have a right to exist and follow their own evolutionary destinies was established in the United States in the Endangered Species Act of 1973. This act has been severely attacked by those who defend the belief that the Earth exists for human use. But the Endangered Species Act still has major limitations. The act includes complex procedures for designating a species endangered, although it rejects the economist's narrow approach of a cost/benefit analysis on each species. Nevertheless, it includes the concept of balance between human needs and species habitat preservation." (Devall and Sessions 1985:126).

The "buts," "althoughs," and "neverthelesses" illustrate a unique aspect of ESA: critical theorists who generally anathematize prohibitive policy see some semblance of wisdom in ESA.

One of the most common criticisms of critical theory is that it has lost what it historically claimed as its distinguishing feature — practicality. Deep ecology may be especially subject to such criticism because it extends the ideal of justice to nonhuman species. The intent of deep ecology is to transcend the dominant worldview, and doing so would require the replacement of anthropocentrism with biocentrism, representative government with consensual policymaking, instrumental rationality with communicative rationality, and economic efficiency with spirituality. These replacement concepts are far from the mainstream of societal thought. They are not impossible but are unlikely to occur within the time frame required to prevent many looming species extinctions. *Deep Ecology* (or similar literature) would probably have to sweep the nation like *Silent Spring* to effect such a conceptual shift, and in the 15 years since its publication, it has not done so.

SUMMARY OF TRADITIONAL ANALYSES

We conducted a comprehensive literature search with Quicksearch, a database linking and referencing program, in April 1996, using "Endangered Species Act" as a key phrase. We found 1,341 ESA articles published in natural science and popular environmental journals and 48 in social science (primarily legal) journals. The Congressional Record Index contained 273 records, corresponding approximately to the number of hearings in which ESA was a primary topic. The American Statistics Index included 42 quantitative publications of federal bureaus and congressional committees. Twenty-five M.S. and Ph.D. theses had been composed with ESA as a primary topic. Using the key words "endangered" and "species," 157 books were indexed, including ten that have been written about ESA or with ESA as a primary topic. An aborted newspaper database search revealed thousands of news articles published on ESA.

Almost all of the journal articles, government reports, dissertations, and books about ESA may be classified under one of the five traditional perspectives, except for a few that simply provide uninterpreted data (e.g., expenditure reports). Many of the congressional reports include testimonial ESA analyses from multiple sources, too, so that there are thousands of policy analyses published on ESA with varying degrees of comprehensiveness. As with most technically challenging policy issues, the majority of ESA analyses are from the policy specialism perspective, as reflected by the preponderance of articles in natural science journals. As with controversial issues in general, pluralistic analyses are common, too. Public choice analyses are also fairly common, because the implications of ESA to private property regulation invites public choice critique. Formal policy science analyses are less common, although many analyses include systematic observations of the institutions and processes associated with ESA. Critical theory analyses of ESA are uncommon because of the bio-

TABLE 2. *Emphases of Traditional Public Policy Perspectives*

Perspective	Dominant Epistemology	Normative Ideals	Primary Role Ascribed to Policy
Pluralism	Behavioralism, deductive theorizing derived from inductive explanation	Political equality, legal primacy, procedural accessibility	Represent and respond to interests
Policy sciences	Value-based deductive theorizing derived from inductive explanation	Efficacy, efficiency, human dignity	Identify and solve societal problems
Policy specialism	Hypothetico-deduction, ostensibly value-free (not linked with normative stance)	Varies with specialty (e.g., preservation of biodiversity)	Base management guidelines on rigorous science
Public choice theory	Broad deduction, methodological individualism	Efficiency, Pareto optimality	Convert individual rationality into collective rationality
Critical theory	Self-reflection, intuition, faith	Elimination of oppression	Engage public in consensual discourse

Sources: Based primarily on Schneider and Ingram (1997), supplemented by Czech (1997a).

centric prerequisites and because critical theorists tend to focus on broader, contextual issues.

As these policy perspectives overlap conceptually (for example, the policy sciences emphasis on cost-benefit analysis providing a link to public choice theory), so do ESA analyses. The most common combinations appear to be those in which ecologists attempt, implicitly or explicitly, to take a new "slant" on ESA by incorporating aspects of political science. Thus, most combinations include a considerable element of policy specialism. For example, Easter-Pilcher (1996) and Scott et al. (1995) incorporated elements of the policy sciences and pluralism, respectively, in assessing decisions pertaining to the listing and recovery of endangered species. Invariably, however, the perspectives from which ESA has been analyzed have been readily identifiable and predominant.

Schneider and Ingram (1997) identified a shortcoming common to the traditional policy perspectives: narrow epistemological and normative foundations support incomplete visions of public policy (Table 2). Also, the distinct perspectives make it difficult to assess the relative merit of policy analyses; comparing a pluralist account with a public choice analysis, for example, is like comparing apples and oranges. Schneider and Ingram argued that a new policy perspective is required for policy analysis to contribute toward solving societal problems and serving democracy, and they called it policy design theory.

Part 2

A Policy Design Analysis of the Endangered Species Act

5

Policy Elements of the Endangered Species Act

Policy design theory assumes that American public policy is supposed to serve democracy in addition to solving technical problems. A good policy has the rationale required to lead efficiently and effectively from clearly stated procedural requirements or incentives to a clearly stated goal. It encourages public participation and enables policy implementers to respond to public needs. It accounts for the social construction of its target groups and seeks to better their lot, being careful to encourage neither cynicism nor deception, or to lead to the oppression of one group by another. In other words, a good policy accomplishes a balance of the goals held in esteem by traditional perspectives and serves democracy in the process (Schneider and Ingram 1997).

The first, most fundamental step in policy design analysis is identification of the policy's legal proclamation and the agents, targets, and goals identified and established by that proclamation. The next step is identification of the rules and tools created by the policy for agents to use in pursuing the policy goals. Those relatively straightforward steps are followed by identification and assessment of the assumptions made and the rationale employed by the authors of the policy.

Identification of policy elements — proclamation, agents, targets, goals, rules, tools, assumptions, rationale — and their relationship to one another enables an assessment of the structural logic of the policy. For example, if it is difficult to identify the policy elements, then successful implementation is unlikely. Identification of policy elements also enables the practice of comparative policy, whereby the element arrangements and structural logic of various policies may be assessed relative to one another. The value of such comparison is suggested by similar pursuits

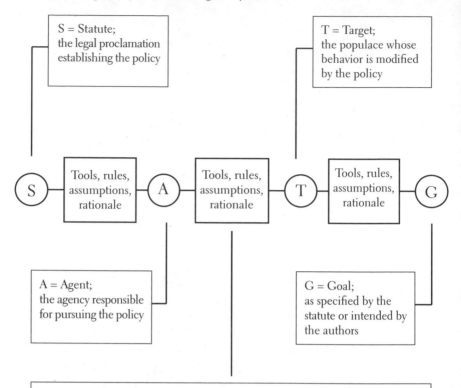

FIG 1. *Template of public policy elements.*

as widely dispersed as comparative anatomy, comparative literature, and comparative government. A template of policy design (Fig. 1) provides a starting point for comparative policy.

Rarely are public policies as simple as the template, however. The policy language does not have to be statutory and may be hidden in obscure court opinions or vague administrative law. Agents are often multiple, and one may or may not be acknowledged as the lead. Sometimes it is difficult to distinguish between agents and targets. Targets and goals may be multiple. The ostensible goal of the policy may be one of many held by the

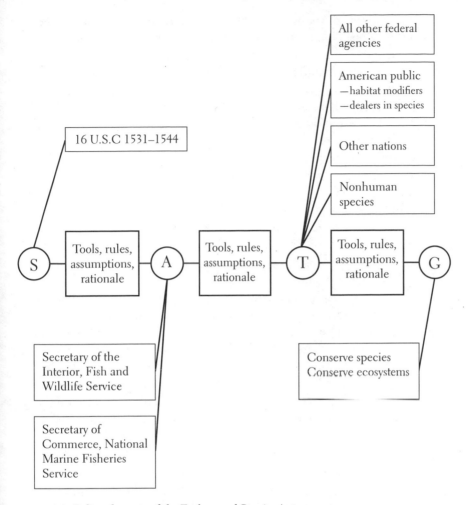

FIG 2. *Policy elements of the Endangered Species Act.*

authors and may even be opposite the goals of some authors, owing to legislated political compromise (Moe 1990). The rules, tools, assumptions, and rationale often encompass a tremendous amount of technical and political complexity that may or may not logically lead from the legal proclamation to the accomplishment of the goal.

The ESA is clearly the focal statute in endangered species policy and is relatively straightforward. Nevertheless, it produces an element structure with several uncommon properties (Fig. 2), notably the targeting of federal agencies in addition to sectors of the American public and a seeming biocentricity of goals. Given the novelty of these aspects and the demands they place on agencies and citizens, it is not surprising that ESA implementation faces challenges from inside the government and out.

Many authors, including those reviewed in chapter 4, have shown how ESA is intended to conserve species and ecosystems through the prohibition of federal and private activities that destroy species and their habitats, overseen by FWS and NMFS. In effect, they have described the agents, targets, and goals of ESA. Some researchers (especially legal scholars) have minutely dissected ESA's statutory language and its associated federal regulations, and have identified the tools and rules applied by the agents (see e.g., Cheever 1996; Lin 1996; Houck 1995; Patlis 1994; Smith et al. 1993; Littell 1992; Yagerman 1990; Rohlf 1989; and Bean 1983). Cumulatively, these authors (especially the legal scholars) have provided a thorough assessment of the rationale connecting these policy elements, with ESA generally receiving high marks. However, the assumptions underlying the design of ESA have been largely ignored.

An assessment of the assumptions underlying the progression of policy elements from statute to goal is essential to the analysis of policy design, because if an assumption is wrong, then the policy may be structurally flawed, regardless of apparent rationality. In formal logic terms, an argument may be valid (its conclusion must follow from its premises) but unsound (its premises are incorrect and therefore its conclusion will not follow). Likewise, a policy may be valid (its goals will be achieved if the assumptions of its authors are correct) yet unsound (the assumptions are incorrect, and therefore its goals will not be achieved). In other words, a valid policy is rational but not necessarily sound and not necessarily destined for success.

Given the copious literature on the other elements of ESA design, we have focused on the assumptions of the authors. The ascertaining of assumptions is not an entirely objective process, and there is no mechanical device with which to measure the accuracy or precision of those undertaking the task. Nevertheless, assumptions can — and for the purposes of policy design analysis must — be ascertained. Legislative history and statements of legislators can provide insight to assumptions, but logical analysis of statutory language is the most objective method. Furthermore, some assumptions are embodied in the logic of statutes and may never have been the topic of discussion among legislators or even consciously derived. Despite the lack of legislative history, these "assumptions in effect" have a direct bearing on implementation and interpretation in the courts.

We analyzed each clause of ESA and ascertained the logically associated assumptions (Appendix 1). We defined an assumption as an implicit premise required to lead from the findings of Congress (Section 2(a)) to the accomplishment of ESA goals (Section 2(b)), or to validate an ESA clause. Some clauses, by their nature, contain few assumptions (such as declarations or definitions). Others essentially constitute assumptions or reveal multiple assumptions. Most of the assumptions are relatively straightforward and eminently sensible. However, several are incorrect or highly debatable and merit further discussion. (Corrective language is suggested in chapter 11.)

INCORRECT OR HIGHLY DEBATABLE ASSUMPTIONS EMBODIED IN ESA

Section 4(b)(2) authorizes the secretary of the interior to exclude an area from critical habitat designation if the economic or other benefits of exclusion outweigh the costs. A species' critical habitat is the area "essential to the conservation of the species" (Section 3(5)(A)). "Conservation" is accomplished when a species is brought "to the point at which the measures provided pursuant to this Act are no longer necessary" (Section 3(3)). The loss of critical habitat to the protections of ESA, then, means that a species will never recover from its endangered status. (Even if a "little bit" of the critical habitat is lost, the species can "never quite" recover.) Since the goal of ESA is the conservation of species, the policy logic of ESA is unsound in cases where the critical habitat exclusion is practiced.

Section 4(b)(6)(B)(ii) stipulates that if insufficient data exists for the petitioned listing of a species even after the 6-month listing extension period provided in Section 4(b)(6)(B)(i), then the listing process is terminated. Congress apparently assumed that in cases of doubt, the disadvantages of listing outweigh the advantages of listing the (doubtfully) threatened or endangered species. That was a faulty assumption for three reasons. First, as Congress itself assumed in Section 4(b)(3)(C)(ii), it is better to err on the conservative side when the existence of a species is in question (Appendix 1). Second, if a species is close to being threatened or endangered (as is probably the case when doubt is involved), it is likely to be truly threatened or endangered in the foreseeable future. In such cases, it is usually more effective to protect the species before it requires more resources to be conserved. Third, the listing of a species costs relatively little — and very little more than what has already been invested by the time Section 4(b)(6)(B)(ii) becomes relevant. Congress would have been more logical to assume that the secretary would formulate relatively uncostly regulations for species of doubtful status.

Section 4(b)(7) allows the secretary to disregard the normal, time-consuming processes of species listing and critical habitat designation in emergency situations. As a federal circuit judge put it, the secretary "was to use his emergency powers less cautiously — in a sense to 'shoot first and ask questions later'" (Littell 1992:92). The emergency clause assumes that the secretary will utilize the clause when emergencies indeed arise, but that assumption is riddled with biological, political, and administrative uncertainty. The field of population genetics has struggled for decades with the concept of genetic viability, which is but one factor in population risk assessment (National Research Council 1995). Where narrow economic interests are at odds with a species' survival, there is political pressure to define the emergency population at a lower level than that defined under purely biological considerations. Furthermore, the secretary of the interior is a political appointee selected by and held responsible to the president. If that president is opposed to ESA implementation, the secretary is bound to be likewise. Thus, during the controversy over listing the Mt. Graham red squirrel, a listing with the potential to halt the construction of an observatory, secretary of the interior Manuel Lujan Jr. told the *Washington Post*, "Nobody's told me the difference between a red squirrel, a black one, or a brown one. Do we have to save every subspecies? Do we have to save [an endangered species] in every locality where it exists?" (Lancaster 1990:A1). In another interview, he expressed the opinion that ESA was "just too tough an act, I think. We've got to change it" (Yaffee 1994a:128). The assumption that every secretary will utilize his or her emergency powers pursuant to section 4(b)(7) is clearly errant.

In section 4(d), the secretary is directed to issue protective regulations for threatened species as for endangered species, except that if a state has entered into an agreement with the secretary for endangered species management, the secretary may not issue takings regulations for resident fish or wildlife species unless the state has corresponding regulations. Unless the ESA authors assumed that a threatened species may recover with no protection — a highly unlikely assumption — they must have assumed that a state's position on a species is more important than species conservation unless the species has reached the point of becoming endangered, in which case species conservation becomes more important. This assumption seems to conflict with Congress's own intent as interpreted by the

Supreme Court in *Tennessee Valley Authority v. Hill*, because "Congress has spoken in the plainest of words, making it abundantly clear that the balance has been struck in favor of affording endangered species the highest of priorities" (437 U.S. 194). It also conflicts with the principle of erring on the conservative side in cases of species survival and with the logic that threatened species are typically on the way to endangerment.

Section 4(f)(1) directs the secretary to prepare recovery plans for listed species "unless he finds that such a plan will not promote the conservation of the species." Congress assumed that the development of a recovery plan can fail to promote the conservation of a species and can perhaps further endanger the species. Although technically inarguable (because there is never a guarantee of success with any plan), this assumption was profoundly cynical. It may entail the more valid assumption that a recovery plan can create a wave of public opposition. However, such opposition can be addressed in a recovery plan, along with strategies to obviate it. Avoiding the problem by abandoning the planning process is no solution.

Section 4(f)(1)(A) directs the secretary, in developing recovery plans, to prioritize species without regard to taxonomy. In addition to assuming that agency budgets would be insufficient to prepare plans for all threatened and endangered species (a realistic assumption), Congress must have either assumed that all taxa are of equal value or that relative values of taxa cannot be ascertained. However, there is strong evidence that the public does not value taxa equally (chapter 6), and there are ecological and evolutionary rationales for prioritizing species taxonomically (chapter 7).

Section 6(i) establishes a "cooperative endangered species conservation fund," into which 5 percent of Pittman-Robertson funds and Dingell-Johnson funds are annually deposited and authorized for expenditure on cooperative programs with states. Congress apparently assumed that 5 percent of the combined funds is enough to successfully administer endangered species cooperative programs with states and that future Congresses would annually appropriate the full 5 percent. The first assumption is debatable, although it may have been more realistic when crafted. However, the second assumption was clearly awry. Clarke and McCool (1996) found that inadequacy of appropriations has long been one of the defining characteristics of FWS. Dwyer et alia reported, "A 1990 audit of the endangered species program by the Department of the Interior's Inspector General noted it would take $4.6 billion to recover all listed species and to list and recover the backlog of candidate species. This total is approximately 50 times recent annual budgets for [ESA] implementation" (1995:738).

Section 7(a)(1) states that all federal agencies shall administer species conservation programs. For FWS and NMFS, Congress provided procedural specifications and appropriations therefor, thus ensuring that those agencies would indeed administer such programs. Congress assumed that the remaining agencies would develop such programs with no procedural specifications and appropriations. Yet for some agencies, the goals of ESA may be impertinent to or even conflicting with their own. Congress may have also assumed that lacking their own species conservation programs, agencies would submit themselves to the scrutiny of FWS and NMFS pursuant to the section 7 consultation process, but that assumption is a dubious application of the honor system to the federal bureaucracy. For example, ever since *Tennessee Valley Authority v. Hill*, the Tennessee Valley Authority has reason to be wary of providing FWS with information on projects, especially any sensitive species information it might control. Agencies face great incentives to expand their programs and budgets, not to voluntarily abandon them at the bequest of another federal agency (Wilson 1989).

Section 7(e)(3) establishes the composition of the Endangered Species Committee, or "God Squad," which is invoked to consider exemptions to the Section 7 prohibitions. The paragraph contains either a faulty assumption or a cognitive error. It states, "The Committee shall be composed of seven members as follows . . . ," and lists six federal officers (subparagraphs A–F of Section 7(e)(3)). For the seventh member, subparagraph G says, "The President, after consideration of any recommendations received pursuant to subsection (g)(2)(B) shall appoint one individual from each affected State, as determined by the Secretary, to be a member of the Committee for the consideration of the application for exemption for an agency action with respect to which such recommendations are made, not later than 30 days after an application is submitted pursuant to this section." With the language "each affected state," subparagraph G acknowledges (as does Section 7(g)(2)(b)) that there are situations where more than one state is affected (e.g., where a contested dam is proposed for a river that forms the boundary between states), but provides no direction for including each state's interest on a seven-member Endangered Species Committee. Congress may have implied that a multistate delegation would be represented by one vote for the purposes of Endangered Species Committee business and counted on the secretary to establish clarifying regulations. It is possible that subparagraph G was an oversight on the part of Congress and its legal staff.

Section 10(d) stipulates that the secretary may only grant a Section 9 exception if such exception "will not operate to the disadvantage of such endangered species." That stipulation reveals the assumption that incidental take may occur without operating to the disadvantage of an endangered species. An endangered species is one in danger of extinction, and it is difficult to imagine a case in which the taking of a specimen, incidental or not, would not operate to the species' disadvantage. From a population dynamics standpoint, that case would only occur if the taking constituted compensatory mortality (mortality that would otherwise occur, if not due to the excepted action). It is doubtful that Congress had compensatory mortality in mind when it crafted Section 10(d). Instead, Section 10(d) seems like a manifestation of political compromise. Furthermore, compensatory mortality has been a controversial concept since it was proposed by Errington (1946), because cases of entirely compensatory mortality are difficult to demonstrate (Smith and Reynolds 1992). Acceptance of the concept would violate the principle of erring conservatively. Finally, even where compensatory mortality was clearly demonstrable, all specimens of an endangered species are valuable for the information they convey to other specimens and to researchers concerned with the species' recovery.

Section 10(f)(5) requires that "no regulation prescribed by the Secretary to carry out the purposes of the subsection shall be subject to section 4(f)(2)(A)(i) of this Act." The most basic assumption is that ESA contains a Section 4(f)(2)(A)(i), but Section 4(f)(2) contains no subparagraphs, and no section of ESA contains a subsection f(2)(A)(i). Perhaps this language is a relic of an early draft and was not corrected in the final version. (Solicitors in the Department of the Interior that we spoke with were surprised by this flaw, which occurs in Title 16 of the U.S. Code and in U.S. Government Printing Office publication 1994-301-134 [14034].)

Section 11(g)(1)(B–C) authorizes citizens to file suit "to compel the Secretary to apply . . . the prohibitions set forth in or authorized pursuant to section 4(d) and section 9(a)(1)(B) of this Act with respect to [takings]," or "against the Secretary where there is alleged a failure of the Secretary to perform any act or duty under section 4 which is not discretionary with the Secretary." Apparently, Congress assumed that listing procedures and taking prohibitions are more important to species conservation than other ESA clauses and that it would be judicially unwieldy to allow citizen suits pertaining to other clauses. The first assumption is reasonable, but the relevancy of the latter assumption is arguable, because that assumption entails a further assumption that judicial efficiency is more important than the effectiveness of species conservation policy. Yet the aforementioned Supreme Court in *Tennessee Valley Authority v. Hill* established the primacy of species conservation ascribed by Congress through ESA. In providing a limited standing to sue, Congress possibly assumed that federal prosecutors would hold the secretary liable for the other clauses of ESA, but that is a risky assumption at best.

SUMMARY

In summary, there were twelve incorrect or highly questionable assumptions made by the authors of ESA in addition to assumptions that may be arguable to some people (Appendix 1). Most dubious assumptions appear to result from political compromise or from underestimating the resources required to administer ESA. A few indicate an ambivalence that developed as Congress reached a conceptual point of diminishing returns in extending the protections of ESA (e.g., Section 3(6)) (Appendix 1). None of the faulty assumptions appear serious enough to undermine the federal program of species conservation established by ESA. However, for some species, the result of one or more of these assumptions will likely lead to extinction. All clauses stemming from questionable assumptions are correctable, however (chapter 11).

In addition to the clause-specific assumptions, ESA — especially Section 4 — reveals a broad assumption that the technical expertise, political willpower, and administrative capacity of FWS and NMFS can stem the tide of species endangerment. This is virtually a "required assumption," as all policies embody assumptions made about the capabilities of policy agents. Nevertheless, it is important to recognize that this assumption may be unfounded. For example, before a species receives ESA protection, it must be recognized via the listing procedure of Section 4, which assumes that FWS and NMFS can identify species that are in danger of becoming extinct, determine the habitat required to allow for a species' recovery, and protect both.

For some species, extinction is a tangible threat, and the listing process of Section 4 should function well. However, there may be numerous cases where species are practically doomed before FWS and NMFS notices or acts, or where FWS and NMFS are remiss in designating sufficient critical habitat. For example, population models have projected the extinction of the northern spotted owl in less than a century because of threats to its habitat, despite FWS's protective regulations (Yaffee 1994a). Although FWS listed the species in 1990 after protracted political suppression, and even if the forest management practices designed to preserve the owl are adhered to, perhaps the critics are right and the owl population is inexorably declining.

Furthermore, if FWS and NMFS had the required technical expertise, political willpower, and administrative capacity to achieve the technical goals of ESA, those very traits could clash with another goal of public policy in general: the strengthening of democracy. Land use would come under increasing control of the FWS and NMFS technocracy rather than the democratic process. It is unclear if the authors of ESA recognized this dilemma between technocracy and democracy (chapter 9).

6

Social Construction of
Endangered Species Act Targets

In policy design theory, special attention is paid to the social construction of policy targets. Social construction is the cultural characterization, virtue, or valence ascribed to a policy target by the general public. The policy target may be portrayed in positive or negative terms with symbolism, metaphor, and fable. In the simplest terms, a policy target may be constructed as good or bad. Social construction is one manifestation of the ontological philosophy of constructivism (Soule and Lease 1995, Hayward 1994).

Perhaps the most blatant application of social construction is the stereotype. The stereotype is a heuristic used to make quick judgments about a member of a societal sector. Unfortunately, the abuses of stereotyping may be more prevalent than the benefits. When a nonhuman taxon is used as a metaphor for stereotyping people, then a double stereotype occurs. For example, if someone says, "Those people from Smithville are sneaky snakes," people from Smithville and snakes are stereotyped as sneaky.

Schneider and Ingram called social construction "an important, albeit overlooked, political phenomenon that should take its place in the study of public policy by political scientists . . . because it contributes to studies of agenda setting, legislative behavior, and policy formulation and design" (1993:334). They also proposed that when social construction is assessed in tandem with political power, prediction of policy design is possible. For an already existing policy, the assessment of construction and power is a tool for interpreting policy implementation. A certain style of policy tends to fit, politically, with a certain construction or power arrangement of a target political group. It follows that if the construction or power of a target group changes over time, a policy may become less politically fit. In nature, the unfit genotype tends toward reproductive failure, and the unfit gene pool toward extinction. In the political arena, the unfit policy element tends toward disuse, and the unfit policy toward congressional oversight, amendment, or repeal.

Schneider and Ingram (1993) proposed four categories of policy targets, based on the interaction of social construction and political power. The "advantaged" (e.g., World War II veterans) have a positive social construction and considerable political power. "Contenders" (e.g., business tycoons) have political power but a dubious social construction. "Dependents" (e.g., mothers) lack political power but enjoy a positive social construction. "Deviants" (e.g., communists) lack political power and are negatively constructed.

Harold Lasswell (1958) defined politics as the process that determines who gets what, when, and how. Schneider and Ingram (1993) essentially defined four categories of who and, for each category, characterized the what and explained the how. Advantaged targets are likely to receive an abundance of policy benefits overtly and have considerable control in designing policy. Contenders have modest control over the policies that affect them, and they receive benefits covertly, while being assigned burdens (including regulations) that are often symbolic. Dependents have little control over the policy process and receive symbolic benefits for which they must grovel in the bureaucracy. Deviants have no control over the policy process; they receive few benefits and many burdens.

For some policies (e.g., comprehensive tax reform), multiple targets run the gamut of social construction and political power. However, it is important to distinguish between a policy subject for which behavior is to be altered in pursuit of a goal, and a policy subject to which benefits or burdens are to accrue in fulfillment of a goal. Of the two policy subjects, the latter is the ultimate target. The former is a proximate target that could also be viewed as a distal agent (Fig. 1). With ESA, the goal of which is to conserve species, the agents are clearly FWS and NMFS (Fig. 2). Proximate targets include all other federal agencies, habitat modifiers, species traffickers, and other nations. The ultimate targets, however, are nonhuman species.

Nonhuman species have distinct social constructions that may be assessed with valuation techniques. Furthermore, although nonhuman species cannot literally participate in the political arena, they do have unsolicited political power held in trust for them by interest groups, which are the fundamental units of political power in pluralist theories of democracy. Save the Redwoods, the Foundation for North American Wild Sheep, and Trout Unlimited are interest groups that wield power in trust.

Assessing the social construction and political power dynamics of non-human species entails at least six questions: Are all types of species equally constructed in the eyes of the American public? If not, then which types are appreciated or valued the most? What types of demographic factors influence species valuation? What traits of species are used by the public in valuing species? What is the distribution of political representation among types of species? Is recovery effort allocation predictable with the social construction/political power model of Schneider and Ingram?

Kellert (1996) summarized answers to the first three questions and speculated on the fourth question. However, Kellert's summary stemmed primarily from survey respondents' 1978 valuation of thirty-three individual species. After two decades of controversial endangered species issues, and with more than a thousand species listed by FWS as threatened or endangered, a suitable assessment required current valuation of broad categories of species. We therefore conducted a nationwide mail survey following the protocol of Salant and Dillman (1994), with the demographics of our survey respondents resembling those of the voting public more than those of the U.S. population at large (Table 3). We shall briefly describe our methodology here; a more thorough assessment of our methods and statistical analyses is found in Czech et alia (1998).

We defined eight types of species (birds, mammals, reptiles, amphibians, fish, plants, invertebrates, and microorganisms) and seven factors for potential use in prioritizing species for conservation (apparent ecological importance, body size, cultural and historical traits, intelligence or behavioral complexity, monetary value, physical attractiveness, and rarity). To determine relative values of species types and prioritization factors, we used visual analog scaling, whereby the respondent indicates value by marking a point along a spectrum ranging from 0 to 100 — from no importance to most importance. Further on in the questionnaire we instructed respondents to rank the same types of species in order of importance, requiring them to prioritize and allowing us to cross-check the scaled data.

For each respondent, we totaled the values ascribed to each species type to create an indicator called "total value," and we tested the effects of demographic characteristics on total value. These characteristics in-

TABLE 3. *Demographic Features of the General Public, Voting Public, and Survey Respondents*

Demographic Feature	U.S. Mean (%)	U.S. Voter Mean (%)	Respondent Mean (%)
Mean age	34.5	46.6	51.6
<30 years age	42.9	22	13
30–44 years age	24.5	38	25
45–59 years age	16	24	32
>59 years age	16.5	16	30
% male	49.1	46	70
Urban:rural	75:25	unknown	73:27
eastern	68.2	68.7	67
western[a]	31.8	31.3	33
high school graduates	82	94	99
college graduates	23	40	43
Democrat	47	38	38
Republican	43	35	35
Independent	10	27	21
unemployed	5.4	2.1	2

Sources: Famighetti (1996), Stanley and Niemi (1995), and U.S. Bureau of the Census (1996).
[a] "Western" means from California, Oregon, Washington, Idaho, Montana, Wyoming, Utah, Nevada, Arizona, New Mexico, Colorado, North Dakota, South Dakota, Texas, Oklahoma, Kansas, Alaska, or Hawaii.

cluded age, gender, region, type of residence, hectares of property owned, education, type of employer, environmental organization membership, and political party membership.

To gauge the political power held in trust for species, we compiled a database of the nongovernmental conservation organizations (NGOs) listed by Gordon (1996) and identified those devoted to the conservation of less than four types of species. We found 126 organizations devoted to one type of species (e.g., Hawk and Owl Trust), and 481 organizations are devoted to broad issues of conservation (e.g., American Conservation Association). Five, however, are devoted to two types of species (e.g., Game Conservation International is concerned with mammals and birds), and one (American Society of Ichthyologists and Herpetologists) is devoted to three types of species (fish, reptiles, and amphibians). No organizations were devoted to more than three types unless they were concerned with wildlife in general (e.g., Native American Fish and Wildlife Society), in which case we classified them as having a broad interest in conservation.

As a measure of recovery effort allocation, we used federal and state expenditure data from fiscal year 1993 — the most recent data available (Babbitt 1995). We transformed relative values of species ascribed by respondents into amounts comparable with endangered species program expenditures for comparison purposes.

SUMMARY OF THE NATIONWIDE SURVEY RESULTS

Plants, birds, and mammals, among which there are no significant differences in public valuation, are valued significantly more than fish, reptiles, amphibians, invertebrates, and microorganisms (Table 4). Fish, however, are valued significantly more than reptiles, amphibians, invertebrates, and microorganisms. Microorganisms are valued significantly less than all other species types. There are no significant differences among reptiles, amphibians, and invertebrates. We detected similar differences among the ranks of the eight types of species (Table 5), except most notably that reptiles were ranked lower than amphibians and no higher than microorganisms.

There is no effect of age, gender, region, type of residence, acres of property owned, education, or type of employer on total value. However, we emphasize that the detection of such effects is limited to the traits defined for each of these factors (Table 6). For example, only two regions, one east of the Great Plains and one from the Great Plains westward, were defined.

Significant effects were, however, associated with environmental organization and political party membership. Not surprisingly, members of environmental organizations value nonhuman species more than nonmembers. Republicans value species significantly less than Democrats and Independents. Respondents defining themselves politically as "Other" valued nonhuman species at an intermediate level not significantly different from the level ascribed by Independents or the two common parties.

The most important factors used by the public in valuing species for conservation are apparent ecological importance and rarity (Table 7). Each of the seven factors listed is significantly different from the others in

TABLE 4. Differences in Importance of Species Types as Rated by the Public

Group A	Mean Importance of A	Group B	Mean Importance of B	Mean Difference of A/B Pairs	t Ratio, Degrees of Freedom	Probability of Type I Error; Reject H_0 if P < (0.05/13) = .0038
Plants	72.19	Birds	71.25	0.93	1.10, 605	0.2723
Plants	72.19	Mammals	70.87	1.36	1.37, 604	0.1721
Plants	72.19	Fish	68.15	4.06	4.83, 603	<0.0001; reject H_0
Birds	71.25	Mammals	70.87	0.43	0.62, 604	0.5353
Birds	71.25	Fish	68.15	3.14	4.37, 603	<0.0001; reject H_0
Mammals	70.87	Fish	68.15	2.95	3.89, 603	0.0001; reject H_0
Fish	68.15	Reptiles	59.32	8.71	9.84, 602	<0.01; reject H_0
Reptiles	59.32	Amphibians	58.51	0.93	1.19, 598	0.2363
Reptiles	9.32	Invertebrates	57.23	2.12	2.73, 603	0.0064
Reptiles	59.32	Microorganisms	52.05	7.42	7.28, 586	<0.0001; reject H_0
Amphibians	58.51	Invertebrates	57.23	1.26	1.67, 600	0.0959
Amphibians	58.51	Microorganisms	52.05	6.20	6.71, 582	<0.0001; reject H_0
Invertebrates	57.23	Microorganisms	52.05	4.85	5.96, 588	<0.0001; reject H_0

TABLE 5. *Differences in Importance of Species Types as Ranked by the Public*

Group A	Mean Rank of A	Group B	Mean Rank of B	Mean B-A Rank Difference	Wilcoxon Sign-Rank Value, N	Probability of Type I Error; Reject H_o if $p < (0.05/9) = .0056$
Mammals	2.66	Plants	3.02	.3549	8659, 510	.009
Mammals	2.66	Birds	3.45	.7843	23361, 510	.000; reject H_o
Plants	3.02	Birds	3.45	.4294	11317, 510	.001; reject H_o
Birds	3.45	Fish	3.74	.2922	9947, 510	.002; reject H_o
Fish	3.74	Amphibians	5.24	1.5039	38693, 510	.000; reject H_o
Amphibians	5.24	Reptiles	5.75	.5098	17536, 510	.000; reject H_o
Reptiles	5.75	Microorganisms	5.98	.2314	5574, 510	.093
Reptiles	5.75	Invertebrates	6.15	.4000	12742, 510	.000; reject H_o
Microorganisms	5.98	Invertebrates	6.15	.1686	1999, 510	.541

TABLE 6. *Effects of Demographic Parameters on Species Valuation*

Demographic Parameter	Traits	N	R Square	F Ratio	Probability of Type I Error; Reject H_0 if $p < (0.05/7) = .0071$
Age	continuous	556	.0030	1.54	.2150
Gender	male, female[a]	573	.0044	2.5151	.1133
Region	East, West[a]	577	.0004	.2583	.6115
Type of residence	urban, suburban, rural	571	.0021	.5926	.5532
Acres of property owned	0, <1, 1–10, 10–100, 100–1000, >1000	571	.0066	.7508	.5857
Education	did not finish high school, high school diploma, some college, bachelor's degree, some graduate studies, graduate degree, technical or trade school	572	.0049	.4599	.8380
Political party	Democrat, Republican, Independent, Other	526	.0274	4.9067	.0023; reject H_0
Environmental organization membership	yes, no	561	.0144	8.1606	.0044; reject H_0
Type of employer	small business, corporation, federal government, other government, state government, self-employed, unemployed, retired, school or university, other	553	.0225	1.3857	.1912

[a] "West" means Washington, Oregon, California, Arizona, Nevada, Idaho, Montana, Wyoming, Colorado, Utah, New Mexico, Texas, Oklahoma, Kansas, Nebraska, South Dakota, North Dakota, Alaska, and Hawaii. "East" means all other states.

TABLE 7. *Differences in Importance of Factors Used to Prioritize Species for Conservation*

Valuation Factor A	Mean A	Valuation Factor B	Mean B	Mean (A–B)	t-Ratio, DF	Probability of A = B; Reject H₀ if p < (.05/6) = .0083
Apparent ecological importance	77.67	Rarity	73.84	3.78	3.57, 597	0.0004; reject H$_o$
Rarity	73.84	Cultural traits	53.05	20.80	15.14, 594	<0.0001; reject H$_o$
Cultural traits	53.05	Intelligence	49.85	2.93	2.30, 594	0.0219
Cultural traits	53.05	Monetary value	32.35	20.67	14.65, 594	<0.0001; reject H$_o$
Intelligence	49.85	Monetary value	32.35	17.61	12.75, 596	<0.0001; reject H$_o$
Monetary value	32.35	Physical attractiveness	29.19	3.22	2.75, 595	0.0062; reject H$_o$
Physical attractiveness	29.19	Body size	28.12	1.12	1.21, 596	0.2268

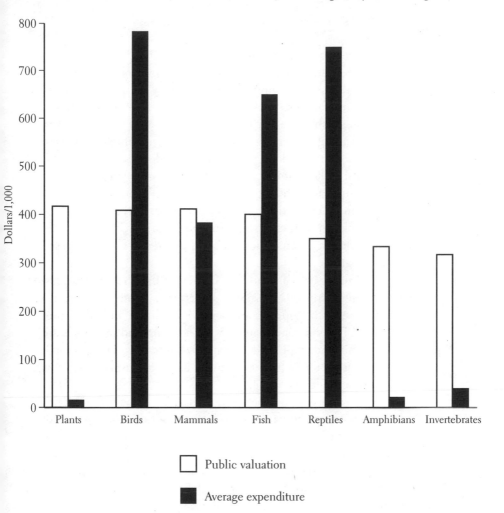

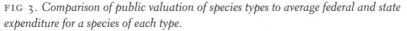

FIG 3. *Comparison of public valuation of species types to average federal and state expenditure for a species of each type.*

its importance for evaluating species for conservation, except for physical attractiveness and body size — the two least important factors.

For plants, amphibians, and invertebrates, spending is far less than that congruent with public valuation (Fig. 3). For reptiles, birds, and fish, spending is far more than congruent.

More political power is held in trust for birds, which are represented by fifty-seven NGOs, than for mammals (40), fish (32), plants (19), reptiles (5), invertebrates (4), amphibians (1), or microorganisms (0).

IMPLICATIONS OF THE NATIONWIDE SURVEY

The demographic profile of respondents indicates that they represent a larger proportion of the voting public than of the general public (Table 3), as expected in surveys pertaining to public policy. Respondents, however, were older and far more likely to be male than either the U.S. population or the voting public. Kellert and Berry (1987) found that males were more concerned about conserving wildlife species and habitats than were females, who tended to be more concerned about domestic animals and individual animal welfare. If that still holds, then males are predisposed to respond to a survey on endangered species — and more likely to consider the topic in electoral decisions. Although our survey results may include a male bias in mathematical terms, they may effectively provide a better approximation of voter values to be considered in the endangered species political arena.

Rating and ranking data support the conclusion that there are two distinct tiers of value ascribed to species by Americans. Plants, birds, mammals, and fish are in the top tier, and are valued higher than the other types of species. The differences among plants, birds, and mammals are practically insignificant, while fish are valued slightly less. There is some evidence that, within the bottom tier, invertebrates and microorganisms constitute a subtier of lowest value.

It is important to distinguish between ambivalence about the prioritization of bottom-tier species and ambivalence about the conservation of species therein. The scaled data indicate that the public considers the conservation of all types of species to be important, regardless of how they are prioritized. Even the lowest-rated type of species (microorganisms) was rated at 52.05 (Table 4). In this respect, the survey results seem inconsistent with Kellert's bar graph (1996:41) portraying the "negativistic" attitude as the third most prominent of the attitudes held by Americans toward nonhuman species. This may indicate a shift in public attitude; Kellert's primary data was gathered in 1978 and supplemented with data from smaller and localized surveys (e.g., Kellert 1993). Our results are more consistent with the claim of Murphy et alia (1994:1) that "we have reached a pivotal moment in history, a time when public understanding and appreciation of biotic diversity is at an all-time high."

Alternatively, Kellert's method for ascribing the "negativistic" attitude may not be consistent with "negativism" in the vernacular. Kellert considered a survey result that "60% reported being afraid to touch a snake" (1980:48) as reflecting the negativistic attitude and reported "an aversion to insects in the home" as well as "a fear of stinging insects, spiders, and scorpions" as evidence for a negativistic attitude (1993:849). Most Americans, however, would probably consider such sentiments natural and appropriate. We do not challenge the validity of Kellert's statistical cluster analyses and subsequent research, but perhaps "negativism" is a misnomer as applied to the cluster it describes. In fact, Kellert's description of the attitude allows for a "healthy distancing and even respect" of nonhuman species (1996:25).

Hayward acknowledged that "values always come socially mediated" but elaborated, "This need not mean taking the view, however, that values are a purely social — and therefore contingent or conventional — construct. For society itself is a part of that non-contingent reality we call nature. So which values get constructed and how is unlikely to be arbitrary, even though the processes involved will be complex and not always easy to discover" (1994:48). In this case, the processes are not even complex: fear and respect are commonly evoked by pain-inflicting species, dangerous species, and species that are difficult for the lay person to distinguish from dangerous species (e.g., snakes in general). Such emotions seem rational and positive. Although truly negative (abusive or irrational) attitudes may be encountered, the portrayal of "negativism" as a dominant theme in the American psyche no longer seems appropriate.

The high rating of apparent ecological importance among the factors used to evaluate species reflects an ecologistic perspective, in which the primary concern is "for the environment as a system, for interrelationships between wildlife species and natural habitats" (Kellert 1980:42). That even the lower tier of species is considered important is further evidence for an ecologistic perspective, as is the high rating of rarity. Despite Kellert's assertion (1996), derived from the past two decades, that the least frequently encountered values of nature are the dominionistic, scientific, and ecologistic, the truth of that statement no longer seems to apply to the ecologistic perspective. A bar chart presented by Kellert (45) that covers the period from 1900 to 1976 shows that the ecologistic perspective was increasing rapidly from the early 1940s on, and nothing indicates a reversal in that trend between 1976 and now. There is a strong ecologistic element in the public view of species conservation, which is not surprising considering the efforts at public education expended by environmental organizations since the 1960s. Perhaps the ascendancy of the ecologistic perspective has usurped psychological territory once claimed by the negativistic perspective.

The clearly distinguished prioritization of birds, mammals, fish, and plants may, however, point to a number of other perspectives. It could suggest an aesthetic perspective, which stresses the "charismatic megaverte-brates" (Kellert 1996:15). It could also suggest a utilitarian perspective, because birds, mammals, fish, and plants are harvested by many people. The data on factors of valuation seemingly contradict both interpretations, because physical attractiveness, body size, and monetary value constitute a lower tier of evaluation factors. Such factors, however, have long been primary determinants of public preferences for species (Kellert 1985; Burg-hardt and Herzog 1980), and it is unlikely that they have been discarded.

There are three likely explanations for the low scores of physical attrac-tiveness, body size, and monetary value. First, people may consider it po-litically incorrect to admit a preference based on appearance or monetary value, because it is politically incorrect to discriminate among humans on the basis of race or class. Second, the low scores may not indicate unimportance as much as they reflect the importance of ecological fac-tors. For example, a respondent who rated rarity at an importance level of 80 may have rated attractiveness at a level of 40, not thinking that attrac-tiveness was unimportant but that rarity was twice as important. The third explanation is based on Kellert's insight that aesthetic perspectives tend to be manifested emotionally, and utilitarian perspectives tend to be "fre-quently expressed and therefore learned as broad belief orientations," whereas ecologistic perspectives are cognitive (1996:212). Responding to a questionnaire (as with voting) is primarily a cognitive event, albeit influ-enced by emotional and subconscious factors.

There is little doubt that the public retains a strong symbolic attitude toward species conservation, an ancient attitude interwoven with human evolution (Wilson 1984). The importance ratings of cultural traits and intelligence support this interpretation, as do the importance ratings of birds and mammals, which are the most symbolically important species (Kellert 1996). The inclusion of fish and plants in the upper tier of species may also reflect a naturalistic perspective, which "often takes expression through . . . birding, fishing, hunting, whalewatching, wildlife tourism, visiting zoos, and the like" (Kellert 1996:12).

More important than determining which perspective is most reflected by the prioritization of top-tier species is to recognize that a number of otherwise conflicting perspectives converge to prioritize these species. The political empowerment availed by such convergence is considerable, and its reflection in policy should be expected and employed by conserva-tionists, especially considering the umbrella qualities of large, wide-ranging vertebrates.

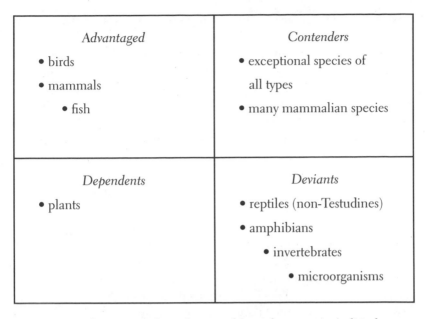

Advantaged	Contenders
• birds • mammals • fish	• exceptional species of all types • many mammalian species
Dependents	Deviants
• plants	• reptiles (non-Testudines) • amphibians • invertebrates • microorganisms

FIG 4. *Types of species as policy subjects in the social construction/political power matrix of Schneider and Ingram (1993). Relative placement conveys information: social construction decreases along the X axis, and political power increases along the Y axis.*

To employ Schneider and Ingram's social construction/political power matrix, the least arbitrary way to separate species based on social construction is to include birds, mammals, plants, and fish in the advantaged/ dependent half. Reptiles, amphibians, invertebrates, and microorganisms are included in the contender/deviant half, recognizing that exceptions may exist.

Political power assessment may be used to finalize the classification, which may then be considered in relation to the allocation of benefits. Plants are represented by only 13 percent (19/148) of the NGOs devoted to the socially constructed upper tier of species. The sharp demarcation between plants and the other highly valued species types justifies the assignment of plants to the dependent category (Fig. 4). As expected for dependents, expenditures on plants are disproportionately less than public valuation (Fig. 3).

Birds, for which 1993 spending was nearly twice the level of public valuation, are represented by fifty-four NGOs and are clearly the most advantaged type. A glance at some of the NGOs associated with birds reveals real political power. Ducks Unlimited, for instance, has a membership of about 550,000 (Gordon 1996), more than seven of the powerful "Group of Ten" environmental organizations (Switzer 1994). Founded in 1937, Ducks Unlimited employs an impressive organization dispersed throughout North America and surely has more political power than all of the combined NGOs affiliated with reptiles, amphibians, invertebrates, and microorganisms.

The political power analysis also helps to explain why expenditures for amphibians and invertebrates are disproportionately less than public valuation. Almost no one has mobilized to support these species exclusively.

The most intriguing data are those associated with reptiles. First, the rating and ranking data indicated some ambivalence or perhaps confusion among the public in how it views reptiles. Considering the negative biblical symbolism involving snakes, the proportion of dangerous species in the reptile class, the evolutionary distance between reptiles and humans' and the unfathomable natural history that distance entails, including poikilothermy (coldbloodedness), it would not be surprising if people had second thoughts about the valence of reptiles.

Relative to the other "deviant" species, reptiles have a political advantage but not enough to justify status as a "contender." Plants have thirteen supportive NGOs, and they were logically placed in the lower level of political support; it would be illogical to categorize reptiles (five NGOs) in the upper level. Benefits are supposed to be disproportionately low for deviants, but spending per species on reptiles exceeds that for all other types except birds (Fig. 3). Meanwhile, reptiles have no ecological features that pose an unprecedented fiscal challenge to researchers or managers, and the types of NGOs affiliated with reptiles would not appear to wield an inordinate amount of political power.

But the list of those NGOs — American Society of Ichthyologists and Herpetologists, Desert Tortoise Council, Desert Tortoise Preserve Committee, Gopher Tortoise Council, New York Tortoise and Turtle Society — reveals that the order Testudines, at least, is well represented in the political arena. Tortoises, especially, evoke an extreme disproportion of political allegiance within their class, far more than other favored groups like waterfowl, bears, and salmonids, and that disproportion is reflected in the distribution of benefits. Of the $23,605,900 spent on the thirty-two threatened and endangered reptile species in 1993, 98 percent ($23,135,500) was spent on the thirteen turtle and tortoise species; almost 66 percent ($15,492,700) on the desert tortoise alone (Babbitt 1995). Turtles and tortoises, then, are worthy of contender status. Even that designation probably underrates the Testudines, however, because if the social construction of Testudines had been assessed in isolation from that of the other reptiles, Testudines would likely be designated as advantaged. They are associated with positive cultural symbols (like the tortoise and the hare), are often kept as pets, and are a common subject of decorative art.

The logical interpretation of the reptile data, then, is that reptiles comprise two distinct tiers of social construction: Testudines and the others. One might even expand the argument by classifying tortoises as advantaged and turtles as strong dependents or contenders, but the evidence gets scanty at that level of distinction. Non-Testudines reptiles, however, are clearly deviants. This strong dichotomy offers an explanation for the higher statistical variance of reptile valuation than of any other vertebrate group (Czech et al. 1998).

The contender concept is problematic as applied to nonhuman species. Whereas a human interest group, even one reviled by the public, can attain political power via diligence and craft, species lacking a positive social construction are much less likely to accrue political power. Nevertheless, the contender category is useful for describing species of contested social construction that generate political activity. Exceptional species from all categories may qualify as contenders, but mammals probably constitute the majority. Although mammals are represented by 25 percent (40/158) of the species-oriented NGOs, they also attract political opposition, especially predators and rodents (Carrier and Czech 1996), which represent a high proportion of endangered mammals.

The consistency with which the eight types of species accrue ESA benefits, as predicted by the social construction/political power model, is remarkable. When non-Testudines reptiles are distinguished from Testudines, only mammals do not receive benefits consistent with the model; that result can be explained by the high number of mammalian exceptions better classified as contenders. Advantaged species receive the most benefits by far; benefits to dependents and deviants are slight.

Of course, social construction and political power are correlated (Czech et al. 1998), and causality is certainly involved. Nevertheless, both are important and harbor distinct implications. For example, an important ratio to consider is that of social construction to benefits. It is possible for a policy subject to obtain enough benefits as to evoke ill feelings among other stakeholders, as when the northern spotted owl controversy erupted in the Northwest. When that happens, a species may decline in status from advantaged to contender, and benefits may subside. Mean-

TABLE 8. *Ratio of Public Valuation to Spending per Species*

Type of Species	Ratio
Plants	4.95
Amphibians	2.32
Invertebrates	1.07
Mammals	0.19
Fish	0.10
Birds	0.09
Reptiles	0.08

Note: Amounts spent per species were divided by one thousand, for analytical convenience.

while, if a species receives few benefits, it may reap proportionally higher benefits from each new political effort. As it moves from the dependent category to the advantaged, or from the deviant to the contender, its benefits will increase. Assuming that is the case, and disregarding umbrella effects, then those concerned with the conservation of species in general may be most efficient at this point by focusing their political efforts on plants and amphibians (Table 8).

Finally, factors other than social construction and political power operate to affect spending practices and to effect spending discrepancies. For example, the logistics involved with migratory fish research and the magnitude of assessment and mitigation projects associated with salmon fisheries in the Northwest are formidable, providing an alternative or supplemental explanation for the relative abundance of expenditures on fish. Dwyer et alia related an unpublished report by Harvard researchers, who apparently found that "species that generate economic conflicts tend to elicit extra political attention and in turn generate spending irrespective of biological or associated priorities" (1995:738). Nevertheless, the social construction/political power matrix provides a helpful tool for interpreting why certain types of species benefit disproportionately from ESA and, perhaps, for developing political strategies for species conservation.

THE SOCIAL CONSTRUCTION OF NATURE

Social construction theory is helpful for understanding how species get listed and how recovery plans are implemented. For the conservationist, however, great care should be taken in propounding and applying social construction theory to the entire biosphere and all activities that occur therein. Lease pointed out, "We and our world may well be real, but intelligible access to that reality is constructed and produced and ultimately incomplete" (1995:5). That is clearly true, but carried to its philosophical extreme, social constructivism posits that reality is indeed nonexistent; entities and events exist only as experienced and interpreted. The number of people subscribing to that ontology caused Shepard to lament, "Intellectuals seem caught up in the dizzy spectacle and brilliant subjectivity of a kind of deconstructionist fireworks in which origins and truth have become meaningless" (1995:21). The danger of such a philosophy to species conservation is its denial of reality and the passivity bred by that denial in the policy arena; species endangerment is deemed unreal, and policies to conserve species are deemed unnecessary.

Recognizing the recklessness of "radical constructivism" in the context of apparent environmental calamity, Hayles proposed a "constrained constructivism" whereby not all interpretations are equally valid. She related how different cultures may have explained gravity and concluded, "No matter how gravity is conceived, no viable model could predict that when someone steps off a cliff on earth, she will remain spontaneously suspended in midair. Although the constraints that lead to this result are interpreted differently in different paradigms, they operate universally to eliminate certain configurations from the realm of possible answers" (1995:52).

In Hayles's constrained constructivism, the claim of truth is replaced by the claim of consistency and is vulnerable to negation. As long as an interpretation of an event falls within constraints, it is deemed worthy of deliberation, at least for the time being. Ironically, this brand of constructivism is virtually identical to the predominant philosophy of science (Popper 1994), which adamant social construction theorists would prefer to dethrone as the most respectable source of knowledge. The "constrained" social construction of a phenomenon is like a hypothesis to be tested and will gradually become like a theory if continually found consistent with knowledge and evidence.

Altruistically inclined social construction theorists strive to deconstruct unjustly constructed images. Like critical theorists in general, they would elevate the maligned and dethrone the advantaged. Their endeavor seems far more laudable than ignoring reality and its attendant problems. Deconstruction too, however, can run amuck. Conservation biologists who propose "equal rights for parasites" (Windsor 1995:1) seem impervious to the broader implications of social construction theory. Policymakers, on the other hand, tend to be lawyers, economists, and others "trained by professors in the humanities and social sciences, many of whom are sympathetic to constructionist views" (Soule 1995:161).

To complicate matters, social construction theory can be bastardized for political purposes, sometimes to the obvious detriment of endangered species. For example, the Wise Use movement argues that extractive industries are just as natural and therefore no less desirable than aboriginal forms of extraction. As Soule (1995) pointed out, the Wise Use movement even argues that industrial activities mimic natural processes and are good for ecosystems. The Wise Use philosopher can argue that the representation of industry as a threat to ecological integrity is a social construction warped by the suburbanized, well-to-do paradigm of the media.

Somewhere between disuse and overuse, however, social construction theory may be productively employed for policy analysis. Page alluded to the same: "I am not arguing here for a pure cultural relativism. Our ecological problems are real, and some ideas about valuation and decision are more useful than others" (1992:99). For species conservation, assessing the social constructions of species is useful — as is attempting to deconstruct harmful myths associated with unjustly classified deviants — but denying nature its existence is not. By employing a constrained constructivism, policy design theory remains consistent with science and critical theory while shunning the demagoguery that both can unwittingly produce.

7

Technical Legitimacy of the Endangered Species Act

Policy design theory views the policy sciences and policy specialism as insufficient foundations for policy analysis and emphasizes that technical legitimacy must be assessed with an eye toward policy context, because technical legitimacy is but a subset of policy legitimacy. For example, designing a breeder reactor that would power half the nation may be technically legitimate. Fiscal and political limitations render much of that technical legitimacy moot, however. The boundaries of policy legitimacy do not encompass the sphere of technical legitimacy (Fig. 5) but, when apparent, should inform the assessment of technical legitimacy, lest the latter result in wasted resources and misleading results. Only within the ambit of policy legitimacy does policy design theory acknowledge the importance of technical legitimacy to sound policy. In this chapter, we consider the technical legitimacy of ESA and what portion of that legitimacy intersects the sphere of policy legitimacy.

A prevalent technical criticism of ESA is that the species is the wrong focus for biodiversity conservation. As Dwyer et alia noted, "Everyone complains about the single species focus of the [ESA]. . . . No one really believes it makes sense biologically or economically to conserve species using a balkanized project-by-project approach" (1995:736). Critics allege that ESA has become unwieldy because there are nearly twelve hundred species listed by FWS as threatened or endangered (Bender 1999), with a burgeoning list of candidates—official or unofficial—to consider. Listing, recovery planning, and critical habitat designation is technically and politically challenging in many cases. Nonetheless, species-based conservation may be more wieldy than the alternatives.

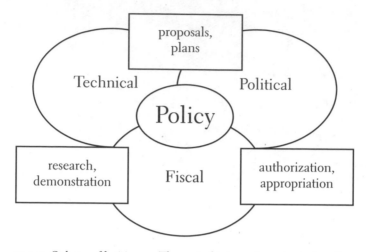

FIG 5. *Spheres of legitimacy. The central intersection represents policy legitimacy. Rectangles represent intermediate results of intersecting spheres.*

Neither species endangerment nor attempts to address it are new (chapter 2), and many of these attempts have been successful (chapter 3). The ubiquity and degree of the problem is new, but the species concept is not. Developed by John Ray and Carolus Linnaeus during the Enlightenment, the species concept was a revolutionary advance in natural science (Boorstin 1983) and has been continually honed ever since Darwin made it a focus of natural science (Cracraft 1989). Discussing the intergenerational transfer of social and ecological models, Worster emphasized, "most of the innovations we have recently made are not likely to survive, that what is old among us is by that very fact worthy of respect and mimicry, that what is *very* old is likely to be wise" (1995:81). The basic unit of ecology, for a very long time, has been the species; perhaps the resulting management focus on species should be given the benefit of the doubt. As Novacek said, "The biological world is a delicate web of connections, a network of species . . . The building blocks of these finely tuned and, as we are increasingly aware, highly vulnerable systems, are the species themselves" (1992:101). The species concept, then, is entrenched in policy and management for legitimate reasons: historical focus and technical pertinence.

Despite the rich academic history of the species concept, the continual honing of species definitions, and the core status of species in natural resources policy, attempts to find management substitutes for the species approach are mounting. Anderson said, "Traditionally, managers have focused on single-species management; however, community management with the concept of biodiversity has become more popular in recent years" (1995:70). Anderson's essay was couched in a history collection illustrating the evolution of natural resources management. Knight and George (1995) followed Anderson's essay on wildlife conservation by proposing three approaches to employ in the futuristic community management: (1) a species approach, (2) an ecosystem approach, and (3) a landscape approach.

The species approach to community management would literally be species management, and hardly new. It would emphasize the importance of species other than those of material value to humans, but that trend is not new either; ESA protects such listed species as the Coffin Cave mold beetle and the Dudley Bluffs bladderpod.

With the ecosystem approach, managers would "focus on ecosystem processes (e.g., tree gap formation, insect diseases, fire). This approach assumes that if ecosystems are properly functioning, then the naturally occurring biological diversity will be intact" (Knight and George 1995:281). Given that native species are the most common gauge of naturally occurring biological diversity, the ecosystem approach would be based on native species monitoring. If a species became endangered, the processes jeopardizing that species would be analyzed and, hopefully, halted in time to preserve the species. That is how ESA functions. After all, the purposes of ESA are to "provide a means whereby the ecosystems upon which endangered species and threatened species depend may be conserved" (Section 2[b]).

Knight and George continued, "A third way to manage for biological diversity is a landscape approach and relies on the principles generated from the discipline of landscape ecology. This strategy manipulates habitat and landscapes in such a way as to collectively influence groups in the desired direction. For example, to maintain songbird communities of late successional stage forests, agencies would want to manage forest stands for large size and decreasing edge and isolation" (1995:282). As with the ecosystem approach, the landscape approach would require an accounting of species (e.g., songbirds) and would prescribe management intended to preserve the ones that become endangered.

Each of the "community management" approaches requires the monitoring and management of species, which requires the management of habitats and therefore other species, as with ESA. The proclivity of alternative management approaches to return to species management is illustrated by the Environmental Protection Agency's (EPA's) experience with pesticide registration. After ESA was passed, and pursuant to Section 7, EPA began evaluating one pesticide at a time and consulting with FWS in cases where the pesticide had potential to jeopardize a species. The process seemed unwieldy, so EPA tried a "cluster approach," whereby pesticides with the same types of uses (e.g., broadleaf herbicides) were evaluated as a group. The FWS would then prepare its biological opinion to include all endangered species that could be affected by the type of use (e.g., forest opening maintenance). The cluster approach was akin to an ecosystem process approach and created a tangle of technical, administrative, legal, and political problems. Frustrated by the complications of the cluster approach, the U.S. Department of Agriculture led the farming community into becoming one of ESA's staunchest detractors (Serfis 1991). Congressional intervention was required, and political capital was consumed by EPA and withdrawn from ESA. Finally, in 1989 EPA developed a "new" approach: endangered species were to be analyzed one by one for their susceptibility to the various pesticides in their environment.

TECHNICAL LEGITIMACY AND POLICY LEGITIMACY

The invocation of landscape ecology, ecosystem management, or any other approach is an understandable attempt to evade the "logistic and financial nightmare of addressing the biological needs of thousands of endangered species and candidates" (Noss 1991:228). Perhaps to the disappointment of many scholars, we believe that the species approach to conservation remains more viable than the ecosystem approach. Critics of ESA and the species approach sense this, too, and stop short of abandoning either the ESA or the species approach to conservation. Rather, they promote a pluralistic approach in which both species management and ecosystem management are joined in a coordinated, comprehensive conservation effort (Kohm 1991). That calling is hard for a conservationist to argue with, but it warrants a closer look.

The ESA was passed with political plaudits and has survived a number of political challenges since. Few in the technical arena deny that, with sufficient resources, it could be implemented to outstanding effect. The policy legitimacy of ESA is proven. Its shortcoming is fiscal; limited appropriations have become more constraining as more species have become endangered (Campbell 1991).

The potential of ecosystem management in the policy arena is less promising. Unlike endangered species, ecosystems have not simultaneously inspired the actions of biologists and politicians. Politicians have supported the majesty of national parks and some level of ecological integrity for other public landholdings, but in no instance have they been roused to action by "a discrete unit that consists of living and non-living parts, interacting to form a stable system" (Allaby 1994:132), because neither has the electorate. However, the most debilitating weakness of ecosystem management, for the purpose of species conservation, may be technical.

A cogent policy dialogue cannot be pursued without agreement on terminology. Czech (1995a) cited a variety of ecosystem management definitions, most of which were too broad to be administratively meaningful. Salwasser noted that ecosystem management "is a hard concept to define and even harder to prescribe" (1991:252). Czech and Krausman called it a "catch-all concept" because "ecosystem" and "management" are comprehensive terms in their own right (1997a:671). Beyond defining the concept itself, there is no widely accepted system for defining the boundaries or key indicators of ecosystems. Ecosystems and communities are neither closed nor static. As Soule noted, "Certainly the idea that species live in integrated communities is a myth. So-called biotic communities, a misleading term, are constantly changing in membership" (1995:143).

From a spatial perspective, environmentalists often recommend that citizens think globally and act locally. From a temporal perspective, perhaps the land manager should think geologically and act administratively. In an administrative time frame, some physical and biological change within the boundaries of any area can be observed. The time for prompt administrative action is when the rate of such change is without precedent in a geological time frame, as it is now in the United States and the world. Ecosystem management, especially as an approach to species conservation, will require a great investment of time to become operational, time during which species will go extinct. Administrative time would be better invested in the up-and-running species approach, or — better yet — in politically addressing the socioeconomic causes of species endangerment (chapter 8).

That doesn't make the species approach any less daunting but suggests that a more appropriate, if bluntly practical, way to battle the complexity of endangered species conservation is to prioritize species for conservation while acknowledging the utility of the species as the focus for management. The ESA prioritizes species — to an extent.

PRIORITIZATION OF SPECIES FOR CONSERVATION

The most comprehensive and proficient technical analysis of ESA was conducted by the National Research Council (NRC) (1995), but we question one of the council's findings. The council noted that ESA fails to protect invertebrates and plants below the subspecies level of taxonomy but protects distinct populations of vertebrates. It judged that division to be arbitrary in a technical sense, a position shared by Murphy (1991) and similar to Grumbine's observation that "the act plays taxonomic favorites, giving animals stronger protection than plants (section 9). This has no justification in conservation biology" (1992:95). However, these authors did not explore the potential justifications of species prioritization.

The boundaries of political and fiscal legitimacy do not encompass every species. That fact is reflected by ESA appropriations history (Campbell 1991). Therefore, numerous conservation biologists have proposed phylogenetic methods to prioritize species for conservation (Crozier and Kusmierski 1994; Faith 1992; Vane-Wright et al. 1991; Williams et al. 1991). Phylogenetics is the study of the evolutionary relationships among species or, metaphorically speaking, the study of the branching patterns of the evolutionary tree of life. Witting et al. (1994), in accounting for phylogenetic diversity and ecological risk (of species loss), broadened the consideration to a more complete scope of biological concerns in proposing a method of prioritization. In doing so, however, they illustrated how a complex phylogenetic prioritization scheme can be made overwhelmingly abstruse by additional variables. In fact, for multispecies prioritization proposals as a whole, the formulae are rather intimidating and the information required to use them is difficult to obtain or substantiate, as Faith (1992) readily admitted. Those are fatal flaws in a democratic policy arena. Furthermore, conservation biologists have neglected two other variables that should be considered when prioritizing species for conservation: the amount of genetic information contained by species and the genetic capacity of species to evolve. We will discuss these relatively simple concepts before returning to the issue of phylogenetic distinctiveness.

One may not freely generalize about species characteristics associated with genetic information. For one thing, the amount of *functional, protein-coding* DNA (deoxyribonucleic acid, the principle constituent of genes and therefore heredity) is not correlated with the *entire* amount of DNA in a haploid set of chromosomes. In other words, the amount of functional DNA is not correlated with genome size, the measurement of which is referred to as "C-value." This counterintuitive phenomenon is called the "C-value paradox" (Li and Graur 1991:207). Nevertheless, Bird (1995) detected a correlation between an organism's complexity and its number of genes, at least. Small and relatively simple members of the animal kingdom (e.g., protozoa) require less DNA to support the limited repertoire of behaviors they exhibit. At the extreme are mitochondria, the cellular components which "de-evolved" from purple photosynthetic bacteria that infected an ancestral host about one billion years ago. Engaged in endosymbiosis ever since, they now perform a literally mindless task (energy production) and have a highly reduced genome (Palmer 1990). In their evolution toward simplicity, the tiny mitochondria retreated from the threshold of autonomous life.

As the number of genes increases, the number of possible tasks — and ways to perform them — does too. But these tasks can only be performed if the machinery to perform them is available. Beaks, horns, trunks, and antlers are examples of machinery that facilitate the performance of niche-widening tasks. Because machinery requires housing, behavioral complexity and genetic information are logically associated with body size. Probably the greatest obstacle to advancing the body size–genetic information relationship from theory to observation is measurement methodology. Genome size is too crude a measure of information because of the C-value paradox, which is probably a result of passively inherited "junk" DNA and actively accumulating selfish genes (Li and Graur 1991).

Species that, within reasonable doubt, contain more genetic information should be prioritized for conservation. In the analogy of the burning library, a large book tends to be more important to salvage than a small book because it tends to contain more information. (Of course, there are exceptions; we emphasize tendency.) The theoretical basis for a correlation of genetic information with body size lends technical legitimacy to the prioritization of vertebrates for conservation, especially in the current triage situation. As Woodwell pointed out, the disregard of evidence and logic by scientists seeking "hyperobjectivity" before tendering management implications "destroys the credibility of science and scientists as a source of common sense" (1989:14).

When rushing into the burning library, the firefighter with common sense would seek not only the large books but also the ones that took a long time to write. Future editions of these more profound documents, even reasonable facsimiles, would be unlikely. Periodicals, which come and go and could be more easily imitated, would receive the least attention. Species also get written, in a sense. Mutation provides a continual source of words, the published arrangement of which results from natural selection.

For two decades after the work of Zuckerkandl and Pauling (1965), it was popular to surmise that mutation rates were constant across taxa. In other words, it was thought that one "molecular clock" determined mutation rates for all DNA (Li and Graur 1991). However, research has begun to distinguish mutation rates among species; one could say that different species have different molecular clocks. Martin and Palumbi (1993:4087) noted, "Body size probably does not control the rate of DNA substitution directly but serves as a convenient guidepost for understanding the biological correlates of molecular rate heterogeneity" (1993:4087). They took data from the literature and illustrated a general trend of DNA evolutionary rate decreasing with body size. For example, they found that the most extreme results were the slow rates in whales and the fast rates in rodents. Their explanation was that species with higher metabolic rates — generally the smaller species — have shorter nucleotide generation times. (Nucleotides are the building blocks of DNA.)

We propose another, hypothetical basis for slower mutation rates in larger animals. Solar radiation is considered to be a significant cause of mutation and perhaps the primary power source that runs the molecular clock, but body tissue absorbs many wavelengths. Generally, and certainly within similar morphologies, the meiotic cells of large-bodied species are less exposed to radiation; they should mutate less frequently. Consider the great difference in astrophysical exposure between whales and rodents, for example.

Soule pointed out that "we are dealing with the problem that the rate of environmental change . . . is several orders of magnitude higher than the rate at which genes are substituted in these populations of vertebrates" (1983:115). Vertebrates tend to be much larger than invertebrates, and larger-bodied species have lower population densities and longer regeneration periods (Calder 1984). Neither recombination nor mutation inheritance events will occur as often in those species as they will in small-bodied species.

Species with slow molecular clocks or with other traits that hamper their molecular evolution should be technically prioritized for conservation, because they are less able to adapt to rapid environmental change without human assistance. There is evidence that large-bodied species have slower molecular clocks, and the life histories of large species render them less capable of prompt molecular evolution. If the relationship with body size is a crude one, it may nevertheless suffice for the crude distinction made by ESA — that is, between vertebrates and invertebrates.

There is no evidence that genetic information or molecular clock speed have been considered by the authors, implementers, or critics of ESA. The congruence of these genetic phenomena with the species prioritization of ESA is a matter of political serendipity. (Recall, from chapter 6, the low social construction/political power of invertebrates and microorganisms.) As we earlier alluded, however, there is widespread concern in conservation biology about the uniqueness of species. As Meffe and Carroll summarized it, "The evolutionary potential of life depends upon the variety of evolving lineages [phyletic variety], not just the number of species [genetic variety]. Lineages that have been evolving separately for long periods of time have many unique genes and gene combinations that would be lost were those lineages to become extinct" (1994:86). A lineage may be viewed as a branch on the evolutionary tree, where its distinctiveness is a function of its distance from other branches. This "distance" may be measured genetically as "the number of nucleotide substitutions per nucleotide site between two homologous DNA sequences that have accumulated since the divergence between the sequences" (Li and Graur 1991).

Genetic distance — and phylogenetic distinctiveness — results from DNA substitution, so the time it takes for a certain distance to be achieved is partly a function of the molecular clock. However, genetic distance should be considered on its own merits because, regardless of molecular clock speed, evolutionary investment may be gauged by it. For example, species A with a molecular clock speed of X may have achieved a genetic distance from its ancestor of Y, while a younger species B, despite a molecular clock speed of 3X, may have only achieved a genetic distance from its ancestor of Y/2 (Fig. 6.A). In this case, based only upon molecular clock speed and genetic distance, it would be logical to prioritize species A for conservation, since it not only has the slower clock but also the more distinct genome.

If, on the other hand, species A with a molecular clock speed of X has achieved a genetic distance from its ancestor of Y, while species B with a molecular clock speed of 3X has achieved a genetic distance from its ancestor of 3Y, the decision for prioritization becomes more difficult (Fig. 6.B). Species B has surpassed species A in genetic uniqueness and, from that standpoint, should be prioritized. But species A merits protection because it is less able to adapt to environmental change.

Furthermore, species B (an endangered species) may have achieved a

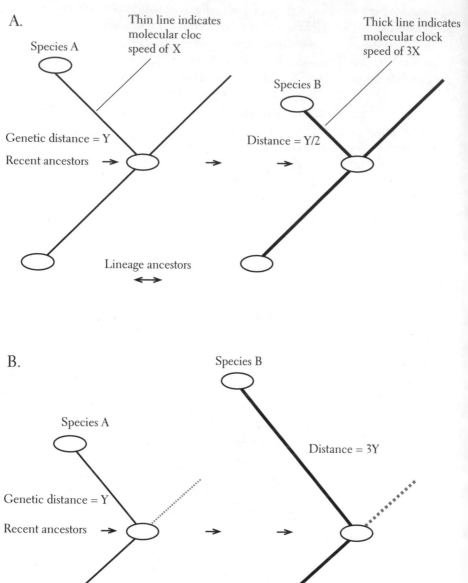

A.

Species A

Thin line indicates
molecular cloc
speed of X

Thick line indicates
molecular clock
speed of 3X

Species B

Genetic distance = Y

Recent ancestors →

Distance = Y/2

Lineage ancestors
↔

B.

Species B

Species A

Distance = 3Y

Genetic distance = Y

Recent ancestors →

Lineage ancestors
↔

genetic distance of X from species A (a common species). In another lineage, species N (an endangered species) may also have achieved a genetic distance of X from species M (a common species). However, the A/B lineage may have originated 50 million years before the M/N lineage. Assuming that there are no intermediary taxa in either lineage, then species B would logically be prioritized for conservation, because the evolutionary investment placed in it would be higher than that of species N. A more difficult choice would arise if species N had achieved a genetic distance of 2X.

Obviously, the use of genetic distance as a prioritization variable can become baffling, especially with whole species assemblages to consider. Multispecies, phylogenetic diversity schemes are prone to confusion, especially at the critical nexus of science and policy. In fact, Ehrlich viewed the genetic distance methods of species prioritization as a "classic example of falling into the rigor trap" (1994:46) and misleading to policy analysts. Once again, body size may be a simple indicator of genetic distance, especially in crude terms of vertebrates versus invertebrates. Large-bodied species tend to occupy the broadest niches. They have greater mobility and larger home ranges (Calder 1984), and they exploit a larger number of food sources. The latter phenomenon has been noted for ungulates (Hanley 1982) and predators (Pianka 1974), and is a basic principle of trophic (i.e., feeding) ecology. Regardless of body size, behavioral complexity facilitates niche breadth. However, if genetic information is correlated with body size (as posited above), and facilitates behavioral complexity and thus niche breadth, then body size and behavioral complexity are not independent. In other words, the correlation of large body size to niche breadth has a genetic foundation. That genetic foundation may greatly simplify the labyrinthine assessments of genetic distance, because a niche demands evolution, which demands genetic distancing.

Whether niche breadth is a physical, physiological, or genetic function, if larger species have broader niches, then it will be more difficult and more evolutionarily time consuming for any other species to fill a niche vacated by a large species. Small species on the brink of extinction are surrounded by close (morphologically if not genetically) relatives that

FIG 6. *Prioritizing species for conservation based on phylogenetic properties.*
A. *Species A with molecular clock speed X and genetic distance Y should be prioritized over Species B with molecular clock speed 3X and genetic distance Y/2.*
B. *Species A should be prioritized because of its slower molecular clock speed, but Species B should be prioritized because of its greater genetic distance from its ancestor.*

are capable of speciating into the vacated niche at a relatively fast pace, aided by the fast molecular clocks of the small relatives. The niche itself will not be as complex and therefore not as difficult to fill by another species.

SUMMARY

Two of the most prevalent technical criticisms of ESA are understandable but misguided. The first, that the species approach to conservation is no longer viable, results from the formidable task of monitoring and managing the burgeoning list of threatened and endangered species. If one assumed that new listings comprise primarily vertebrates, then perhaps the managerial prospect would be hopeless indeed. However, plants and invertebrates have made up an increasing proportion of listings, reflecting to some extent the preponderance of such species owing to trophic-level structure and the fact that most top-level carnivores are already listed. The more recent listings put less of an administrative burden on FWS and less of a regulatory burden on the pubic than listings of vertebrates. Even were that not the case, however, the species approach to management would continue to be the most workable alternative. Proposed management concepts intended to replace or supplement species management inevitably return to a focus on species. Much of the effort invested in these concepts would be more productive if redirected toward strengthening the species approach to management in the political and fiscal spheres of policy legitimacy.

Meanwhile, the preponderance of imperiled plants and invertebrates has spawned the second technical criticism — that there is no basis for prioritizing listed vertebrates for conservation efforts. However, there is a conceptual genetic basis that happens to correspond with political and fiscal bases. The proposition that all species should be equal under the law would only find legitimacy in nontechnical philosophy, such as biocentrism, where each species has an inherent right to exist. Much of the effort invested in promoting taxonomic equity would achieve more conservation if redirected toward the preservation of politically advantaged species or toward species with a high ratio of public value to program spending (Table 8).

Technically, with regard to the species concept and the prioritization of species, ESA is legitimate policy. Species and the species concept are

88

fundamental to ecology and conservation. Unfortunately, species are like books in a burning library — in a city with an undermanned fire department. We would prefer to save them all, and perhaps in a biocentric utopia we could. In the United States, we can try to save them all, but we will be drastically remiss if the tomes of antiquity burn in the process.

8

Context of the Endangered
Species Act

O ne of the weaknesses of traditional policy analysis has been the inadequate consideration of context. Traditional analysts do not ignore context, but their narrow visions for the role of public policy lead to narrow contextual foci. For example, Yaffee (1982) had much to say about the political context of ESA, Clark et alia (1994) about the bureaucratic context, the National Research Council (1995) about the scientific, Simmons and Kay (1997) about the economic, and Devall and Sessions (1985) about the psychospiritual. Legal scholars and historians provide contextual analyses from their perspectives, too.

We have described the historical context for ESA, incorporating ecological, social, and legal phenomena (chapters 2–3). We concluded that ESA signified the peak of the environmental movement. With ESA, Congress responded to the public's concern over environmental degradation, a concern that had burgeoned after the publication of *Silent Spring*. Politically and psychologically, ESA was eminently sensible in its historical context, as indicated by the landslide vote with which it was passed. Ecologically and technically, it was a logical step toward correcting the problem of species endangerment. However, policy is not limited in time to the date of its enactment but is an evolution of language, interpretation, and action. Context changes, too. The focus of this section is the context of ESA at the dawn of the twenty-first century.

The purpose of contextual analysis is not an impossible one of describing the entire social, technical, and metaphysical world in which a policy exists. That world must indeed be scanned by the policy design analyst, but the analysis is focused on identifying inconsistencies between a policy and its context, and examining the implications. Any common theme running through the inconsistencies is of particular interest, as it may indicate a profound policy design flaw. Alternatively, a common theme may indicate a problem in the context itself that warrants treatment in the policy arena.

By its nature, ESA affords an efficient analysis of contextual inconsistency. A species becomes listed only upon examination of its status and the threats thereto, so the proximate causes of a species' endangerment are generally known and are published in the *Federal Register*. Each cause may be considered a contextual inconsistency with ESA.

We used a multivolume compendium by Lowe et al. (1990), Moseley (1992), and Beacham (1994), to compile a database of endangered species and causes of species endangerment. The compendium contains accounts of the 877 American species listed through 1994. It does not contain a comprehensive publication list for any species and relies heavily on FWS reports. However, we tested the compendium against the *Federal Register* for the reliability of its data and found inconsistencies in less than 5 percent of the species accounts. Furthermore, these inconsistencies were always slight, with only one or two causes of species endangerment listed by one source but not the other. Finally, the compendium is the only individual source that lists the causes of endangerment for each species.

We identified eighteen categories of causes that have jeopardized species since the passage of ESA (Table 9). In many cases, the original causes for a species' decline are not the same as the current causes. We do not address the amount of endangerment historically attributable to each cause.

Species are rarely endangered by only one of the eighteen causes. For most species, it is easier to determine the causes of endangerment than it is to determine the relative importance of each cause. To state that a species is endangered by a cause does not imply that the cause is the only or even the primary cause of endangerment. By the time a species is endangered, any loss of individuals is important, so that the "relativity" of importance loses relevance. In some cases, however, an individual cause is clearly the predominant factor in the species' decline.

Some causes are strongly associated with others (Czech et al. 2000). Association exists in two basic forms: supportive and incidental. Supportive association occurs when one cause of endangerment supports another (e.g., road construction supports recreational traffic). Incidental association occurs when a species is endangered by independent sources. Inde-

TABLE 9. *Causes of Endangerment for Species Classified as Threatened or Endangered by the U.S. Fish and Wildlife Service*

Cause	Species Endangered (including Hawaiian and Puerto Rican species) and Rank of Frequency		Species Endangered (excluding Hawaiian and Puerto Rican species) and Rank of Frequency	
	No.	Rank	No.	Rank
Interactions with non-native species	305	1	115	8
Urbanization	275	2	247	1
Agriculture	224	3	205	2
Outdoor recreation and tourism development	186	4	148	4
Domestic livestock and ranching activities	182	5	136	6
Reservoirs and other running water diversions	161	6	160	3
Modified fire regimes and silviculture	144	7	83	10
Pollution of water, air, or soil	144	8	143	5
Mineral, gas, oil, and geothermal extraction	140	9	134	7
Industrial, institutional, and military activities	131	10	81	12
Harvest, intentional and incidental	120	11	101	9
Logging	109	12	79	13
Road presence, construction, and maintenance	94	13	83	11
Genetic problems	92	14	33	16
Aquifer depletion, wetland draining or filling	77	15	73	15
Native species interactions, plant succession	77	16	74	14
Disease	19	17	7	18
Vandalism (destruction without harvest)	12	18	11	17

pendent sources often produce the same effect (e.g., riverine species can be endangered by farming, mining, logging, and other practices that cause erosion and siltation).

To detect regional trends of endangerment, we assigned each endangered species to a state based on the distribution maps in the compendium. Most endangered species exist in only one state; indeed, many exist in only one county (Dobson et al. 1997). Species existing in more than one state were assigned to the state in which the species remains most numerous. If that information was unavailable, then the species was assigned to the state encompassing the estimated geographic mean of the species' distribution.

We distinguished natural from unnatural endangerment. Götmark said, "In its most common usage, naturalness reflects degree of human influence — the lower the influence, the more natural the site" (1992:455). Grumbine defined a natural ecosystem as "an ecosystem whose species and ecological structure and function remain largely unaffected by human activity" (1992:278). These definitions are consistent with American vernacular (Kempton et al. 1996). We concluded that naturalness is a relative concept and does not require the absence of hominids but that causes of endangerment emanating from industrialized society are unnatural. For species in the heavily industrialized United States, this definition is easy to apply. Native American tribes exist politically and are important ecosystem managers (Czech 1995b, 1999), but even they no longer function with aboriginal methods.

CAUSES OF SPECIES ENDANGERMENT

In this chapter we discuss each of the eighteen causes of species endangerment in order of increasing frequency. We also address prominent socioeconomic factors related to the causes. We conclude by considering a phenomenon — an ultimate cause, as it were — underlying the individual causes.

Vandalism

The relatively small number (twelve) of species impacted by vandalism reflects the pathological nature of such activity. However, the documented cases of vandalism may represent a small fraction of actual occurrences. Species and their habitats are sometimes vandalized by landowners attempting to evade the provisions of ESA's Section 9. For example, Lowe et al. (1990:60) reported that vandals have been responsible for driving the adult population of Virginia round-leaf birch down from fourteen to four since its listing in 1978, "presumably because of a fear that the federal government will use the trees as a reason to intrude on the rights of local landowners."

Disease

Disease is known to endanger nineteen species: eleven birds, seven mammals, and one reptile. Disease is magnified in importance by the very endangerment it contributes to. For example, canine distemper has been an important factor in nearly driving the black-footed ferret to extinction in the past two decades (Reading et al. 1996). Were ferrets not already limited in distribution by the decline of prairie dogs (their primary prey), disease may not have been as threatening. After all, disease is a natural occurrence in the evolution of species.

All diseases are unnaturally endangering when they threaten the existence of a species that has been decimated by other unnatural causes, but some diseases are clearly less natural than others. For example, pox and malaria have contributed to the endangerment of forest birds in Hawaii. These diseases are carried by mosquitoes that evidently were introduced to the islands in the 1820s by the Polynesians (Kuykendall and Day 1948; Kirch and Sahlins 1992).

Native Species Interactions

In a sense, most species endangered by habitat modification decline due to native species interactions, since native food or cover species are usually the depleted habitat components. Placement in this category, however, is limited to species for whom native prey are lacking, species that are being preyed upon by native species at unprecedented levels, or species missing a critical life-cycle process due to the absence of a native species. For example, some plant species in Hawaii are endangered partly because native insect pollinators have declined.

Abundant in the tropical Americas, the wood stork is a species besieged by problems in the United States, including interactions with native species resulting from historical and ongoing non-natural pressures. Wood storks nest in cypress and mangrove swamps adjacent to lakes and rivers in the Southeast. Their primary foraging habitat is nearby wetlands that flood in spring. Loss of habitat to urban and agricultural development is the major historical cause of the stork's decline (Kushlan and Frohring 1986). Today the species is endangered partly by a lack of prey, which constitutes a native species interaction. However, the lack of prey is a function of unnatural water flow (Ogden 1985).

Another native species interaction contributing to the stork's endangerment is raccoon predation. In 1981, water levels at a rookery in Hillsborough County, Florida, dropped low enough to allow access to raccoons, which then destroyed all 168 stork nests (Lowe et al. 1990). Such raccoon predation could hardly be considered natural, however. In Florida, human demands on water have altered ecosystem composition, function, and structure, while raccoon populations have proliferated in areas where agricultural development abuts swamplands.

As the wood stork illustrates, the endangerment associated with native species interactions is subsumed by its own context of unnatural causes. Of the seventy-seven species endangered by native species interactions, only four appear to be endangered primarily by those interactions: Hawaiian monk seal, Florida salt marsh vole, Shenandoah salamander, and cave crayfish. A fifth, the Aleutian shield fern, may also belong in this category (it was rare upon discovery by Christensen [1938]), but it remains endangered today at least partly by the grazing of non-native reindeer.

If one considers the historical threats to species, however, then only one or two species appear to have been endangered naturally. Moseley concluded that the decline of the Florida salt marsh vole "appears to have been caused by naturally occurring climatic changes that have gradually turned coastal prairie habitat into woodland unsuitable for voles" (1992:1388). The Shenandoah salamander, which is endangered by competition from the red-backed salamander (Jaeger 1970), may be another such species, but its historic range is unknown and there is little information on its life history and ecology.

Although the Florida salt marsh vole is naturally endangered, it is prevented from a natural chance at recovery by development surrounding its remaining range. To some extent, the same could be said about the Shenandoah salamander, which is known to exist only in Shenandoah National Park. Furthermore, the native species interactions may be undetectably unnatural. For example, the Hawaiian monk seal was historically reduced by harvesting and habitat conversion. Today, with its remaining range protected by the Hawaiian Islands National Wildlife Refuge, it is endangered primarily by shark predation. Given the ichthyological up-heaval caused by pollution and overfishing, however, shark populations may plausibly have reached unnaturally high levels in the oceans.

Aquifer Depletion, Wetland Drainage, and Filling

As the human population expands, agricultural needs increase. Efforts to meet these needs include irrigating drylands and draining wetlands to make them tillable. Wetlands are also filled for construction. These activities modify hydrological processes, and plant community structures are modified in turn. Species composition changes accordingly. Seventy-three of the seventy-seven species endangered by aquifer depletion and wetland loss live on the mainland, especially in Florida and coastal and central California, where wetland drainage and filling are rampant, and in the arid Southwest, where groundwater pumping depletes aquifers.

One species serves to illustrate the two problematic ends of the hydro-logical spectrum. The Amargosa niterwort is endangered because much of the wetlands it inhabits in Nevada were drained for peat mining. Since then, groundwater pumping for irrigation has reduced the spring flows that feed the remaining wetland. Succumbing to the increased discharge and decreased recharge, the niterwort now exists at only two sites and is vulnerable to demographic and genetic stochasticity (i.e., events of random chance in the population dynamics and genetic evolution of the species).

Genetic Problems

Genetic problems are known or suspected to threaten ninety-two species. Most of the genetics problems documented thus far inflict fish and plants. Unlike causation that is *exacerbated* by species endangerment (e.g., disease), some genetic problems are a direct mathematical *function* of endangerment. Nevertheless, once a genetic problem inflicts a species, it becomes a distinguishable and noteworthy threat. The main problems are loss of genetic variability through drift and inbreeding depression (Li and Graur 1991; Falconer and Mackay 1996).

Hybridization, which has the effect of diluting a species' genetic integrity, is another genetic problem that afflicts an increasing number of species as ecological barriers are disrupted by human activities (Levin et al. 1996). Hybridization is exacerbated by lowered numbers.

There is also the potential for unnaturally high mutation rates in areas of environmental contamination, but we found no reference to this for any endangered species. Lack of reference may be correlated with lack of evidence, which in turn may be correlated with difficulty of detection.

Genetics problems are difficult to detect, and analyses have only been conducted with a small number of species. By the time a species is endangered, genetic sampling of the remaining specimens is difficult and perhaps imprudent, depending on the methods required. Furthermore, genetic drift is likely to be underestimated in populations that have experienced severe bottlenecks (Richards and Leberg 1996). Cause and effect is difficult to ascertain in cases of inbreeding depression and deleterious mutations, especially in wild populations. Finally, although hybrid sightings are often reported, the act of hybridizing is rarely observed in the field.

Genetic problems are particularly ominous because of their permanence and the suddenness of their phenotypic effects. While an aquifer can be recharged once water conservation is implemented, a depleted genome may never regain its integrity. Levin et alia noted, "For a rare species, contact with a cross-compatible congener may constitute an environmental perturbation whose consequences are soon irreversible" (1996:14). Frankham demonstrated "a threshold relationship between inbreeding and extinction. There may be little warning of impending extinction due to inbreeding"(1995:797).

For species like the Florida panther, which numbers less than fifty and exhibits signs of inbreeding and genetic invariability (Roelke et al. 1993; Maehr and Caddick 1995), it is probably too late to salvage a vigorous genotype. Likewise for other species, such as the red wolf, which could be hybridized out of recognition by increasing coyote populations (Brownlow 1996).

Road Presence, Construction, and Maintenance

Roads weave the fabric of American economy and culture, bringing food to nearly every table and people to nearly every major event. Roads range from two-track Jeep trails to eight-lane interstate highways and they pose a variety of problems for species. The effects of road presence, construction, and maintenance can go undocumented, but roads are known to endanger ninety-four species.

Mammals like the San Joaquin kit fox that nocturnally hunt along habitat edges are run over by automobiles, as are reptiles like the blunt-nosed leopard lizard that are attracted to warm roadbeds. Roadbeds and ditches contribute to the siltation that endangers a number of darters in the Southeast. Right-of-way mowing destroys habitat for the elfin tree fern and others. The dwarf lake iris is endangered by chemicals used in right-of-way maintenance and road salting, while the building of roads in anakeesta shale results in sulfuric acid runoff that endangers the Smoky madtom. Movements are interrupted by the presence of roads, even for fish species like the Kendall Warm Springs dace, where culverts take the place of natural streams. Several sites of Minnesota trout-lily were simply obliterated by road construction, while road improvements were sufficient to destroy some patches of San Diego Mesa Mint.

Roads are supportively associated with urbanization, logging, mining, agriculture, and recreation. It is virtually impossible for these categories to intensify without simultaneous road building, maintenance, or use.

Logging

Forests cover 32 percent of the land area in the United States (Cubbage et al. 1993), and logging endangers 108 species. Logging is generally conducted for timber extraction purposes but may be incidental to agricultural, residential, and industrial development. Logging not only entails road construction and improvement, fire suppression, and silvicultural practices that endanger species but also contributes to pollution and siltation problems plaguing some species.

Logging has played an important role in the nation's economy since the late 1800s, and many regions have experienced the boom and bust of nonsustainable logging. The upper Midwest underwent some of the most drastic economic and ecological transitions in the process, including some of the most extreme conflagrations in history, for example, Wisconsin's Peshtigo Fire of 1871. It is reasonable to infer that species restricted in range to the northern hardwood forests went extinct prior to their identification, and likewise for species restricted to southern baldcypress swamps prior to the pullboat logging thereof (Vileisis 1997).

The most recent timber economy boom occurred in the Pacific Northwest in the 1980s, when President Reagan's policies included one of the highest rates of timber extraction in American history (Hirt 1994). The federal government manages 39 percent of forest land in the United States, and the United States Forest Service manages most of the remaining old growth forests of the Northwest. On the one hand, it could be argued that the spotted owl controversy is largely a result of federal forest management. After all, wherever the Forest Service manages timber, similar controversies exist (e.g., over the Mexican spotted owl in the Southwest and the red-cockaded woodpecker in the Southeast). On the other hand, the fact that the national forests still have significant populations of spotted owls suggests that the Forest Service has been more successful than other landholding entities. In the northeastern states, for example, similar controversies have been avoided only because the peak logging days were over long ago; the forests were privately owned and readily converted to higher economic uses (Cronon 1983).

Harvest

Harvest is the primary threat for only a small fraction of the 120 species it endangers. However, it is increasingly problematic to plants (chapter 2), 59 species of which are already endangered by it. It also threatens a disproportionate share of charismatic megafauna. For decades, when the number of bald eagles was brought to low levels primarily by DDT and other organochlorine contamination, harvesting was a complementary threat to the national bird. Harvesting remains a critical factor for the thick-billed parrot, the Snake River chinook salmon, and numerous sea turtle and whale species. It also threatens reintroduction efforts for the Rocky Mountain gray wolf. Harvested specimens often enter the black market economy.

Industrial, Institutional, and Military Activities

This category includes industrial development and operations, military practices, and a few instances of rural development of government facilities. These activities endanger 131 species, including 81 on the mainland. Of the 50 Hawaiian and Puerto Rican species placed in this category, more than half were placed there because military exercises in Hawaii cause threatening fires on and off the military reservations.

On the mainland, the threat is more typically related to industrial construction and subsequent operations, which often pollute water and deplete aquifers. Pollution is a simultaneous source of endangerment for almost half (38) of the mainland species endangered by industrial development.

Industrial development is strongly associated with urbanization, a simultaneous cause of endangerment in sixty-six cases. For example, eleven populations of Bradshaw's lomatium remain, and 90 percent of the individuals are within a 16-km radius of Eugene, Oregon. Eugene is a rapidly expanding city, and two of the larger populations of Bradshaw's lomatium are endangered by industrial and residential development plans.

Steamboat buckwheat is one of the few examples of a species endangered by rural development of government facilities. In the late 1970s, after ESA was passed but before the buckwheat was listed, one acre of the remaining buckwheat range in Nevada was lost to the construction of a post office.

Mineral, Gas, Oil, and Geothermal Extraction or Exploration

No other non-urban habitat modification is as stark as mining. Stewart Udall noted that "the land legacy of any mining operation is, necessarily, a pit, a shaft, or a hole" (1988:59). In the case of strip or open-pit mining, entire landscapes are simply peeled away as their constituent parts are rendered in quarries, chemical pools, and smelters. And for every viable mine, a great deal of exploration must occur. Mining is also unique in that it threatens not a single species in Hawaii and only 6 in Puerto Rico, so that almost all of the 140 species threatened by mining exist on the mainland. The rank of mining in endangerment frequency therefore jumps from ninth place nationwide to seventh place on the mainland. In two regions mining is particularly problematic: the Southeast, and the Southwest as extended to the Great Basin and central California.

More species are endangered by mining in Tennessee, Georgia, Alabama, Arkansas, Louisiana, and Florida than in the rest of the United States combined. This is due to high levels of mining and to high levels of biodiversity and endemism in the Southeast (Lydeard and Mayden 1995), and to the suceptibility of riverine systems to mining-related degradation. Most of the species endangered by mining in the Southeast are mussels or fishes that are plagued by a host of problems related to water quantity and quality. Mining contributes to siltation, turbidity, and chemical contamination. Silt buries the gravelly substrates that mussels anchor themselves to and that many fishes spawn in. Mussels are filter feeders; turbid water clogs their feeding apparatus, while toxic chemicals become concentrated in their tissues.

Almost all of the remaining species endangered by mining are located in California, Nevada, Utah, Colorado, New Mexico, and Arizona. Most of them are plants. Because the arid Southwest hosts many specialized endemic plants, mining conflicts with their survival in direct proportion to the area mined and explored. For example, the dwarf bear-poppy exists in one area near St. George, Utah, where gypsum deposits are prevalent. Not much mining has occurred, because the market for gypsum is not amenable to the strip mining that would be required. However, mining claims are continually assessed (entailing off-road driving and assaying columns of earth), damaging the dwarf bear-poppy and its habitat in the process.

Pollution of Water, Air, or Soil

Of the 144 species endangered by pollution, 85 are found in a southeastern region expanded to include the Carolinas, Virginias, Kentucky, and Tennessee. All except 18 of these species are fish and mussels. Most of the rest are plants, snails, and other invertebrates of aquatic or otherwise mesic environments. Mining, logging, farming, factories, and urban developments constitute the collective source of pollution. Two rapidly populating states, California and Texas, account for 19 of the 57 species endangered by pollution outside of the Southeast. Texas hosts a number of mesic caves with endemic species endangered by seepage from residential and commercial development.

Perhaps the most infamous pollution in terms of species endangerment is organochlorine contamination of raptors. For decades, organochlorines such as DDT and DDE caused eggshell thinning and therefore low reproduction (Heintzelman 1979). Bald eagles and peregrine falcons were especially hard hit. Since the banning of DDT and other organochlorines pursuant to *Environmental Defense Fund, Inc. v. Ruckelshaus*, most raptors have recovered remarkably. The northern aplomado falcon is an example of one that did not. By the time protections went into effect, its range had already receded southward from the United States owing to pesticide use, loss of habitat to overgrazing, modified fire regimes, and other factors (Hector 1980). Sightings in the United States have become rare.

Modified Fire Regimes and Silvicultural Practices

Widespread and consistent modification of a natural fire regime can modify selection pressures enough to remove the competitive advantage of fire-adapted species. Where this process takes place in a short period of evolutionary time — as when caused by managerial decisions such as fire suppression — fire-adapted species may go extinct. The infrequent but related endangerment causes of wildfires and silvicultural practices are included in this category. Cumulatively, these causes are implicated in the endangerment of 144 species.

Czech (1996b) identified ten factors that support a powerful firefighting institution in the United States: reaction to fuel buildup resulting from past fire-suppression efforts, firefighter conflict of interest, federal budget anomalies, concern for neighboring landowners, political pressure (national and local), an expanding urban-rural interface, a misled public, institutional reaction to zealous pro-wildfire land managers, smoke concerns, and economies of scale. These factors constitute a veritable juggernaut that draws a massive fireline around the backcountry of the United States, a fireline that is periodically breached by unnaturally intense wildfires as fuels continue to build up.

Nearly half of the species endangered by fire suppression cling to survival in Florida. Of those, almost all are plants of the slash pine, pine rockland, and sand pine communities, which evolved to the rhythm of frequent, light intensity fires (Myers 1985, 1990). Moreover, the expansion of urban development into rural areas places intense political pressure on fire crews to suppress wildfires. This pressure is only likely to increase after the devastating Florida fires of 1998.

Reservoirs and Other Surface Water Diversions

As with mining, there is nothing subtle about the endangerment caused by reservoirs. When species are geographically limited to an inundated area, they are obliterated. This phenomenon spurred the biggest controversy in ESA history. The snail darter was only known to live in an area to be impounded by Tellico Dam, so Section 7 was invoked to prevent the Tennessee Valley Authority (TVA) from completing construction. The issue was supposedly settled by the Supreme Court in 1978 via *Tennessee Valley Authority v. Hill* but was then skirted by a congressional rider two years later (Bean 1983). In a somewhat anticlimactic outcome, the dam was built and other populations of snail darter were discovered nearby.

Another blatant problem posed by reservoirs (or dams) is that they block movements of species that need access to other portions of rivers for parts of their life cycles. Even fishes may be blocked from spawning grounds by massive pools of water lacking a discernible, consistent main current.

The distribution of species endangered by reservoirs and other surface water diversions is very similar to that of species endangered by mining, where the Southeast and Southwest are most heavily affected. The historical context of river impoundment, especially in the Southeast, is rooted in the New Deal policies of President Franklin Roosevelt's administration (Clarke 1996). The Tennessee Valley Authority, Roosevelt's first effort to join natural resources planning with economic growth, likewise joined a substantial share of Southeast species endangerment with economic growth. The Tennessee Valley Authority and other New Deal water development programs ushered in a new era of pork-barrel politics that created strong resistance to sustainable water use (Ferejohn 1974).

Although the intensity of water development in the West never rivaled that of the TVA region, it is perhaps more important per capita to the Southwest–Great Basin economy. When the Bureau of Reclamation was created in 1904, it marked the beginning of a decline for many western riparian species. One of them was the cui-ui, a large sucker found in the Truckee River drainage of Nevada that was an important food source for the Northern Paiute Indians. One of the bureau's earliest efforts, the Newlands Project (including the construction of Derby Dam), drastically altered the cui-ui's ecosystem. Since the project began in 1907, Pyramid Lake has receded to the lowest levels in about four thousand years (Benson 1978). Although the cui-ui still inhabits Pyramid Lake, the Newlands Project caused its extirpation from Winnemucca Lake, which had been the only other portion of its range (Buchanan and Coleman 1987).

The Tellico Dam and spotted owl controversies could soon pale in comparison to that developing along the Columbia River (Lee 1993). Barker thought that ESA "could put salmon protection above all other uses of the Columbia and Snake rivers. Flows through the eight federal hydro-electric dams between Idaho and the ocean would have to change. The Bonneville Power Administration, Army Corps of Engineers, Bureau of Reclamation and Pacific Northwest utilities would have to revamp the largest coordinated hydroelectric system in the world and bring the complicated treaties and contracts that govern it into compliance with the act" (1993:96).

Domestic Livestock and Ranching Activities

Livestock grazing has been a source of species endangerment since the 1800s. Fleischner, noting that 70 percent of the West was grazed, called livestock grazing "the most widespread influence on native ecosystems of western North America" (1994:630). Carrier and Czech (1996) identified habitat degradation, predator control, reduction of competitors, accidental mortality, trophic effects, disease, parasites, and chemicals as outcomes of or activities related to grazing that contribute to the endangerment of species.

More than 180 species are endangered by livestock grazing, and 79 reside in part or entirely on federal land, including about 74 species on Bureau of Land Management lands (National Research Council 1994). Most of the species endangered by grazing outside of federal lands reside in Hawaii, Texas, and the Southeast, where grazing complements the myriad of factors contributing to siltation. In California, the mainland state with the greatest number (29) of species endangered by grazing, a nearly equal mix reside on federal (16) and nonfederal (13) land. (These figures distinguish only between those that live entirely or partly on federal land from those that live entirely on nonfederal but possibly other public land.)

This category does not include those species endangered by the grazing of native species or feral livestock. If those were included, many would be added to the list from the Hawaiian Islands alone, where feral livestock are especially problematic.

Outdoor Recreation and Tourism Development

This category includes disturbance associated with hikers, hunters, fishermen, horseback riders, skiers, rock climbers, dirt bikers, four-wheel drivers, tourists, and the construction of facilities for any of these. It represents a spectrum of human activity ranging from solitary wilderness pursuits to organized social pleasures, blending into the category of urbanization when the construction of tourist facilities endangers species in urbanizing areas. Associated categories include road construction and reservoirs; roads are built to bring people into recreational areas and reservoirs attract a variety of outdoor enthusiasts.

This category has one of the highest proportions of species that live on federal land, indicating the prominence of outdoor recreation thereon. On the mainland, 150 species are endangered by outdoor recreation, 92 of which live on federal land. The management of federal land is especially subject to public prerogative and ESA regulation, and some concessions have been made for endangered species. For example, the dwarf bearpoppy is endangered by development activities and off-road vehicles in Utah; the bear-poppy recovery plan calls for a closure to off-road vehicles on lands administered by the Bureau of Land Management (U.S. Fish and Wildlife Service 1985).

California hosts the greatest number (32) of species endangered by recreation, followed by Hawaii (26) and Florida (19). In terms of ecosystems, the Mojave Desert and the Great Basin are areas of high recreation impact. Twelve species in Utah and Nevada (and several from eastern California) are endangered by recreation. These ecosystems are a mecca for dirt bikers and four-wheelers due to their openness, topographic variety, and dry substrates. Unfortunately, these are also some of the most "brittle" — and therefore most challenging for restoration purposes — environments in North America (Savory 1988). Smaller, widely distributed ecosystems with similar traits including sand dunes, shale barrens, and limestone hills, are subject to recreational traffic and resulting endangerment.

The majority (125) of species endangered by recreation and tourism are plants. This reflects the prominence of trampling in this category, as plants are incapable of evasion. Other species endangered by recreation and tourism include twenty-three invertebrates, nineteen mammals, six reptiles, six fishes, five birds, and two amphibians.

Of the mammals, the order Chiroptera is particularly susceptible. Bats hibernate in caves and, when disturbed by spelunkers, lose calories required to carry them through hibernation. The largest caves (with the greatest hibernation capacities) are usually developed as tourist attractions. For example, some of the largest colonies of the endangered gray bat were destroyed by commercialization (Tuttle 1979).

Agriculture

The threats of agriculture are as numerous as the varieties of agriculture practiced. Most obvious is total liquidation of a species' habitat, as when forested areas are cleared for tillage. Less obvious are habitat modifications that threaten a species more gradually than outright destruction of all habitat elements. Some species coexist with farming to a degree, but incidental take can occur, as when a farmer plows through the shallow burrow of a kangaroo rat.

Agriculture is such a prominent aspect of American geography and economy that it is associated to some degree with every other category of endangerment (Czech et al. 2000). In supportive association with agriculture, roads are built, wetlands are drained, aquifers are pumped, dams are constructed, exotic species are introduced, urban areas are developed, and processing plants are built. Agriculture, meanwhile, is supportively associated with pollution, and more than half (76) of the 144 species endangered by pollution are endangered by agriculture. Agriculture is incidentally but frequently associated with mining, because both contribute to the siltation that endangers riverine species, especially in the Southeast.

As a region, the Southeast has the greatest number (98) of the 224 species endangered by agriculture. California has 43, tying it with Florida for the most number of species endangered by agriculture in a state. These areas have been identified as endangered species "hotspots" (Dobson et al. 1997). However, agriculture is also the most ubiquitos of endangerment sources, endangering species in thirty-five states and Puerto Rico.

Urbanization

When a minimum density of 1,000 people per 1.6 square kilometers reside in a contiguous area with at least 50,000 people, the area is classified by the U.S. Bureau of the Census as urban (Edmondson 1991). As of 1990, there were 396 urban areas in the United States, accounting for 158 million people or 64 percent of the population. However, the rapid connection of these officially urban areas with urban-like suburbs or large tracts of commercial development has created a situation whereby a greater proportion of the population is urban in the vernacular (Diamond and Noonan 1996).

Urbanization endangers species by replacing habitat directly and by depleting nearby resources needed to support urban economies. Urbanization is supportively associated with several other causes, too. Dams are often built to control flooding and to supply water and electricity to urban areas. Road building emanates from urban areas, and outdoor recreation tends to be heaviest near urban areas. Urbanization also has many subtle effects, the threat of which have not been assessed. For example, most U.S. cities of more than 200,000 residents can expect unnatural, significant warming by the year 2035, with the average expected to be 0.19 degrees Celsius (Viterito 1991). This warming will be site specific and in addition to whatever global warming may occur. Temperature affects species assemblages in a myriad of ways (Saunders et al. 1991), so that seemingly minor differences in temperature can translate into major differences in species assemblages.

Next to agriculture, urbanization is the most ubiquitous threat, endangering 275 species in thirty-one states and Puerto Rico. Sixty-four species are endangered in Florida, 61 in California, and 26 in Texas — three of the most rapidly urbanizing states. In contrast, urbanization endangers only two species in the combined area of Utah, Nevada, and Idaho, largely because most of the Great Basin is owned by the public and unavailable for urban development. Urbanization in the United States also endangers 132 plants, 46 invertebrates, 33 mammals, 24 birds, 21 fishes, 15 reptiles, and 4 amphibian.

Interactions with Non-native Species

When a species suddenly appears in an ecosystem, as when introduced by humans, it can create selection pressures that extirpate native species. If the native species are also endemic, then extirpation is equivalent to extinction. Usually the introduced species are called "exotics" because they were introduced from another country. Here we classify as exotics non-native species and a much smaller set of species that are native to North America but have become established in ecosystems outside the limits of their natural range, or have rapidly become prominent in areas where they were historically rare and relatively unimportant (e.g., brown-headed cowbirds in some areas).

Hawaiian and Puerto Rican species are more prominent in this category than in any other. While this category is the most prevalent for the United States as a whole, it is only the eighth most important factor of endangerment on the mainland, where urbanization endangers more than twice as many species as non-native species do. However, species endangerment caused by non-native species is proliferating on and off the mainland (Devine 1999).

Non-native species endanger 182 species on Hawaii, almost all of which are plants (156) and birds (25). Most of the problems in Hawaii involve grazing by feral pigs, goats, sheep, and cattle. Other problematic exotics include rats, mongooses, feral house cats, axis deer, mynas, mosquitoes, phibiscus snow scale, water hyacinth, strawberry guava, and various hymenopterids (mainly parasitic wasps and predaceous ants) (Lowe et al. 1990; Moseley 1992; Beacham 1994). A number of less notorious exotic plant species and insects have a large cumulative effect.

The Hawaiian vetch is an example of a species endangered by exotics via multiple pathways. It lives on the big island, where feral goats and pigs have denuded large areas of native plants and effectively tilled the soil, enabling introduced weeds to invade. Meanwhile, forest birds — the chief pollinators of Hawaiian vetch — depend on a variety of native plants for food and cover and therefore have declined precipitously.

FRAGMENTATION AS AN EFFECT OF SPECIES ENDANGERMENT CAUSES

No discussion of species endangerment would be complete without addressing habitat fragmentation. Fragmentation is often treated as a separate cause of species endangerment, and some consider it the most glaring problem for species preservation (Noss and Csuti 1994). Saunders et alia (1991) pointed out that fragmentation threatens species not only through the processes of island biogeography but also by causing physical changes in the environment that result in modification of remaining habitat.

We do not consider fragmentation as a separate cause of species endangerment because it is caused by the other habitat-destroying factors. Collectively, the habitat destruction factors constitute the major cause of both fragmentation and endangerment. Nevertheless, those who treat fragmentation as a cause of species endangerment make a point that should be emphasized: species are not endangered proportionally to the amount of habitat lost, especially once numbers are critically low. A threshold level of habitat loss can be reached whereby the viability of a population is lost. No matter how many nonviable populations exist, if they are reproductively isolated by fragmentation, the species is bound for extinction.

TRENDS IN THE SOCIOECONOMIC CONTEXT OF ESA

With the possible exception of overharvest, which for animals is decreasing, all causes of species endangerment appear to be intensifying. Recent rates of activity have decreased for some causes, most notably wetland drainage (Vileisis 1997) and logging on public lands (Hirt 1994) — largely because of the protections afforded by ESA — but absolute prevalence and effect are still increasing, especially when fragmentation is accounted for. Urbanization and agriculture, the two most prevalent causes of species endangerment on the mainland, best illustrate the intensifying inconsistency between ESA and its socioeconomic context.

For demographers, urbanization usually refers to the increase in the proportion of people living in cities. Urbanization in the United States has occurred in three major stages (Monkkonen 1988). From the American declaration of independence until about 1830, there was a slow and gradual migration from rural to urban areas. Next followed a century-long period of steady and rapid migration. Since about 1930 the rate of migration has tapered off, especially to the largest cities. However, demographic urbanization continues when smaller cities are taken into account.

At one time, the proportion of people urbanized was thought to have a major influence on America's ecological conscience and conservation ethic, with urban residents generally characterized as disconnected from nature and therefore uncaring and ignorant of conservation issues. Sociopolitical trends now cast doubt upon this portrayal; the conservation ethic of urbanites has exceeded that of rural people in some respects. Kellert (1996) ascribed this transition to a tendency toward *suburbanization* (vs. urbanization *per se*) and to the increasing level of outdoor recreation practiced by urbanites. Many suburban people live next to nature, and ease of travel has made the countryside readily accessible to the vast majority of true urbanites. Meanwhile, although rural people in some areas resist urban development for cultural reasons, the Sagebrush Rebellion and the Wise Use movement have been manned, at least on the front lines, primarily by rural people. These groups are intensely utilitarian and anti-protectionist (Echeverria and Eby 1995).

Kellert also found "no significant variations in knowledge of nature and animals" between urban and rural people (1996:57). However, Kellert also found that "young Americans appear increasingly to get their knowledge of the natural world from books and schools" (46). It is logical to suspect a major difference in experience-based knowledge between rural and urban people. The likely outcome of a rural existence, especially for those who work outdoors, is a greater awareness of ecological processes and components, including nonhuman species. For the purposes of species conservation, perhaps the most productive sociopolitical sector on a per capita basis consists of people who simultaneously possess a conservation ethic and firsthand knowledge of the land. To the extent that the latter is diminished by demographic urbanization, urbanization is a contextual challenge to ESA.

While the impact of demographic urbanization on species conservation is questionable, the impact of physical urbanization is not. With the possible exception of large industrial and institutional developments, cities represent the furthest departure from natural ecosystems and the most thorough liquidation of wildlife habitat. Like demographic urbanization, the growth of American cities has occurred in distinct stages.

At the dawn of European colonization, there was a widespread loss of Native American population centers, especially in the East and South, as Native Americans were devastated by epidemics that swept ahead of the colonists (Cronon 1983; Stannard 1992). These Native American settlements were not cities in the modern industrial sense, but they abutted major agricultural developments and their residents accounted for a large annual harvest of wild plants and animals. Some scientists have come to view the plenitude of wildlife during frontier times as a function of Native American population reduction during the preceding decades of epidemic (Martin and Szuter 1999). Nevertheless, there is no evidence for plant and animal exploitation at levels that endangered species during late Holocene, pre-Columbian times, especially north of what is now Mexico (Czech 1999).

During the colonial and frontier periods the number of cities grew slowly, but growth increased rapidly toward the end of the nineteenth century. The growth in number of large cities has tapered off noticeably, but the appearance of towns with populations greater than 2,500 has not. "The age of the big city is over, but the age of cities continues with greater vigor than ever" (Monkkonen 1988:74). Furthermore, this proclamation of the big city's demise is accurate only in political terms. More small cities are incorporating, but they are usually connected to big cities physically. The age of the political big city may be over, but the age of the gargantuan physical city has just begun. Metropolises like New York, Chicago, and Los Angeles are contiguous with vast tracts of urban appendages, and megalopolises are expected to evolve along the Atlantic and Pacific seaboards.

Not all new cities are appendages of bigger ones. City building in isolated areas is still common, especially in the West. Trying to assess the ecological threat of metropolitan expansion relative to the ecological threat of an increase in the number of isolated cities is like the inverse of the SLOSS controversy, whereby ecologists argue about whether to preserve "single large or several small" natural areas. While metropolises have formidable environmental features, like dangerous concentrations of pollutants and microclimatic warming (Viterito 1991), isolated developments entail more infrastructure, much of which connects larger cities and fragments surrounding ecosystems.

While this inverse SLOSS controversy has dubious implications for species conservation, the cumulative growth of the urban environment is clearly a problematic context for ESA. Consistent with the ecological principle of competitive exclusion, the conversion of more natural ecosystems to cities means that people replace nonhuman populations and endanger species in the process (Czech 2000a). Cities and industrial areas occupy about 6 percent of the continental United States (Odum 1989), and the percentage is steadily increasing.

The impact of physical urbanization is far from exclusively direct. Urban areas require some natural resources from within, but many more from without (Rees 1992). Detailed studies of this phenomenon are complex, expensive, and seldom performed, but Odum (1989) estimated that the urbanized 6 percent of the U.S. mainland entailed the appropriation of natural resources from an additional 29 percent. By this estimate, American urbanity requires approximately 35 percent of the land base of the mainland United States. Rees and Wackernagel (1994) estimated that industrial areas with densities of more than three hundred people per square kilometer use ten to twenty times more land for food and forest products and to produce biomass energy equivalent to that consumed in the form of fossil fuels (which are replenished through the fossilization of biomass). Different types of ecosystems have different ratios of urban to supportive lands. Folke et alia (1996) found that the twenty-nine major cities of the Baltic Sea basin appropriate an amount of wood, paper, fiber, and food that requires a land base two hundred times the size of the cities. None of these studies accounted for the export demands placed on natural resources by the urban populations of other nations. The economy of Hong Kong, for example, is fueled by natural resources from other nations. For nations that serve as international sources of raw materials, including the United States, the demands on certain resources exceed those associated with the national population. In other words, global urbanity requires more than 35 percent of the land base of mainland United States.

In addition to the usurpation of natural habitats, urban areas produce massive quantities of waste that enter the environment, contributing to the pollution that endangers 144 species. Sewer systems are probably the most important vehicle for distributing these pollutants, mostly into surface waters. These pollutants include pesticides such as malathion, atrazine, and chlordane; other organic chemicals such as fluorene, pyrene, and naphthalene; heavy metals such as lead, zinc, and chromium; pathogenic genera such as *Salmonella, Shigella,* and *Pseudomonas*; chloride salts; and nitrates (Pitt 1996). Urban economies also drain wetlands to make room for development and drain aquifers for residential and commercial water needs, thus contributing to the depletion of wetlands and aquifers that endangers seventy-seven species. Urbanization also reduces the permeable soil surface through which groundwater is recharged. Aquifers underlying urban areas are often recharged from septic tanks, industrial waste injection wells, and nonsewered stormwater that has absorbed the aforementioned pollutants.

The trend toward physical urbanization in the United States is culturally supported by a set of distinctly American attitudes (Yeates 1980). The first is that landowners should be allowed to do whatever they wish with their land, including subdividing and developing. Second, citizens have come to desire second-home recreational developments. Third, no matter where they live, Americans have come to expect a level of services that are similar to those provided in large cities, so that small settlements, including recreational developments, have taken on the infrastructural characteristics of cities. Finally, each of these trends are viewed as rights, contributing to the rights revolution discussed by Landy (1993).

Ultimately, the primary feature of urbanization that attracts participants is the economic advantage provided thereto (Dunn 1983). Certainly, physical and perhaps demographic urbanization is likely to continue as long as the American population increases. Even if the population stops growing, urbanization may effectively continue as long as per capita consumption continues to increase. The manifestations of increased per capita consumption may include larger houses and lot sizes, larger corporate structures and lots, larger vehicles, more infrastructure, and more public facilities.

The growing urban economy is reflected in the American countryside that nourishes it. There were about 6.5 million farms operating in 1920, with an acreage of approximately 958 million (Cramer and Jensen 1994). Despite technological advances and a decline in farm numbers to about 2.1 million, by 1992 the acreage was up to 981 million, which exceeds the combined acreage managed by the Bureau of Land Management, Forest Service, Fish and Wildlife Service, National Park Service, and Army Corps of Engineers. Increases in acres of production and production per acre were required to meet the demands of a larger population, a more affluent population, and a much larger export market. These figures reveal a threefold increase in average farm size and a tendency toward corporate monoculture.

Farms have always entailed ecological change, but family farms were historically beneficial to an assortment of economically and culturally valuable animal species (Leopold 1966). The farm was a mosaic of plant communities, primarily domestic yet prevalently wild. The mosaic farm often provided far more edge than the preexisting ecosystem. Wide fence rows, often wooded, provided security cover and connectivity within and among farms. They provided alternative food sources and an array of special habitat needs, like perches and nesting cavities. Small wetlands and ponds were skirted by the plow and provided year-round habitat for a diversity of invertebrates, amphibians, and small mammals. These wetlands were also stopovers for migratory waterfowl and were frequently visited by large mammals and upland gamebirds. Woodlots were often retained as a source of firewood and fenceposts, simultaneously serving as host to woodland plant and animal species. Tilled areas were kept in productive seral stages and provided supplemental or even primary food sources. Harvesting methods were imperfect enough to leave a pile of corn cobs here, a bushel of oats there. Tilled areas were generally left in stubble over winter and provided enough cover to support wintering populations of gamebirds and small mammals. Fields were left fallow on a rotational basis and hosted much higher densities of wintering animals than did the stubble areas. A countryside of family farms comprised a biologically rich, uncultivated matrix within which food was produced in patches — intentionally for humans and incidentally for wildlife.

Cramer and Jensen's data (1994) indicate that the acreage encompassed by farms has increased by 23 million acres since 1920. However, fencerows have simultaneously been usurped, wetlands have been drained, and woodlots have been converted for the sake of production and efficiency. If such efficiencies have added 10 percent to the 1920 farm base, then the additional acreage put into production has been nearly 96 million acres, or 119 million acres if new farmland is included. Meanwhile, harvesting and tillage methods have become ultra-efficient. Little grain is left in the fields after harvesting, fall plowing eliminates winter security cover, and fallowing is seldom practiced, as fertilizer is depended on to enrich the soil. Efficiency has also been improved by removing fencerows and amalgamating formerly separate fields into vast tracts of production.

Thus, the cumulative effects of increased agricultural production on native species have been threefold: habitat has been lost via expansion of the farm base, habitat within the farm base has been degraded via increased farming efficiency, and the connectivity of habitat has been lost via both. These trends continued throughout the twentieth century; Aldo Leopold (1949) lamented them fifty years ago. Due to the political efforts of conservationists, some federal programs have evolved to reclaim the conservation values of farmland, most notably the Conservation Reserve Program established by the Food Security Act of 1985 (Farm Bill). Under this program, which is administered by the Agricultural Stabilization and Conservation Service, farmers are paid to retire limited amounts of highly erodible lands. The continually evolving Farm Bill also has sodbuster and swampbuster provisions that deny subsidies to farmers who plow highly erodible land previously out of production or convert wetlands to croplands. Two related programs, the Wetlands Reserve Program and the Wildlife Habitat Incentives Program, operate on a much smaller scale.

These conservation programs and provisions apply to limited acreage, cumulatively ranging from 35 to 50 million acres, depending on Farm Bill amendments and appropriations. They have often been mismanaged or compromised in the field and face perpetual political pressure (Zinn and Copeland 1996). Although they have reclaimed some wildlife habitat, they have not stemmed the tide of agricultural expansion. The most rapidly expanding sector of agriculture is comprised of corporate-sized (if not corporately structured) farms, or those farms that tend toward monoculture. The number of farms with annual sales of more than $100,000 rose from 271,000 in 1980 to 326,000 by 1991 (Cramer and Jensen 1994).

Furthermore, the increasing size of the agricultural sector entails a concomitant increase in the agribusiness complex, which overlaps with other causes of endangerment. Farming is served by industries that provide fertilizer, petroleum products, machinery, and chemicals. In other words, an expanding agricultural sector is directly related to an expansion of industrial activities, oil exploration and extraction, mining, and pollution. As increasingly marginal, arid lands are turned to for agricultural production, additional irrigation is required. For example, irrigation accounts for about 90 percent of all human water consumption in Arizona and New Mexico (Sabol et al. 1987). Irrigation usually entails dam-building or aquifer depletion and thus contributes to the endangerment of 161 and 77 species, respectively (some of which are endangered by both causes). At the other end of the hydrological spectrum, where marginality is imposed by waterlogged soils, agricultural expansion requires drainage. Although wetland drainage has been slowed by the likes of ESA, the Clean Water Act, and the Farm Bill, it continues (Vileisis 1997).

With so much of the economy tied to agriculture, it is easy to see why the French physiocrats of the late 1700s insisted that agriculture was the only true source of economic production (Galbraith 1987; Czech 2000b). Two centuries later, it is just as easy to see why agriculture is the most ubiquitous cause of species endangerment: it is caught up in fueling an economy that grows at the competitive exclusion of wildlife in the aggregate (Czech 2000a).

SUMMARY

Conservation biologists and others who have claimed that the current wave of species endangerment is unnatural are clearly correct. Only by employing an esoteric concept of naturalness could one claim otherwise, as one might in a "degenerative policy context" characterized by manipulative and deceptive rhetoric (Schneider and Ingram 1997). The Florida salt marsh vole is the only probable case of natural endangerment, and its capacity to survive adaptation and evolution is undermined by unnatural phenomena surrounding its remaining range.

The two major causes of endangerment on the mainland — agriculture and urbanization — encompass the vast majority of the American socioeconomic context. Americans dwell in cities and their food requirements are met principally through agriculture. As the U.S. population increases, urbanization and agriculture will expand to support the population. Even if the U.S. population stabilizes, physical urbanization and agriculture may increase, depending on trends in per capita consumption and global markets.

With a growing economy — the synthesis of population, per capita consumption, and exports — the only alternative to increasing urbanization is for higher population densities or greater affluence to occur in rural environments. Generally, that means more or bigger ranches, farms, logging communities, mining towns, and "bedroom towns," which require more roads and increase automobile pollution. As the economy grows, threats to species increase, whether the threats are urban or other (e.g., ranching, logging, mining). Ultimately, as rural areas become populated to a saturation point, they will become urban.

With a growing population and agricultural exportation, the only exception to increasing the spatial scale of agriculture is when agricultural efficiency increases at a faster pace than the synthesis of population and export demand. However, much of the potential for increased efficiency is gone because the best lands are already under production or urbanized (Ayers 1998). Furthermore, the productive capacity of agricultural land tends to decline as soils are eroded and minerals depleted in step with demand. Clearly, economic growth constitutes a formidable policy context for ESA, or for any law intended to conserve species.

Hypothetically, economic growth could ensue without threatening species if the development of ecologically sound technology kept pace with the rate of overall growth. This hypothesis is an implicit corollary of neoclassical theories of economic growth, which depend heavily on technological improvement (Ekelund and Tollison 1988; Mankiw 1992). Ultimately, however, there would still be biophysical limits to the scale of human economy (Daly 1993; Czech 2000b). And given the principle of competitive exclusion, the history of species endangerment in the United States is incontrovertible evidence that economic growth has perennially outpaced — and continues to outpace — the development of ecologically sound technology.

9

Implications of the Endangered Species Act for Democracy

As Lineberry pointed out, "Democracy is a much overused word. So utterly positive are its connotations today that the word could have been invented by a public relations firm. It takes its place with words like freedom, justice, and peace as a value that almost everyone favors but no one examines very carefully" (1980:36). Its connotations were not always so positive, however. Even some of the Constitution's authors were somber about the democracy they pondered. John Adams, for example, warned, "Remember, democracy never lasts long. It soon wastes, exhausts, and murders itself. There never was a democracy yet that did not commit suicide. It is in vain to say that democracy is less vain, less proud, less selfish, less ambitious, or less avaricious than aristocracy or monarchy" (1851:484). Nevertheless, policy design theory prescribes the serving of democracy as one of the fundamental purposes of public policy. It follows that an assessment of the current social construction of the term "democracy" is in order.

DEMOCRACY AS AN AMERICAN INSTITUTION

Democracy is nearly as broad a topic as ecology or economy, and it invokes different images among Americans (Adler 1991). Some view democracy as representative government made possible by the institution of voting. To others, any government that protects individual freedom qualifies. Most Americans probably have a distinctly American vision of democracy, one shaped by their elementary school acquaintance with the U.S. Constitution and its founding fathers, and by other great American statesmen like Abraham Lincoln. Thus, "Most Americans would probably say that democracy is 'government by the people'" (Lineberry 1980:32), and *Webster's Ninth New Collegiate Dictionary* defines it precisely that way.

Is government by the people an end or a means? Schumpeter posited, "Democracy is a political method, that is to say, a certain type of institutional arrangement for arriving at political — legislative and administrative — decisions and hence incapable of being an end in itself" (1976:242). Lineberry asserted, "Democracy is a means of selecting policy makers and of organizing government to ensure that policy represents and responds to the public's preferences" (1980:33). To Popper, democracy was a type of government "in which the governed can get rid of their rulers without bloodshed" (1994:220).

To others, like President Woodrow Wilson (1901), the concept of democracy embodies certain principles, and "a" democracy is a state that subscribes to those principles. The essential principles of democracy are equality, freedom of information, participation, representation, and majority rule (Lineberry 1980). To the extent that democracy protects and serves those principles, the institution of democracy may be seen as an end. Perhaps democracy is best perceived as an end requiring particular means.

We used the survey instrument described in chapter 6 to investigate the public's attitude toward democracy relative to species conservation and toward other related concepts and institutions. Not surprisingly, democracy has not lost favor among Americans since Lineberry found its connotations "utterly positive." In fact, Americans value democracy significantly higher than economic growth, property rights, and the conservation of species (Table 10). On the other hand, democracy is rated no higher than ecosystem health, and neither of these are rated as highly as resources for posterity.

Because democracy encompasses a number of esteemed principles, its high ranking relative to other institutions is not surprising and lends credence to the position of policy design theory — that public policy should serve democracy as well as solve technical problems. To ascertain the implications of ESA to democracy and vice versa, we consider the relationship of ESA to the major democratic principles identified above.

Equality

As applied to ESA, equality is an unwieldy topic, because nonhuman species are the ultimate targets. Only about 20 percent of our survey respon-

TABLE 10. *Relative Values of Selected Institutions*

Institution A	Mean Value of A	Institution B	Mean Value of B	Mean A–B[a]	t Ratio, Degrees of Freedom	Probability of Type I Error; Reject H_o if $p < (.05/6) = .0083$
Resources for posterity	85.80	Democracy	82.54	3.32	3.88, 601	<.0001; reject H_o
Democracy	82.54	Ecosystem health	80.54	1.86	2.10, 600	0.0366
Democracy	82.54	Conservation of species	76.47	5.92	5.67, 605	<.0001; reject H_o
Ecosystem health	80.54	Conservation of species	76.47	4.05	6.26, 601	<.0001; reject H_o
Conservation of species	76.47	Property rights	76.26	0.19	0.16, 609	0.8720
Conservation of species	76.47	Economic growth	75.4	0.10	0.90, 609	0.3709

Not all mean differences between A and B are consistent with differences calculated from columns 1 and 3, because some respondents failed to evaluate each of the six institutions.

dents saw little or no (≤ 5%) difference in importance among all species types for conservation, and many among that 20 percent considered all nonhuman species to be of little importance or of less importance than humans. Only a slight minority (5%) who valued all types of species at the maximum importance level of 100 could safely be considered biocentric.

Even though the public is not biocentric, nonhuman policy targets cannot be summarily removed from issues of equality. For example, some policies target corporations. Although the public presumably values humans more than corporations, and probably values some types of corporations more than others, all corporations are supposed to be treated equally under rule of law. In fact, corporations are people for the purposes of law (Pope 1996; Roush 1995). But it is easy to imagine a policy on cars that treats them as decidedly unequal, based, for example, on safety features. From a legal perspective, species probably fall somewhere in between. They are not people for the purposes of law, but public-interest lawyers often think of species as their clients (Cheever 1996).

At Orwell's animal farm a sign read, "All animals are equal but some animals are more equal than others" (1987:90). Although Orwell's animals are metaphors for human classes, his profound statement of social reality is no less applicable to the animals themselves. Indeed, all species are not treated equally by ESA. Some are not recognized at all, including those belonging neither to plant nor animal kingdoms (e.g., blue-green algae). The ESA protects distinct populations of vertebrates but not invertebrates and plants, and Section 9's protections are stronger for animals than for plants.

Equality is an ideal, which then, by definition, cannot fully be attained. In striving for the ideal, however, logic need not be abandoned. There are genetic and ecological rationales (chapter 7) that correspond to the political rationale (chapter 6) for distinguishing vertebrates from the other taxa. Therefore, perhaps the current arrangement—which treats vertebrates equally, plants and animals similarly, and disregards microorganisms—reflects the summation and distribution of equality that Americans are willing to offer other species via other principles of democracy, especially majority rule.

Freedom of Information and Public Participation

If one is careful to distinguish freedom of information from public participation, it would be difficult to deny that ESA is a veritable bastion of the former. The distinction is problematic, however. Information may be freely obtained but voluminous and difficult to understand, thus limiting to participation. Nevertheless, ESA requires that agency information on endangered species be generally available to the public (Section 4(b)(3)), solicits public scrutiny of endangered species management decisions (Sections 4(f)(4); 4(h)(4); 7(g)(2)(B)(ii); 7(g)(8); 7(l)(2); 9(f); 10(c)), and allows ample time for citizen response (Section 4(f)(5)). Sections 6(c)(1)(E) and 6(c)(2)(D) require states desiring cooperative endangered species management agreements with FWS to have public participation protocol established beforehand. Even the meetings and records of the God Squad must be open to the public (Section 7(e)(5)(D)). Furthermore, ESA mandates judicial review of citizen suits pertaining to the listing process (Sections 4(b)(3)(C)(ii), 4(b)(6)(B)(ii)), exemption decisions of the God Squad (Section 7(n)), and the enforcement of takings prohibitions (Section 11(g)).

Despite its liberal information and participation provisions, ESA has been a target for criticism from participation advocates and adversaries alike. Rarely can a true adversary of participation be found, but given the urgent nature of species preservation, the generous participation clauses of ESA are criticized by those less sympathetic to the democratic process than to species conservation. In other words, democratic participation may be important to almost everyone, but species conservation competes with democratic participation for relative importance. With uncanny application to endangered species conservation, Trotsky observed, "There is a limit to the application of democratic methods. You can inquire of all the passengers as to what type of car they like to ride in, but it is impossible to question them as to whether to apply the brakes when the train is at full speed and accident threatens" (1974:177–78).

Nevertheless, for adamant advocates of democratic participation, ESA implementation is just another example of technocratic suppression. Technocracy is a system of governance in which academic experts rule by virtue of their specialized knowledge and position in dominant scientific institutions (Fischer 1990). Endangered species policy has been noted as particularly prone to technocratic domination (Czech 1997b). Because the genetic, evolutionary, and ecological theory involved in species conservation is highly complex, the general public is virtually inconversant in much of the endangered species policy arena; even more threatening to democracy, so are legislators, judges, presidents, and bureaucratic generalists. That is why endangered species recovery teams have become so influential in the judicial branch of government (Cheever 1996).

All this may explain why critical theorists, who by definition are preoccupied with rooting out the sources of oppression, are generally silent or ambivalent about ESA (chapter 4). The ESA protects one class of oppressed (endangered species) but does so with a technocratic program. While critical theorists tend to support the biggest underdogs, the list of which would probably include nonhuman species, the technocratic form of oppression is a primary target for their enmity.

Just as one should not rush to judge a policy without considering its context, however, one should not rush to judge the effect of technocracy without considering its context. Ironically, technocracy may serve democracy in some policy contexts, albeit with the disclaimer that the end, not the means, is the aspect of democracy served. Such may be the case in degenerative policy contexts, where the democratic process has been manipulated by parties interested more in economic gain than in freedom of information or public participation.

Not all degenerative contexts can benefit from technocracy; technocrats may be the same advantaged manipulators that degenerate the context to begin with. In cases where technocrats are closely aligned with the public interest, however, and where nontechnocratic manipulators not pursuing the public interest have mastered the political process, technocracy offers hope for a democratic outcome. In other words, there are cases where hyperpluralism may be restored to a healthier pluralism by an injection of technocracy.

The endangered species policy arena is an example of a degenerative policy context. Ehrlich and Ehrlich said, "Sadly, much of the progress that has been made in defining, understanding, and seeking solutions to the human predicament over the past thirty years is now being undermined by an environmental backlash." They called this phenomenon "brownlash," which they said "has produced what amounts to a body of anti-science—a twisting of the findings of empirical science—to bolster a predetermined worldview and to support a political agenda" (1996:11–12). That agenda consists of dismantling environmental regulations—with ESA as a key target. Brownlash makes a mockery of democratic participation but effectively reduces the freedom of information, too. Degenerative agendas are seldom revealed, and brownlash misinformation interferes with productive conservation dialog.

The extractive industries and the Wise Use movement are primary sources of degeneracy in the environmental policy arena (Lewis 1995; Roush 1995; Deal 1993), but popular journalism exacerbates the degeneracy (Williams 1996). Ehrlich and Ehrlich (1996) observed that whenever there is virtual scientific consensus on an issue (e.g., that global warming is a serious threat), popular journalism refuting such consensus sells better than journalism that simply adds to it. Since popular journalists write for a living and are not as constrained by the peer review process as authors in academia, they have incentive and license to criticize the scientific consensus that species endangerment has reached proportions unprecedented in human history. Accordingly, they have.

The majority of species endangerment is caused by economic growth (chapter 8; Czech et al. 2000), which requires capital. Logically, then, the wealthy will confront ESA's prohibitions most often and with most at stake. There are exceptions, of course, but convincing examples support this logic (e.g., timber and mining corporations). By definition, a degenerative subset of wealthy contenders strategize and hide agendas when ESA stands in the way of profits. Journalists, economists, and even scientists may be recruited into the degenerative agenda. Although the public may value species more than do industrialists who liquidate natural capital for profit, they probably value species less than do the conservation biologists who dominate the endangered species technocracy. To the extent that the outcome represents a compromise between profiteering capitalists and abstruse technocrats, it may correspond with the public interest — the pluralist model of public policy is not devoid of merit.

An advantage of a policy arena in which technocracy and degenerative forces are on opposite ends of a spectrum, with the public interest in between, is that the public need not invest as much time in the process. Of course, such efficiency may be a Pyrrhic victory if citizenship atrophies and public learning opportunities are foregone. Critical theorists view such atrophication as one of the greatest threats to democracy. Nevertheless, with a strong endangered species technocracy to protect the public interest, citizens have more time to participate in other policy arenas that are less degenerative. In that case, citizenship may benefit.

Arguably, another problem with technocracy is its unwillingness to view anything but science as the basis of knowledge. Popper was probably more open-minded than most scientists when he stated, "I regard scientific knowledge as the best and most important kind of knowledge we have — though I am far from regarding it as the only one" (1994:3). Other forms of knowledge include mathematical proof, logic, memorized experience, common sense, and intuition. There are also metaphysical claims to knowledge (Oelschlaeger 1994). There are no clear guidelines for prioritizing or legitimizing any of these thought processes in the policy arena, but science does have one clear advantage: science is the systematic employment of rational self-criticism, which makes it quite ironic that some of the loudest protests of science in the policy arena have come from critical theorists such as Dryzek (1990) and Fischer (1990).

In the case of endangered species policy, it may come down to comparing two imperfect scenarios: meaningful democratic participation overshadowed by a technocratic and degenerative dialectic, or unlimited democratic participation in a non-technocratic context rendered meaningless by degeneracy. Scientific knowledge and reactionary brownlash would dominate the former scenario; knowledge of any type would be difficult to verify in the latter. There appears to be a tradeoff, in other words, between freedom of information — including the accuracy thereof — and public participation.

Representation and Majority Rule

An old adage states that democracy is the recurrent suspicion that more than half of the people are right more than half of the time. For many people, majority rule is indeed synonymous with democracy. However, for large groups, majority rule is virtually impossible to attain without representative government, and then only imperfectly. Furthermore, both are potentially dangerous principles that can conflict with democracy at large. Roush asserted, "Tyranny of the majority has caused some of this country's most shameful missteps from the straight way of democracy" (1995:9). There is a fine line between the liberating function of majoritarian government and the "mutual coercion" prescribed by Hardin (1968) to obviate the tragedy of the commons. As for representation, John Adams asked, "Is not every representative government in the universe an aristocracy?," then answered, "Representation and democracy are a contradiction in terms" (1851:462).

Our bicameral Congress was created so that the legislature would answer to people, not to states, but also to safeguard citizens from the dangers of popular government (Davidson and Oleszek 1994). Yet, to many who occupy large states of little population, neither House nor Senate may seem representative. That is not a result of ESA; all American domestic policies are subject to the strengths and weaknesses of representative government.

Nonetheless, real and perceived imbalances in representation affect the political fitness of ESA and the ability of bureaucrats to administer ESA. A shortage of representation perceived by rural westerners is one of the motivating forces behind the Wise Use movement, the members of which would prefer the disposal of public land and the revocation or weakening of ESA (Echeverria and Eby 1995). As an alternative to programs that operate under the auspices of federal agencies (e.g., grazing leases), privatization would provide rural westerners with relief from Section 7 regulation; that is, the legislated political reach of easterners would not extend to the farms, ranches, and mines of the West.

Unfortunately, privatization has many technical pitfalls for species conservation, including the application of ESA. If the public lands protections of Section 7 were lost to privatization, the protections of Section 9 would take their place to some extent, but Section 7 is a preventive measure, whereas Section 9 is reactionary. Section 7 embodies a planning approach to species conservation, an approach more likely to meet with technical and political success than the prohibitory approach of Section 9. On such a large scale, Section 9 would require a generous faith in the motives of people subject to it or a massive law enforcement program. The rhetoric of Wise Use warrants no such faith in the former, and the history of FWS budgets offers no hope for the latter. Furthermore, Section 7 results in the generation of a great amount of ecological knowledge and awareness through the process of biological assessment; Section 9 does not. Finally, maintenance of a public land base requires the concomitant maintenance of a public technocracy that may protect the public interest from the subversion of degenerate political actors.

Most relevant to American democracy, however, is that the majority would lose a great resource through privatization. Every year millions of hunters, fishermen, birdwatchers, sightseers, and outdoor recreationists travel to public lands for which they have paid taxes. To others, the existence of public lands is valued whether they visit those lands or not. Large-scale public land disposal, which was legally abandoned with the Federal Land Policy and Management Act of 1976 and practically abandoned since passage of the Taylor Grazing Act of 1933, would not readily become politically palatable. The existence of public lands and ESA may not represent the preference of all individuals, but it apparently indicates the preference of the national voting public. With majority rule to consider, privatizing in order to better represent a vocal minority in the rural West would be like robbing many Peters to pay one Paul. Therein lies a dilemma, though, as Roush noted, "We cannot have local people making unilateral demands on resources of national importance. Yet we also cannot have national policies forced down the throats of local people" (1995:9). The only solution to such a dilemma is to create a situation where the cumulative demands are low enough to enable an acceptable compromise. The prospects for such a solution are considered in chapter 11.

The representation issue also involves levels of American government—federal, state, and local. With the possibility of privatization seeming so remote, the Wise Use movement is sympathetic to the "next best thing"—local government takeover of federal land. Indeed, many Wise Use members are leaders in local government (Williams 1995). Many of the problems stemming from privatization also apply to local takeover, however. Local governments are generally more concerned with economic growth and political expansion than with natural resources conservation or species preservation (Platt 1996). The growth of local economies is often based on natural resources extraction, and political expansion usually proceeds concurrently with urbanization. Given the primacy of urbanization and extractive activities as causes of species endangerment (chapter 8), greater influence of local government is likely to exacerbate the problem.

The widespread desire to charter county governments is disturbing in this respect. Until recently, county officials have been relatively satisfied to perform the duties prescribed by their states' governmental leaders. Most states have a constitutional amendment that allows all or certain of their counties the ability to charter their own governments, but only 125 charters had been incorporated prior to 1990 (Cowan and Salant 1999). From 1990 to 1998, seventy-six counties drafted charters for voters to consider, of which twenty-four were approved by voters. A county charter typically establishes executive offices, describes powers and duties of officers, and lays out a financing system. Charter government gives counties more growth potential than that provided by state legislatures to traditional county governments.

States tend to fall between federal and local governments in terms of the relative emphasis given to conservation versus economic growth. That states place a greater emphasis on species conservation than local governments do is not entirely a function of political economy, however. States simply have wildlife jurisdiction that local governments lack. The wildlife jurisdiction possessed by states peaked around 1900 (Czech 1996a), with inroads made thereafter by federal (Bean 1983) and later tribal governments (Czech 1995b; Czech 1999). The federal government has historically taken the lead role in preventing extinction and promoting recovery of endangered species. Today, states and tribes have jurisdiction over most game species, while the federal government has jurisdiction over migratory birds and endangered species.

The political history of ESA indicates that the public has overwhelmingly viewed species extinction as a threat to the national interest. Nevertheless, the ESA authors accommodated the federalist principles of American government, and Section 6 is devoted to cooperation with states. Section 4(b)(5)(A) requires that affected states (and counties) must receive special notice of proposed listing regulations and must be solicited for their opinion on such regulations. If the secretary makes a decision contrary to a state's opinion, the secretary must provide that state with a written justification (Section 4(i)). Even in emergency situations, when the listing process may be expedited, states must receive special notice (Section 4(b)(7)(B)). For threatened species, the secretary cannot engage Section 9 prohibitions within a state that has an ESA cooperative agreement unless that state also adopts such prohibitions (Section 4(d)). Section 8A(e)(4) even ensures that states' authority over resident fish and wildlife may not be usurped by the Convention on Nature Protection and Wildlife Preservation in the Western Hemisphere.

Partly due to ESA's Section 6, forty-five states have their own endangered species acts (George 1998). The state acts are generally much weaker, providing only for the listing of species and the prohibition of take. A few states, however, have emulated ESA — most notably California.

We have discussed the standard geographic and political aspects of democratic representation, as have many others. The temporal aspect of representation, however, is often disregarded in public policy. To the extent that Americans hold the nation and its resources in trust for future generations, however, they should represent those generations in the policy arena. In a temporal sense, ESA is uniquely representative. Given that many species, once endangered and protected by ESA, will not recover for many decades, many of the benefits accrue only to future generations. The ESA represents the interests of posterity by calling for a monetary sacrifice of the extant; a concern for temporal justice represents an investment in posterity.

SUMMARY

The ESA adheres strongly to the principles of democracy. It was passed and is retained via principles of majority rule and representation, and its authors respected the American, federalist system of democracy. The measure of equality granted to species in ESA language and in ESA implementation is consistent with that granted by the majority and with biological principles. The ESA authors embraced freedom of information and public participation, although the latter is limited by the technical complexity of species conservation. However, the endangered species technocracy serves the public interest, considering the degeneracy of the endangered species policy arena. A more important threat, at least to the freedom of information, is that FWS is perennially one of the most severely underfunded natural resource agencies (Clarke and McCool 1996). A skeletal budget cripples the information-dissemination abilities of an agency in a number of ways; for example, fewer personnel are available to disseminate information, printing and publishing declines, and less data are gathered or transformed into information. Skeletal budgeting is a politically derived fiscal restraint, however — not an ESA flaw.

10

Property Rights and the Endangered Species Act

The relationship of private property rights to democracy is puzzling. Friedman (1962) claimed that private property was a necessary condition for democracy, but Sunstein (1993) posited that tightly held private property rights can disempower democracy. Both offered compelling arguments; perhaps democracy owes some of its derivation to a dialectic in which efforts to secure private authority over property are pitted against efforts to communize. If this is so, one might expect a capitalist democracy (e.g., the United States) to prevail where the libertarian spirit is stronger, and a "socialist democracy" (e.g., Sweden) otherwise (Adler 1991). In this view, it is not democracy *per se*, but constitutionalism that keeps nations from moving to the extremes of anarchy or totalitarianism (Sunstein 1993).

By its nature, however, constitutionalism tends to serve democracy and result in democratic government. The Constitution of the United States, for example, embodies and employs the five principles discussed in chapter 9. Perhaps the pivotal document of democracy in the world, the Constitution upholds other principles too, including private rights to real property. The Fifth Amendment to the Constitution states, "No person shall be . . . deprived of life, liberty, or property, without due process of law; nor shall private property be taken for public use, without just compensation."

Scholars argue that, with the property clause, the Constitution's authors were motivated by concerns for economic efficiency as well as equity (Lazarus 1993). As statesmen versed in William Blackstone's *Commentaries on the Laws of England* (1766), they believed that property rights would be the heart of the agricultural society they wished to engineer. They also were formulating their ideas in the wake of Adam Smith's *The Wealth of Nations* (1776) and thus were convinced that sharply defined, readily transferable, and lawfully protected property rights would ensure the optimum allocation of resources. They held this belief at a time when economic growth was a universally cherished goal, whether by the old means of mercantilism or the new means of capitalism (Rostow and Kennedy 1990).

Furthermore, the Federalists subscribed to John Locke's natural law as set forth in *Two Treatises on Civil Government* (1690), by which the rights to life, health, liberty and possessions were deemed inalienable (Hamilton et al. 1961). They perceived of their task as one of explicating the "social contract" by which government was legitimized, a contract that protected the individual's inalienable rights from infringement by other individuals or government. In the tradition of natural rights, "that government is best which governs least . . . government's role is to help convert natural resources into private property, and then to protect that property" (Roush 1995:2).

Epstein (1995) noted the similarity between constitutions and covenants, the former being distinguished by their societal scope but not by their susceptibility to the "doctrine of changed conditions." This doctrine holds that a restrictive covenant is no longer enforceable when the social and environmental conditions existing when the covenant was created no longer apply. Similarly, from the perspective of policy design theory, although the Constitution is the foundation of government and policy in the United States, it is itself a policy—upon which the importance of context is not lost. For example, the nation has struggled with the interpretation of the Second Amendment, which established the right to keep and bear arms. Surely, at the time the Constitution was drafted, arms were not foreseen as fully automatic, much less nuclear, weapons. Whether they were foreseen as semiautomatic assault rifles, however, is a topic of heated debate.

Likewise, the question has arisen of what constitutes "property" and the taking thereof. No one doubts that a deeded parcel of land is property, nor that eminent domain constitutes a taking that must be compensated for. But landowners whose activities have been affected by environmental statutes have asserted that the ability to conduct certain affairs on their property constitutes property itself, and that the regulation of that ability constitutes a taking that must be compensated for. Claiming constitutional high ground, they base their assertion on Locke's philosophy of natural rights. Locke proposed that every man naturally had a property right to his person and that the work of his hands were naturally his as well. When the concept of work extended to include thought, then the plans of a person became that person's natural property too.

Furthermore, thought contributes to identity; which is a constituent of personhood and therefore private property in the Lockean sense. As Radin described it, "If an object you now control is bound up in your future plans or in your anticipation of your future self, and it is partly these plans for your own continuity that make you a person, then your personhood depends on the realization of these expectations" (1995:11–12). This philosophy helps to explain the adamancy with which some landowners defend their plans as property. It also helps to explain why property law, especially Fifth Amendment takings, has become "one of the most vibrant, varied, and contested fields of legal scholarship" as environmental regulations have intensified (Ellickson and Rose 1995:xiii).

REGULATORY TAKINGS V. NUISANCE PREVENTION IN THE FEDERAL COURTS

The concept of regulatory takings has been recognized by the Supreme Court at least since 1922 via *Pennsylvania Coal v. Mahon* (Dwyer et al. 1995). The Pennsylvania Coal Company owned the mining rights under Mahon's house, and Mahon had signed a contract releasing the company from liability for subsidence due to mining activity. Afterward, the state of Pennsylvania forbade mining that caused residential property to subside. The company filed suit, claiming that its right to the coal beneath Mahon's residence had been taken. The Supreme Court concurred, surprising some observers in light of earlier Court opinions (Dwyer et al. 1995). In *Hadacheck v. Sebastian,* for example, a ban on brickmaking to protect encroaching residences was not ruled as a taking of a brickmaker's property. And in *Mugler v. Kansas,* a prohibition of alcohol sales was not ruled as a taking of a brewer's property. However, whereas the earlier cases involved regulated properties that remained available for other economic activities, the Pennsylvania Coal Company's subsurface mineral rights were rendered essentially worthless by the Pennsylvania law.

While *Pennsylvania Coal* established a precedent for requiring compensation to landowners whose property rights are rendered worthless by government regulation, the facts of the case were unique, and the Court quickly returned to its pre-*Pennsylvania Coal* form. Six years after *Pennsylvania Coal,* the Court upheld a Virginia law in *Miller v. Schoene* that allowed the state, with no liability for compensation, to eliminate a land-owner's stand of ornamental trees to curb the spread of disease to a nearby orchard. In *Bailey v. Holland* (1942), the Court found that a ban on hunting near a wildlife refuge did not constitute a taking, despite Bailey's claim that the ban rendered his land "practically worthless" (Dwyer et al. 1995:731).

Not until 1978, with *Pennsylvania Central Transportation Co. v. New York*, did the Court explicate criteria for settling takings cases (Buck 1991). The Court first provided that if there was a physical invasion of property, a taking had almost certainly occurred. This criterion follows readily from the Constitution and had long been employed in the courts. It was reiterated in *Pennsylvania Central*, presumably for the sake of comprehensiveness or to provide a starting point of certainty from which cases of lesser certainty could proceed. In 1982 the physical invasion criterion was established as a "per se" takings rule in *Loretto v. Teleprompter Manhattan CATV*, meaning that a plaintiff would not need to address any other criteria to establish the fact of taking, once physical invasion was established.

Next, the *Pennsylvania Central* Court established that if a land use regulation did not produce widespread public benefit, it probably constituted a taking. Historically, courts generally adhered to the principle that if a regulation was enforced to benefit the public, it was probably a taking, but if the regulation was enforced to prevent a private party from harming the public, it was a legitimate exercise of police power (Buck 1991; Dwyer et al. 1995). In many cases, however, preventing harm is practically indistinguishable from providing benefit. With *Pennsylvania Central*, the Court essentially retired the benefit/harm test and assumed that government regulations were intended either to benefit the public by preventing harm or to prevent the harm of neglecting beneficial regulations. However, if the regulation in fact provided little benefit (or prevented little harm), it could be ruled a taking. Furthermore, if a substantially beneficial regulation was not applied equally among properties in similar situations, it could qualify as a taking of the properties to which it applied most severely.

The *Pennsylvania Central* Court also provided that the extent to which the property owner was restricted from earning a reasonable rate of return on his or her investment in the property had to be considered. Consistent with *Pennsylvania Coal*, total elimination of economic value constitutes a taking. In 1992, this principle was established as a per se rule in *Lucas v. South Carolina Coastal Council*. The value of Lucas's coastal property was practically eliminated when South Carolina passed a law prohibiting beachfront construction; the Court found that it needed not to assess any other *Pennsylvania Central* criteria to rule that the prohibition was a taking. The Court has not ruled that partial loss of value cannot constitute a taking, but a taking via partial loss cannot occur per se: the other criteria for establishing takings must also be considered.

Application of the total loss criterion is not simple. Even if Lucas's property was worth only a dollar after construction was prohibited, its value was not literally eliminated. The courts must decide on a case-by-case basis, in other words, if the proportional magnitude of the loss is great enough to engage the per se *Lucas* rule.

Finally, the *Pennsylvania Central* Court established that an investment in a project would not be ruled taken via regulation if it had been unreasonable to expect the project's fruition when the investment was made. The Court applied this criterion in 1984, when the chemical company Monsanto had secret information that it claimed was "taken" via federal disclosure law. In *Ruckelshaus v. Monsanto Company*, the Court ruled that in a highly regulated industry like chemical manufacture, companies should continually expect new regulations. In so ruling, the court found it unnecessary to consider other taking criteria; that is, the reasonable investment-backed criterion may be used per se in a no-taking ruling.

The case law on regulatory takings has been consistent with a larger body of jurisprudence called "nuisance doctrine." As Buck explained, "There is a general rule at common law that no one may use his property to impair the right of another person; that is, no one may create a nuisance. There are two kinds of nuisance: private and public . . . A public nuisance is an activity that adversely affects the health, morals, safety, welfare, comfort, or convenience of the public in general" (1991:61). In a sense, nuisance doctrine constitutes a Fifth Amendment for neighbors, protecting their rights to "possess" integral components of life, liberty, and private property in the form of personhood. Nuisance doctrine, then, stands powerfully juxtaposed to natural rights in land.

Most of the nuisance jurisprudence associated with natural resources has been meted out in state courts, which show considerable variance in their interpretations of what constitutes nuisance (Sax 1993). Describing a trend toward the incorporation of nuisance doctrine in property law, however, Lazarus asserted, "Both public and private nuisance doctrine easily extend to the safeguarding of environmental and natural resource concerns" (1993:202). The high value attributed to species conservation by the public supports the argument that endangered species habitat destruction is a public nuisance. Furthermore, as more species go extinct or become endangered, the possibility of widespread ecological and there-fore economic collapse increases, along with the propriety of classifying habitat destruction as a public nuisance.

Habitat destruction might qualify as private nuisance in some cases. If a landowner's action contributes to the extinction of a species, it may "take" from the mental health, morals, and personal identity of people (Wilson 1984), especially neighbors who otherwise would have experi-enced the species' presence. This application of biophilia stretches the meaning of private property, much like the concept of including a land-owner's plans stretches the meaning of personhood. The landowner's plans are more readily gauged in economic terms than the public's bio-philia, but that may simply demonstrate the naïveté of public choice the-ory (Schelling 1995).

WILDLIFE AND PROPERTY RIGHTS IN THE FEDERAL COURT SYSTEM

Cases involving compensation for Fifth Amendment private property tak-ings are heard in the Court of Federal Claims and may be appealed to the Supreme Court. Until 1997, no ESA-related takings cases had been adjudicated by either court, although the Supreme Court came near the issue in 1995. In *Sweet Home v. Babbitt*, the Court supported the FWS' interpretation of "harm" (i.e., to a threatened or endangered species, as prohibited in Section 9 of ESA) as including habitat destruction. *Sweet Home* was a "facial" case; it settled a dispute over the meaning of a law without considering the facts of the case (Flick et al. 1996). If the Court had determined that the FWS interpretation was unlawful, then FWS, in order to prevent habitat destruction, would have had no recourse but to practice eminent domain and compensate the landowner in the process. The Court's approval of the FWS interpretation of "harm," in combina-tion with ESA's clear prohibition of harming listed species, implied that there is no taking of property necessitated when FWS prohibits a land-owner from destroying endangered species habitat. Instead, FWS is prac-ticing legitimate police power vested in it by ESA. *Sweet Home* did not, however, imply that an FWS regulation cannot constitute a taking if, for example, it triggers one of the *Pennsylvania Central* per se rules.

On August 22, 1997, an ESA takings case was decided by the Court of Federal Claims in *Good v. United States*. Judge James F. Merow's thirty-five-page opinion provides an account of the statutory and case law pertinent to ESA takings cases. *Good* is also a fairly typical example of a controversy involving the ESA and a developer, so the opinion and the finding offer substantial information pertaining to how the courts will treat ESA takings cases.

On October 8, 1973, Good purchased a set of properties in the Florida Keys, including a parcel called Sugarloaf Shores. Sugarloaf Shores contained about 13 hectares of wetlands (including salt marsh and freshwater sawgrass marsh) and 3 hectares of upland. Good intended to develop a 54-lot subdivision with a 48-slip marina. The development would entail excavation, drainage, dredging, and filling. The property contained habitats for several species that were eventually listed as endangered, including the Lower Keys marsh rabbit and the silver rice rat. Most of the property was periodically submersed in the tidal, navigable waters of Upper Sugarloaf Sound. The Clean Water Act had been passed the previous year, and ESA would be passed later that year. Other federal and state environmental laws more or less directly related to development in the Keys had been passed, and the purchasing contract stated, "The Buyers recognize that certain of the lands covered by this Contract may be below the mean high tide line and that as of today there are certain problems in connection with the obtaining of State and Federal permission for dredging and filling operations" (39 Fed.Cl. 85).

In 1980, Good hired Keycology, a consulting firm, to obtain the county, state, and federal permits required for development. Keycology was to be paid $24,000 for its efforts and an additional fee if the permits were indeed obtained. Although the lack of any permit could halt the project, the focus of *Good* was on the permitting role of the Army Corps of Engineers and the influence exercised by FWS under ESA. The Corps is responsible for regulating dredging, filling, and discharge in navigable waters in the United States via the Rivers and Harbors Act of 1899 and the Clean Water Act. The Corps is also required to coordinate its activities with FWS pursuant to the Fish and Wildlife Coordination Act, and it is required to consult with FWS on projects with the potential to harm threatened and endangered species pursuant to Section 7 of ESA.

In 1983, Good received a Corps permit that was valid for five years but was unable to obtain the requisite county and state permits during that period. He received two Corps extensions, and the Corps issued a new permit in 1988 after incorporating some newly developed regulations designed to conserve rare wetland types. Meanwhile, Keycology obtained for Good a state permit that was conditioned upon receipt of a county permit. The Monroe County board of adjustment, however, which classified Good's proposal as a major development, had established a moratorium on issuing major development approvals. Good convinced the Monroe County Commission to overrule the Board of Adjustment. The Florida Department of Community Affairs appealed the commission's action to the Florida Land and Water Adjudicatory Commission. While this appeal was pending, Monroe County adopted stricter regulations on the dredging and filling of salt marsh. Good filed suit in state court, claiming that the state's actions had prevented him from developing his property before the county adopted stricter regulations. This case was settled by a stipulation that entitled Good to have his county permit applications be considered on the basis of the earlier county guidelines for major development reviews.

The county's major development review process entailed that Good obtain a surface water management permit from the South Florida Water Management District, which denied the application. The district noted that the property provided habitat for two species listed as endangered under state law: the Lower Keys marsh rabbit and the mud turtle. The district also noted that Good had failed to provide for mitigation of impacts on these species' habitats. Good declined to reapply to the district and filed for final development approval with the county without the district permit. That attempt failed, and the county permit expired on May 9, 1991.

Good's 1988 Corps permit was not set to expire until 1993. However, Good informed the Corps on June 14, 1990, that he needed a new permit. Apparently, he intended to obtain a Corps permit that would account for the state and county regulations he had encountered prior to pursuing the county permitting process further.

The Lower Keys marsh rabbit was listed under ESA on June 21, and FWS initiated consultation pursuant to Section 7. Based on Good's 1990 proposal, FWS opined in February 1991 that Good's development would not jeopardize the marsh rabbit. The FWS did, however, recommend denial of the permit based on its mandate under the Fish and Wildlife Coordination Act, a toothless law (chapter 3) that altered the outcome of neither the permitting nor the adjudicatory process.

Good reconsidered his decision to file for a new Corps permit. On May 14, 1991, despite his failure to obtain the requisite county permit, he informed the Corps that he would proceed according to the 1988 Corps permit. Judge Merow's opinion does not address Good's motivation. Perhaps Good planned to approach the county commission and skirt the county permitting process, as he had done with partial success before. Or perhaps he had begun to strategize for a takings case and chose to pursue the 1988 permit because it would demonstrate greater economic potential of his property. The silver rice rat had been listed fifteen days prior. It must have been obvious to Good, an ex-attorney, that permits were going to be harder to obtain.

The FWS prepared new biological opinions based on the 1988 and 1990 permit applications. New data showed further decline in the marsh rabbit population, and FWS noted that a fire on another of Good's properties may have destroyed marsh rabbit habitat. The FWS sought permission to evaluate Good's properties. Good denied, and FWS opined that, based on the available evidence, the 1988 and 1990 permits would jeopardize the marsh rabbit and the rice rat. The FWS recommended that the Corps deny the 1990 permit and provided "reasonable and prudent alternatives" to the 1988 permit pursuant to Section 10 of ESA. These alternatives restricted development to the upland portion of Sugarloaf shores.

Good refused to participate in the development of the alternatives. Instead, he hired an environmental consultant and mammalogist, Dr. Larry Brown, who contested FWS's jeopardy finding. Brown asserted that Sugarloaf Shores was not marsh rabbit habitat and that the rice rat did not inhabit the property. The Corps asked FWS to reinitiate consultation: FWS declined, restating its biological opinion of jeopardy. On March 17, 1994, the Corps denied Good's 1990 permit application and noted that his 1988 permit had expired but indicated that the alternatives provided by FWS were permissible.

Good clearly began, if he had not already done so, to strategize for a takings case. On May 27, 1994, he responded to the Corps with a letter asserting that any development of Sugarloaf Shores would violate ESA. He attached a two-page report from Dr. Brown, who now claimed that even the upland portion of the property could not be developed without violating ESA because all of the property constituted a "unit of natural habitat which is a functioning ecosystem, necessary for the continued survival of the Key's marsh rabbits which live on the site" (39 Fed.Cl. 93). On July 11, 1994, Good filed suit against the United States. He claimed that the Corps' denial of his permit application deprived his property of all economic value because ESA required that his entire property be maintained in its natural state.

In its defense, the United States pointed out that the commerce clause of the Constitution grants the federal government the power and duty to regulate the navigable waters of the United States. This navigational servitude inheres in the title of all property. Good's development was dependent on access to navigable waters, so there was no inherent value of the development and therefore no taking. Merow disagreed: "It cannot be said that plaintiff's statements relate strictly to values reserved to the federal government pursuant to the navigational servitude. Accordingly, taking the facts most favorably for plaintiff, defendant has not shown that all economically relevant limitations on plaintiff's use of Sugarloaf Shores inhered in his title" (39 Fed.Cl. 97).

Merow also disagreed, however, with Good's claim to a *Lucas* per se taking. First, he found that ESA did not require Good to maintain Sugarloaf Shores in its natural state. He pointed out that Good, in his letter to the Corps asserting that any development would violate ESA, had failed to recognize the Section 10 exemptions to the Section 9 prohibitions of taking endangered species. Merow added, "Those exemptions were added to the Act in 1982 to resolve precisely the tension between section 7 and section 9 that plaintiff seizes upon to support his *Lucas* claim" (39 Fed.Cl. 99). The FWS had provided for exempting Good of incidental take in its reasonable and prudent alternatives. (We surmised in chapter 5 that the Section 10 exemptions were a political compromise with dubious biological merit. However, our recommendation in chapter 11 for improving Section 10 would remain consistent with Judge Merow's opinion if FWS were able to demonstrate that Good's project would result in no additive mortality to the species' population and that individual marsh rabbits taken via Good's project would be of insignificant ecological or scientific value to the species' conservation in their living state.)

Good claimed that even if ESA did not require him to maintain Sugarloaf Shores in its natural state, his limited development options were not economically viable, and therefore a *Lucas* per se taking had still occurred. Although this argument was for a *Lucas* per se ruling, it also invoked the *Pennsylvania Central* criterion of reasonable investment-backed alternatives. But Merow quoted from the 1934 opinion in *Olson v. United States*: "Elements affecting value that depend upon events or combinations of occurrences which, while within the realm of possibility, are not fairly shown to be reasonably probable should be excluded from consideration, for that would be to allow mere speculation and conjecture to become a guide for the ascertainment of value" (39 Fed.Cl. 104).

While acknowledging the general propriety of the *Olson* opinion, Merow nonetheless noted that ongoing litigation (*Florida Rock Industry v. United States*) appeared to be refining the opinion. He then considered the United States's proposition that property value assessment may only account for uses permissible under state and county law. He found that proposition untenable because it would "exclude from consideration the possible existence of a market of investors speculating on a future development for Sugarloaf Shores." Without mentioning the substantial irony therein, he proceeded with the observation, "The possibility that such a market could exist is evidenced by plaintiff's own representations relating to Sugarloaf Shores. In his 1980 contract with Keycology, for example, after acknowledging the dim prospects for obtaining the necessary permits to develop Sugarloaf Shores, plaintiff nonetheless speculated that the property had a worth of $350,000.00 in its undeveloped state without those permits." Thus, the United States could not refute Good's *Lucas* per se claim by pointing to the state or county regulations, but neither could Good claim that any regulations had totally devalued his property. Speculative market values were likely to fall within the range of reasonable investment-backed expectations.

Merow elaborated on the reasonable investment-backed expectations of Good and further investigated the property values of Sugarloaf Shores pre- and post- investment. Basically, he found that a reasonable investor would have concluded that development of Sugarloaf Shores was a speculative endeavor and that a significant value remained in the post-investment property. In the absence of total loss of property value, he clearly placed more import on the reasonable investment-backed criterion. Merow concluded that land development at the time of Good's purchase "was a highly regulated business, and plaintiff's sought uses for Sugarloaf Shores were subject to restriction or prohibition under that regulatory regime. While plaintiff was free to take the investment risks he took in this regulated environment, he cannot look to the Fifth Amendment for compensation when such speculation proves ill-taken" (39 Fed.Cl. 114).

Although *Good* provides a fairly comprehensive illustration of Fifth Amendment takings jurisprudence as applied to ESA, legal scholars are disappointed that *Good* failed to clarify several issues (M. Bean, Environmental Defense Fund, pers. comm.). For example, Merow ruled that the United States failed to demonstrate that the limitations to Good's development inhered in his title (because of the navigational servitude), but he did not indicate what would constitute a successful demonstration. Later, when Merow concluded that "state and county restrictions at issue in this case may not validly be asserted to effect a total defense to a *Lucas per se* claim" (39 Fed.Cl. 105), he did not state what distinguished "this case" from others.

We would also point out that the United States neglected to argue that limitations on wildlife consumption inhere in the title to land ownership. Although the limitation of private rights to wildlife are seldom expressed in terms of inherence, it is clear that American landowners have never had property rights to free-ranging wildlife or species (Rolston 1991). States have generally reserved those rights, with federal and tribal governments accruing a greater share in the twentieth century. The concept of regulatory takings assumes that a property owner has a bundle of rights, one or more sticks of which are taken by regulation, thus requiring compensation. Regulating the taking of a species or a live specimen by a landowner is not a taking, in the sense that a species or a live specimen was never a "stick" in the bundle of rights. Furthermore, if ESA took one stick that arguably belonged in the bundle (a "natural right" of land management) so that a stick (a species) belonging to the public was preserved, it would do so to prevent a public nuisance. Perhaps these principles are manifest in the statutory and case law employed in *Good*, but explication of these principles may help to clarify ESA takings cases.

PRINCIPLES OF DEMOCRACY AND THE FUTURE OF ESA TAKINGS CLAIMS

As economic growth endangers more species, economically motivated landowners are likely to file for Fifth Amendment compensation more frequently. As takings case law indicates, there will be no easy legal solution to the ESA–property rights conflict. Compounding the legal complexity is biological uncertainty in cases where little is known about a species and its habitat on private property (Frank 1993). In *Nollan v California Coastal Commission* (1987), the Court opined that a regulation must have an "essential nexus" to the impacts caused by the regulated development (Dwyer et al. 1995:733). That criterion will probably increase the influence of the endangered species technocracy on the judiciary.

In cases like this, where it is unreasonable to hope that the technocracy will be consistently correct and the courts perpetually prudent, society has little choice but to fall back on the holistic system of democracy established by the Constitution and characterized by the five aforementioned principles. Concerned citizens, equal under the law and free to become informed, may participate to form a majority that is then represented in the legislature. If the resulting legislation is deemed unconstitutional by the judiciary, however, then the majority must become strong enough to amend the Constitution in order to pursue its agenda. The only other recourse may occur if the issue is contested within the judiciary. In that case, political influence on the composition of the courts may result in the outcome desired by the majority seeking change (O'Brien 1993) — assuming that majority has persisted throughout the long process of judicial turnover. In fact, judicial turnover may affect ESA implementation, because today's federal judges tend to be more sympathetic to landowners' rights than they have been in recent decades (Dwyer et al. 1995). That trend reflects the fact that Ronald Reagan was the most successful court-packing president since Franklin Roosevelt (O'Brien 1993).

We used the survey instrument introduced in chapter 6 to determine where Americans stand on the issue of property rights as related to endangered species conservation. On an agreement scale from 0–100 (where 50 indicates neutrality), the respondents agreed at a level of 61 with the statement, "Landowners should not have the right to use their property in ways that endanger a species." Respondents disagreed at a level of 41 with the statement, "Endangered species protection should not interfere with a landowner's right to develop property." These straightforward statements represent different sides of the same coin but were used in tandem for verification purposes. The answers total to almost exactly 100, and the agreement levels are uncanny indicators of majorities. For example, while the agreement level for the first statement was 61, 61 percent of respondents agreed to some extent (rated their agreement with the statement at > 50) with the statement (Table 12). These results indicate that the public has a well-defined stance on this issue.

On the other hand, respondents agreed at a level of 58 with the statement, "Landowners prevented from developing their property because of endangered species laws should be paid for any lost income by the public." Again, the level of agreement is practically the same as the proportion of respondents that agreed with the statement (Table 11).

These data shed some light on the ESA–property rights dialectic. Apparently, the public supports the implementation of ESA on private lands and also supports the compensation of landowners for losses incurred by the implementation of ESA. However, these results convey vastly different implications.

The ESA is a statute. Barring its amendment, endangered species protection will affect landowners' rights to develop property. The public supports that effect, which means ESA should not be modified to excuse private landowners from species conservation responsibilities, through the democratic principles of majority rule and representation. If the majority felt otherwise, then ESA would be bound for repeal. The Fifth Amend-

TABLE 11. *Levels of Agreement with Stances on Property Rights and Species Conservation Law*

Statement	Mean Agreement Level	Agree (%)	Neutral (%)	Disagree (%)
Endangered species protection should not interfere with a landowner's right to develop property	41.26	33.3	7.8	58.8
Landowners should not have the right to use their property in ways that endanger a species	60.54	61.0	6.2	32.8
Landowners prevented from developing their property because of endangered species laws should be paid for any lost income by the public	57.51	56.6	6.9	36.6

ment, however, is not so accessible for modification. The majority opinion that landowners should be compensated is not sufficient for a constitutional amendment. To be passed by Congress, an amendment requires a two-thirds majority in both houses (or a national constitutional convention requested by legislatures of two thirds of the states) and ratification by legislatures of three fourths of the states (or by a convention called for by three fourths of the states).

Furthermore, many people in favor of compensation would probably not be in favor of amending the Constitution to effect such compensation. Even if all such people favored an amendment, and assuming accurate representation by Congress, an additional 10 percent of the population would need to be convinced for a two-thirds majority to be attained. The survey results suggest that those favoring compensation — not necessarily amendment — hold a majority in only twenty-nine of the required thirty-eight states. The relative weakness of the majority in favor of compensating landowners for losses ascribed to ESA suggests that a constitutional amendment to mandate such compensation is an unlikely prospect for the foreseeable future.

Furthermore, support for compensating landowners is positively correlated with age (Czech 1997a), and there are two plausible explanations. The public may be getting less concerned with preserving the inviolability of property rights and more concerned with protecting the public from the activities of private landowners, as it sees a gradual erosion of the natural resources base and increasing numbers of imperiled species. Indeed, Lewis quoted a law professor who called the Wise Use movement "the last powerful gasp of a land-use ethic that is becoming obsolete" (1995:19). Alternatively, people may become more concerned with property rights as they age and acquire property. Perhaps both explanations are true; the correlation is strong and highly significant. If both are true, then the majority will gradually diminish (unless life expectancy increases interminably). These survey data support the opinion of Meltz (1994), who predicted that the challenges to ESA by property rights advocates will fail.

Of course, there are no constitutional barriers to mandating compensation via amendment to ESA itself. Five states have passed laws requiring state and local governments to compensate landowners for significant property value reductions resulting from state and local regulations (Zhang 1996); Congress could do likewise for federal regulations. If the current majority holds and is, per capita, as participatory and politically astute as the minority, then an ESA amendment to compensate landowners is foreseeable and democratically appropriate. However, the window of opportunity may be closing. Support for the statement that, "landowners should not have the right to use their property in ways that endanger a species" is strongly and negatively correlated with age (Czech 1997a).

SUMMARY

The doctrine of changed conditions is of principal importance to property rights cases involving ESA. Several relevant phenomena have not changed since the Constitutional Convention. A deeded parcel of land qualifies as property, physical invasion of landed property is clearly a taking, and property rights facilitate economic growth. The condition that appears to have changed most relevantly is the propriety of economic growth. Economic growth is increasingly seen as an anachronistic goal of—and even as the major threat to—Western society (Douthwaite 1992; Daly and Cobb 1994; Ayers 1998; Czech 2000b). While the equity principles underlying the Fifth Amendment property clause may be timeless, the economic motivation apparently is not. If this is correct, then ESA's indirect effect of slowing economic growth by diminishing property development rights (public and private) serves not only endangered species but also the general welfare of the United States.

11

Summary and Recommendations

The history of the United States is a concurrent history of species endangerment. As the nation's preoccupation evolved from conquest to settlement to economic growth, the causes of endangerment changed from harvest to habitat destruction to ecosystem-wide degradation. The concern for species conservation is not new — nor is the concern for conserving habitats and ecosystems — but political efforts to stem the tide of extinction were more effective against the clearly visible problem of overharvest. Today, although many more species are known, and the public has become increasingly concerned with noncharismatic taxa, the problem is far more formidable and elusive.

Informed by the ecological sciences, academic and bureaucratic institutions became prominent participants in the wildlife policy arena. Statutory law evolved to reflect and further that participation, and jurisdiction over species became increasingly federal. Along with the public, and affecting the public, the wildlife profession expanded its scope of concern far beyond game species.

The ESA represents the natural product of these social, professional, and political developments. Given the widespread popularity as well as the regulatory impact of ESA, it became a frequent subject of policy analysis. Policy analysis, however, has been a controversial occupation in its own right. Theories and perspectives of policy analysis have fallen short because of epistemological, philosophical, methodological, and ideological myopia. Pluralism, policy sciences, public choice theory, and critical theory have produced analyses characterized by a lack of normative content, preoccupation with reductionist methods, illogical optimism in a free market, and little practical application, respectively. Policy specialism has succumbed to each of these weaknesses in various combinations, depending on the specialized paradigm of the analyst.

Policy design theory was developed to address the shortcomings of traditional policy analysis perspectives. It recognizes strengths in each of the traditional perspectives and employs the same. More important, it also recognizes the importance of an orderly and logical arrangement of policy elements, the social construction of target groups, the technical legitimacy of a policy, and the socioeconomic context of policy. Most distinctively, it attaches to all policy the normative duty of serving democracy.

The application of policy design theory to ESA illuminates some logical errors of ESA structure, including thirteen incorrect or highly dubious assumptions of the ESA authors. It helps to explain the allocation of benefits to species and reveals opportunities for more effective conservation efforts in the political arena. It provides a holistic view of the species approach to conservation. It reveals an incredibly challenging socioeconomic context to any policy that would conserve species, no matter how logical that policy would otherwise seem. Finally, it shows that ESA embraces the principles of democracy. Ironically, that very finding provides an opportunity for improving policy design theory itself, as we will show. First, however, specific recommendations for the improvement of ESA are made possible by the analysis of the assumptions underlying ESA.

RECOMMENDATIONS FOR CORRECTING FAULTY ASSUMPTIONS OF ESA AUTHORS

Policymakers may improve the logical soundness of ESA that was diminished by the incorrect or highly questionable assumptions of the ESA authors. For example, the first sentence of Section 4(b)(2) states, "The Secretary shall designate critical habitat, and make revisions thereto, under subsection (a)(3) on the basis of the best scientific data available and after taking into consideration the economic impact, and any other relevant impact, of specifying any particular area as critical habitat." Because the loss of critical habitat to the protections of ESA means, by definition, that a species will never recover from its endangered status, the latter part of this statement is not consistent with the policy logic of ESA (chapter 5). The phrase beginning "and after taking into consideration the economic impact" should be deleted. By deleting that phrase, the contradiction of this clause with the goal of ESA, in light of the definitions of "critical habitat" and "conservation," is avoided.

The first sentence of Section 4(b)(6)(B)(ii) states, "If a proposed regulation referred to in subparagraph (a)(i) is not promulgated as a final regulation within such one-year period (or longer period if extension under clause (i) applies) because the Secretary finds that there is not sufficient evidence to justify the action proposed by the regulation the Secretary shall immediately withdraw the regulation." Congress assumed that in cases of doubt, the disadvantages of listing outweigh the advantages of listing the (doubtfully) threatened or endangered species. That was a faulty assumption for reasons pertaining to error philosophy, foreseeability of endangerment, and cost reduction (chapter 5). The sentence should instead state, "If a proposed regulation referred to in subparagraph (a)(i) is not promulgated as a final regulation within such one-year period (or longer period if extension under clause (i) applies) because the Secretary finds that there is sufficient evidence that the action proposed by the regulation is unnecessary to conserve the species, the Secretary shall immediately withdraw the regulation. Otherwise, the Secretary shall immediately publish as final the regulation in the Federal Register." This correction would distinguish between cases of doubt and cases where it was demonstrated that a species was not threatened or endangered, and would remain consistent with the logic of erring on the conservative side. Error in this case would amount to assuming and obviating the likelihood that a species of questionable status, if not quite "fully" threatened or endangered, is likely to become so in the relatively near future. It would also produce a more cost-effective conservation strategy than the more desperate measures that would be required to save the species later.

Section 4(b)(7) allows the secretary to disregard the time-consuming processes of species listing and critical habitat designation in emergency situations: "Neither paragraph (4), (5), or (6) of this subsection nor section 553 of title 5, United States Code, shall apply to any regulation issued by the Secretary in regard to any emergency posing a significant risk to the well-being of any species of fish and wildlife or plants." The phrase "shall apply to any regulation issued by the Secretary in regard to any emergency" implies that the secretary may proceed immediately with an emergency regulation — but also may not. The assumption that the secretary will proceed (a necessary assumption for the policy logic of ESA), however, is subject to considerable uncertainty (chapter 5). The problematic phrase should be modified to state, "When any emergency poses a significant risk to the well-being of any species of fish and wildlife or plants, and notwithstanding paragraph (4), (5), or (6) of this subsection or section 553 of title 5, United States Code, the Secretary shall immediately issue a regulation to effect the conservation of the species." (The succeeding subparagraphs, A and B, would have to be linguistically modified to accommodate this change.) In the improved scenario, the secretary would only have discretion regarding what constitutes an emergency but no discretion regarding whether to proceed immediately in cases of emergency. A more elaborate correction would devise a system for ascertaining emergency status that was also independent of secretarial discretion, for example, by engaging a committee of scientists.

The second sentence of Section 4(d) states, "The Secretary may by regulation prohibit with respect to any threatened species any act prohibited under section 9(a)(1), in the case of fish or wildlife, or section 9(a)(2), in the case of plants, with respect to endangered species; except that with respect to the taking of resident species of fish or wildlife, such regulations shall apply in any State which has entered into a cooperative agreement pursuant to section 6(c) of this Act only to the extent that such regulations have also been adopted by such State." Congress's assumption that a state's position on a threatened species' conservation is more important than the species' conservation is inconsistent with the policy logic of ESA and with the Supreme Court's interpretation thereof (chapter 5). The portion of the sentence beginning with, "except that with respect to the taking of resident species of fish or wildlife," should be deleted. This correction would also make Section 4(d) consistent with the logic of erring on the conservative side and with the logic that threatened species are typically on the way to endangered status (in which case the controversial clause would no longer apply anyway).

Section 4(f)(1) directs the secretary to prepare recovery plans for listed species, "unless he finds that such a plan will not promote the conservation of the species." The profoundly cynical assumption indicated by this clause (that a recovery plan can create a wave of public opposition) is, if not inconsistent with the policy logic of ESA, unproductive as employed in the problematic clause (chapter 5). The clause should be deleted, and a sentence should be added: "A recovery plan shall not contain information likely to be used to the detriment of any endangered species, and, when necessary, will include a strategy for obviating any potentially destructive use of information contained in the plan." This correction addresses the problem that the problematic phrase was meant to obviate without abandoning the planning process that is crucial to species recovery.

Section 4(f)(1)(A) directs the secretary to prioritize species for recovery planning "without regard to taxonomic classification." Neither the assumption that all taxa are of equal value, nor that relative values of taxa cannot be ascertained, are legitimate (chapters 6 and 7). The problematic clause should be deleted, and the consideration of taxonomy in prioritizing species for recovery planning should be discretionary.

Section 6(i)(2) states, "[The previously specified] Amounts deposited into the special fund are authorized to be appropriated annually." This wording should be replaced with, "Amounts deposited into the special fund shall be appropriated annually," to correct the faulty assumption that the authorized funding would be appropriated. Dedicated funding should also be mandated by Section 15, which is the major ESA fiscal provision.

The second sentence of Section 7(a)(1) states, "All other Federal agencies shall, in consultation with and with the assistance of the Secretary, utilize their authorities in furtherance of the purposes of this Act by carrying out programs for the conservation of endangered species and threatened species listed pursuant to section 4 of this Act." Congress's assumption that the "other" (i.e., non-FWS or NMFS) agencies would develop such programs with no procedural specifications and appropriations took no account of bureaucratic politics (chapter 5). The sentence should be replaced by, "Every other Federal agency shall employ an endangered species coordinator whose sole occupation shall be to direct a program, in coordination with the Secretary, for the conservation of endangered species and threatened species listed pursuant to section 4 of this Act."

Section 7(e)(3)(G) states, "The President, after consideration of any recommendations received pursuant to subsection (g)(2)(B) shall appoint one individual from each affected State, as determined by the Secretary, to be a member of the [Endangered Species] Committee." This clause produces potential for an organizational conundrum (chapter 5), and should instead state, "The President, after consideration of any recommendations received pursuant to subsection (g)(2)(B) shall appoint one individual to represent the affected State(s), as determined by the Secretary, on the Committee." The improved clause would ensure that the committee is indeed composed of the intended number of members (i.e., seven).

Section 10(d) authorizes the secretary to grant a Section 9 exception that, "if granted and exercised will not operate to the disadvantage of such endangered species." That stipulation, to remain consistent with the policy logic of ESA, requires that the dubious process of compensatory mortality be engaged (chapter 5). It should be changed to "can be demonstrated with the best scientific evidence to result in no additive mortality to the species' population, and when individuals taken pursuant to such exception are of insignificant ecological or scientific value to the species' preservation in their living state." By applying a burden of proof and reducing secretarial discretion as to what constitutes a disadvantage to an endangered species, this correction would reduce the considerable chance of the secretary mistakenly concluding that the loss of individual members of an endangered species may occur without operating to the disadvantage of the species. It also would reduce the politicization of Section 9 exceptions.

The last sentence in Section 10(f)(5) requires, "No regulation prescribed by the Secretary to carry out the purposes of the subsection shall be subject to section 4(f)(2)(A)(i) of this Act." That sentence should be deleted, because there is no section 4(f)(2)(A)(i). In fact, no section of ESA contains a subsection f(2)(A)(i), and it would be impertinent to speculate from the context what the phantom section may have addressed.

Section 11(g)(1)(B–C) authorizes citizens to file suit "to compel the Secretary to apply . . . the prohibitions set forth in or authorized pursuant to section 4(d) and section 9(a)(1)(B) of this Act with respect to [takings]," or "against the Secretary where there is alleged a failure of the Secretary to perform any act or duty under section 4 which is not discretionary with the Secretary." Subparagraphs B and C should be consolidated into a subparagraph B that states, "to compel the Secretary to apply prohibitions set forth in or authorized pursuant to this Act, or against the Secretary where there is alleged a failure of the Secretary to perform any act or duty mandated by this Act." This would correct the faulty assumption that judicial efficiency is more important than species conservation (chapter 5).

Taken together, these recommendations would improve the policy logic of ESA. Of course, some of the "incorrect assumptions" we have noted may simply represent political compromise. Nevertheless, from the perspective of policy logic, they are assumptions in effect. The ESA is a valid program for species conservation; it would function as intended if the assumptions of its authors were correct. Therefore, with all of its assumptions met, ESA would be sound and effective, although political and fiscal limitations will always influence ESA implementation.

RECOMMENDATIONS FOR PRIORITIZING SPECIES FOR CONSERVATION

The only common arguments about the prioritization of species come from two extremes. One is that we should not bother with anything not charismatic or monetarily valuable. The other is that all species are equal in value and equal in their rights to exist. In political terms, these perspectives generally correspond to the far right (i.e., conservative) and the far left (i.e., liberal), respectively. As such, they represent the typical environmental policy dichotomy (Hayward 1994).

The conservative approach is exemplified by Wise Use champions like the American Farm Bureau, which "claims it is being victimized by toads, owls, chubs, suckers, rats and bats, bugs and weeds, whose extinction it is perfectly willing to countenance" (Rauber 1996:31). The Wise Use movement is served in Congress primarily by western Republicans like Representative Don Young (R-Alaska), chairman of the House Resources Committee, who said of the Tipton kangaroo rat, "It's a pest. It's nothing. It has no value" (Williams 1996:122). Although Young voted for ESA, he later asserted that Congress "envisioned trying to protect, you know, pigeons and things like that. We never thought about mussels and ferns and flowers and all these subspecies of squirrels and birds" (Bergman 1995:54). The conservative approach is inherent to public choice theory, because the market welcomes only the tangible monetary value associated with large, charismatic species.

The liberal approach is inherent to a critical theory of species conservation but is also prevalent in policy specialism. In Congress, there is no Don Young analog to the left on ESA, but Democrats have been the most consistent supporters of ESA since it was introduced to the House by Representative John Dingell in 1972. The support for ESA provided by Democrats in Congress is consistent with the aforementioned survey results (chapter 9), via the democratic principle of representation. The liberal approach is championed, however, by environmental organizations, the most extreme of which is Earth First! The Earth First! internet site stated: "Earth First! does not believe in compromise. We set forth the hard-line position of those who believe the Earth must come first. . . . Earth First! is different from other environmental groups. We believe in using all the tools in the tool box, ranging from grassroots organizing and litigation to civil disobedience and monkeywrenching . . . [Earth First!] is not an organization, but a movement. . . . It is a belief in biocentrism, or Deep Ecology, and a practice of putting our beliefs into action" (May 13, 1997).

There is a curious absence of political advocacy from the middle ground, although one does find some academic exploration therein. The middle ground is associated mostly with the policy sciences and, to a lesser extent, with policy specialism, including the prioritization schemes mentioned in chapter 7. Pluralism would predict endangered species policy to rest on the middle ground, but pluralism does not generally recognize a public interest and therefore prescribes little except the integrity of political procedure (see chapter 4).

From a policy design perspective, the middle ground should be advocated. That is not to say that policy design theory always, or even generally prescribes pluralistic compromise. In terms of prioritization, however, all species may be important to preserve, but some are clearly more valuable to humans than others. Policy design theory does not say that value to humans is the only value to consider but acknowledges its exceptional importance. If it came down to a choice between saving the peregrine falcon or the smallpox virus, humans would save the falcon. If the choice was between the peregrine falcon and the giant carrion beetle, the choice would still be clear to a strong majority. If the choice was between the peregrine falcon and the black-footed ferret, the choice would be difficult, and if between the peregrine and the aplomado falcon, more difficult still.

One may argue philosophically that where making a choice entails considerable doubt, and where the goal of each alternative is similar and contributes to a common larger goal, then the outcome is not likely to matter very much, and little should be invested in resolving the issue. Assuming that there is indeed a slight difference in each such instance, but that we are unable to predict that difference or even measure it once it occurs, then we are likely to be right half of the time by simply flipping a coin. To fine tune a prioritization system so that we can always ascertain which alternative is better may require so much time and money that we may lose net conservation benefits in the process.

The recommendation for policymakers, then, is to move quickly in all cases, regardless of academic controversies over prioritization. When it is obvious what species should be prioritized for conservation, conservation programs for those species should commence immediately. When it seems impossible to decide which species are more important for conservation, a set of them should be selected based on criteria of speed. By moving quickly, we ensure that conservation, not argumentation, is the prominent activity.

Of course, there will always be some argument over what is obvious and what is impossible to decide. Therefore, we propose the following rule of thumb for policymakers and bureaucrats: where there is no obvious basis for prioritizing species, then a taxonomic preference should be engaged that corresponds with the social construction/political power dynamic (chapter 6). Species should be prioritized as follows, from most to least important: birds and mammals, fish, plants, reptiles, amphibians, invertebrates, and microorganisms (Fig. 4). When there is additional information available about a taxon's social construction or political power, a species may be prioritized differently than it would be based on this rule of thumb. For example, amphibians should be prioritized over non-Testudines reptiles, raptors over rice rats, and butterflies over scorpions: in each case, the social construction/political power combination is clearly greater for the former taxa.

No doubt the preceding recommendation will draw fire from biocentrists and some conservation biologists, but it is important to consider its precepts. First, prioritization is a distasteful but necessary chore. Second, by "going with the flow" socially and politically, conservationists will be more effective and a greater number of species will be conserved, regardless of type. Third, the prioritization of species in the order listed provides a considerable umbrella effect due to body-size-related ecological phenomena. Fourth, the social construction/political power prioritization of species corresponds roughly with evolutionary rationale, because genetic information and phylogenetic diversity increase from the bottom toward the top of the list, while molecular clock speed decreases. Finally, to maximize effectiveness, conservationists should increasingly focus on contextual issues — such as economic growth — rather than investing time in more complex, esoteric strategies for species prioritization.

Finally, the ratio of public valuation to fiscal allocation (Table 8) is a promising parameter for prioritizing political action. When people value species far more than those species benefit from policy, the political opportunities to effect conservation for those species are great. When spending has reached higher levels than public valuation, however, additional political support is unlikely to effect as much conservation per unit effort. Activists may find surprisingly fertile ground in organizing support for plants and amphibians, but they should be mindful of social construction distinctions within those widely varying types.

RECOMMENDATIONS FOR IMPROVING ESA CONTEXT

A policy design analysis of ESA reveals the overwhelming impact of human economy on species conservation (chapter 8), indicating a formidable inconsistency of ESA with its context. Other policy perspectives recognize the inconsistency, too, but produce vastly different prescriptions. Public choice theory emphasizes the importance of making ESA fit the socioeconomic context; policy science does likewise but to a lesser extent. Pluralism would predict that ESA will evolve to fit that context, regardless of what happens to endangered species. Critical theory, however, and policy specialism to a lesser extent, directs its prescription to the context itself.

Compared to the traditional policy perspectives, our policy design analysis provides a comprehensive foundation from which to consider the implications of the ESA/context inconsistency. We concur with legal analysts that ESA is, with some exceptions because of faulty assumptions, an internally logical and generally sound policy. The ESA's concurrent protection of ecosystems and endangered species has been criticized, but the critique doesn't pass muster. The rhetoric of ecosystem management is a symptom of or a reaction to the ESA/context inconsistency but not a superior approach to conservation. Essentially, nothing within ESA appears to be the source of the inconsistency.

Perhaps the very goal of ESA is questionable, but that would be a paradoxical conclusion to the results of our analysis. Although species types vary in their social construction, all types of species are valued by society. Furthermore, species conservation is valued as highly as such revered institutions as property rights and economic growth. And ESA has weathered a political storm ever since its well-received passage — an inconceivable outcome if the goal of ESA was inconsistent with the principles of American democracy. Unlike wealthy industries that are able to stealthily "capture" agencies, to the public detriment (Wilson 1989), ESA is dependent upon the popular majority for its survival. That ESA upholds principles of public participation, freedom of information, and equality (to its applicable extent) complements the propriety of its goal in explaining its political prestige.

All of this encourages a closer analysis of the other component of the contextual inconsistency — context. Although the causes of endangerment are unnatural (chapter 8), they are rarely malicious or criminal. If one were forced to distill the causes of endangerment into an ultimate cause in the managerial time frame, it would be economic growth, which is a function of population size, per capita consumption, and, less directly, exportation. Following the ecological principle of competitive exclusion, the human economy grows at the expense of the economy of nature, including its ecosystems, habitats, and species (Czech 2000a).

Species are not endangered in a linear relationship to the amount of habitat lost. A threshold level of habitat loss can be reached whereby the viability of a population is lost. No matter how many nonviable populations exist, if they are reproductively isolated by fragmentation, the species is bound for extinction. Thus Noss and Csuti (1994:262) called habitat fragmentation "one of the greatest threats to regional and global biodiversity." However, caution is required when considering the relationship of fragmentation to species endangerment. Fragmentation, like species endangerment, is an effect caused by the other, habitat-destroying factors, and there is a potential danger in confusing the cause and effect relationship.

If fragmentation becomes widely portrayed as a cause of endangerment in its own right, policymakers will tend to disregard the effects of economic growth, believing that proper spatial arrangement associated with economic growth — "smart growth" — is the key conservation strategy. Such a strategy, however, is already difficult to pursue because of the demands on natural resources created by human economy. If it gains momentum, this strategy will complicate conservation efforts far into the future. It will distract policymakers from addressing the real causes of endangerment (Table 9), as well as the ultimate cause (economic growth) and its functional components (primarily population and per capita consumption).

If population size and per capita consumption are not addressed in the policy arena, then unnatural extinctions and associated environmental problems will clearly proliferate. All other efforts — mitigation, environmental assessment, and triage, to name a few — can only prolong extinction for a short period of evolutionary time. Expending energy in those efforts is a negative-sum game whereby the energy is lost and the results remain elusive. The implication is clear. As a past board member for the National Wildlife Federation, the American Forestry Association, and National Parks and Conservation Association, Carl Reidel exhorted more than a decade ago, "It is no longer enough to limit the focus of our 'professional' concern to traditional natural resource management issues. . . . It is time to recognize that population policy is natural resource policy writ large" (1988:48). The same goes for consumption policy and, collectively, economic growth policy.

Yet, the context of ESA is a nation that not only fails to address population and per capita consumption but propounds economic growth politically, legislatively, and bureaucratically. For example, during the nationally televised vice-presidential debate of October 9, 1996, twenty-two topics were debated (including introductory and closing statements), only three of which directly pertained to the economy. Nevertheless, Republican candidate Jack Kemp interjected fourteen calls for faster economic growth in thirteen of the topical categories, including discussions of the environment, political civility, and the Family and Medical Leave Act. Kemp exhorted emphatically, "We should double the rate of growth, and we should double the size of the American economy," and argued that "what has to be discussed is how we as a nation are going to create the size of an economy, create a national wealth that would at least double this $6 trillion or $7 trillion economy. We [under a Dole/Kemp administration] would have $6 trillion in 15 years extra wealth for the American people" (*Washington Post* 1996:A26). Although less adamant, the Democratic incumbent, Al Gore, nevertheless sanctioned the economic growth race: "Well, the economy is growing very strongly right now. . . . The average growth rate is also coming up. It is higher than in either of the last two Republican administrations" (*Washington Post* 1996:A26).

In her annual report for fiscal year 1992, Republican president George Bush's secretary of commerce, Barbara Hackman Franklin said, "Recognizing that commerce has supplanted military and security issues as the main concerns among nations, the 14 diverse agencies that make-up [sic] the Commerce Department rallied around a new banner — 'commerce is America's new front line' — to advance a seven point agenda for fostering economic growth and creating jobs in the United States" (1992:1). In his annual report for fiscal year 1994, Democratic president Bill Clinton's secretary of commerce, the late Ronald Brown said, "The activities of the Department - promoting economic growth through civilian technology, export growth, sustainable development, economic development, and economic information and analysis — have worked in strategic harmony to provide increased economic security for all Americans. . . . Strong public-private sector partnerships — recognizing business as the engine of economic growth and government as a facilitator — have enabled tough economic challenges to be addressed more successfully" (1994:III).

Discussions about economic growth invariably broach the dubious concept of sustainable development. Ecological economists distinguish between growth and development; the former refers to the "quantitative increase in the scale of the physical dimension of the economy," the latter to the "qualitative improvement of the structure, design, and composition of the physical stocks and flows" (Folke et al. 1994:7). Unfortunately, the concepts are probably undistinguished in the American vernacular. In fact, as used in government programs, nationally and internationally, "development" has long been a cryptic term highlighting the benefits of economic growth while hiding the costs (Willers 1994; Robinson 1993). Berger emphasized this unfortunate phenomenon while discussing the evolution of the terms "growth," "modernization," and "development":

The problem of definition is most complicated with regard to the third term, that of development. Often it is used as an equivalent of one or both of the other two. In that case, the utility of an additional concept is open to question. However, the notion of development, in its general usage, has a much stronger undertone of positive evaluation than is implied by the other two terms . . . while growth and modernization can rather readily be defined in a value-free way, such definition is much more difficult with development. Usage of the term usually implies a general improvement in the well-being of the population undergoing the process . . . Put simply, development means *good* growth and *desirable* modernization (1974:35).

Even in agencies that play an active role in natural resources conservation, economic growth may supersede or suffuse agency missions. The Army Corps of Engineers, the oldest natural resource agency in the federal government and responsible for much of the nation's water quality and wetlands conservation, has since the 1970s defined its mission in terms of four programs: national economic development, regional economic development, environmental quality, and social well-being. In 1983, consistent with President Reagan's emphasis on regulatory impact assessment, the Corps prioritized economic development. Graves explained that "the primary objective of any project would be to 'maximize net national economic development benefits.' The new guidelines defined the 'Federal objective' as 'contributing to national economic development' . . . the recommended plan would be the one that offered the greatest net economic benefit consistent with the other considerations"(1995:219).

Because we inhabit a biosphere of limited natural resources and space, and because human economy requires the consumption of natural resources and space to store byproducts, it is biophysically impossible for economic growth to be sustainable (Daly 1993; Jansson et al. 1994; Czech 2000b). A given economic level, as gauged by consumption, may be sustainable, but not growth per se. Thus Botkin referred to sustainable development as "an oxymoron if strictly interpreted"(1990:156).

Alternatively, one could subscribe to the position of Holling et al: "Both the ecological and social components of these problems [natural resource depletion and the attendant economic blight] have an evolutionary character. That is why the phrase 'sustainable development' is not an oxymoron" (1994:71). In other words, because societies change in their values and political structures, and because ecosystem structures change, there may be a constant reallocation of resources and therefore continual "development." Holling et alia proposed that fact to restore cogency to the phrase "sustainable development." Unfortunately, that rather esoteric rendering is likely to be overlooked. We take the position that sustainable development is indeed an oxymoron, if not when esoterically rendered, then in the vernacular.

As with all species in the economy of nature, the only sustainable human economy is one in which neither the population nor its stock of capital perpetually grows, and where the production of waste does not exceed the assimilative capacity of the ecosystem. Daly called this a "steady state economy" (1993), in which natural capital is withdrawn only at the rate of its replenishment, with the stock of man-made capital reaching sustainable equilibrium. The principle of a balanced natural capital account is embodied in the strategy of sustainable yield — a supposed focus of the U.S. Forest Service since its creation in 1905 (but see Hirt 1994). Czech (2000b) noted the similarity of natural resources and natural capital but defended Daly's terminology because of its higher likelihood of arousing mainstream economists and economic policymakers. In any event, a limited amount of development is possible prior to the establishment of a steady state economy, but "limited development" and "sustainable development" are essentially antonyms.

At most, "sustainable development" would be a viable phrase only when preceded by the word "a." A sustainable development, in economic terms, would be an individual development; for example, a farming community. The community would be developed, development would terminate, and a sustained existence would ensue. Furthermore, the nation and the Earth could support only a limited number of sustainable developments; the collection of such developments would constitute a steady state. Sustainable development is not used in that sense, however (Ayers 1998). It is rarely preceded by the word "a"; rather, it is used to refer to the continual economic growth of a political state, as in the preceding citation of Commerce director Brown.

The paradox of ESA, then, is that the same government that created and implements it also embraces — politically, legislatively, and bureaucratically — the core phenomenon that endangers species. In a sense, the government endangers species and then protects them. If accounting for natural capital (including biodiversity) was standard government practice, then policymakers would concur with Daly and Cobb (1994) that current policies of maximizing the productivity and accumulation of man-made capital are no longer economic, even in the most traditional sense. Unfortunately, current measures of economic growth (e.g., gross national product) are based entirely on man-made capital (Heilbroner and Thurow 1987).

Government is not the sole or even primary source of economic growth and attendant species endangerment. Were government not instrumental in perpetuating economic growth, growth would nevertheless continue in a capitalist democracy. After all, citizens are bombarded by exhortation and advertisement that urges them to consume more. Furthermore, a complex relationship between natural selection and motivational psychology predisposes humans to conspicuous consumption (Czech 2000b). With these powerful forces at work, elimination of the Department of Commerce, for example, would not go far toward solving the problem of species endangerment. Nevertheless, government — especially local government — plays a leading role in fueling economic growth. Furthermore, government can be described in terms of what it does not do as well as what it does. To the extent that one views the lack of a population/consumption policy as a government position, then government is a proponent of economic growth even without its economic development programs and subsidies.

Were the economy sustained at a level low enough that no species were endangered, the policy context of ESA would be irrelevant because ESA would be unnecessary or nonexistent. Furthermore, were government not facilitating economic growth, ESA would better fit its policy context, regardless of the level of economy. As it is, with ESA in the context of government-led economic growth, the policy/context relationship is a paradox. With a public perennially steeped in economic growth by its political leaders, encouraging development while upholding ESA is futile at best, and dangerously hypocritical at worst.

There are only two possible policy recommendations for alleviating the ESA/context paradox: abandon the goal of ESA or abandon the goal of economic growth. Unfortunately, neither choice would be politically viable, because both goals are treasured by the electorate. The only solution, then, is to modify the political viability of one or the other, a challenge that is doomed to failure without political activism from outside the policy arena. In fact, political activists from both sides are already involved with this agenda. However, that is not to remove the onus from policymakers to lead. Policymakers, not activists, hold the public interest in trust for the present and future. Political activism is a necessary but insufficient condition to effect the modification of political viability and to incorporate that modification in public policy.

First, however, policymakers and political activists must reach consensus or a strong majority on which of these treasured goals to abandon. Perhaps the most enlightening voice in the debate comes from ecological economics, the classic works of which have been compiled and condensed by Krishnan et al. (1995). The bottom line of ecological economics is that not only species but also the economy itself is ultimately endangered by economic growth. A steady state economy is the only mathematically sane prospect for humans and their economy.

Finally, then, the only logical policy implication of the ESA/context paradox appears: policymakers should work toward reducing the political viability of economic growth, with the goal of establishing a steady state economy. They should prudently invest political capital in exhorting the public to reconsider what economic growth entails, being careful not to lose office to candidates less knowledgeable about ecological economics. They should educate the public about the basic principles of population size, per capita consumption, exportation, resource finiteness, and standard of living. They should use every available opportunity to illuminate the causal connectivity of humanity's great problems, including war, poverty, and crime, with resource shortage and, in turn, the connection of resource shortage with population growth and per capita consumption. They should emphasize that a halt to economic growth does not entail a lower standard of living if population is stabilized. They should portray good citizenship as that which conserves, and bad citizenship as that which wastes and wantonly accumulates wealth at the expense of posterity. They should, perhaps, lead and not follow the "steady state revolution" described by Czech in *Shoveling Fuel for a Runaway Train* (2000b).

As public knowledge about the implications of economic growth builds, policymakers should gradually replace incentives for economic growth with barriers to economic growth. To the extent they are successful, ESA will become consistent with its socioeconomic context. Ironically, one of their most potent tools in effecting this transformation may be ESA itself. The ESA has been helpful in checking the effects of several of the causes of endangerment, especially those associated with rural land use: agriculture, mining, logging, grazing, recreation, reservoirs, roads, and aquifer depletion/wetland draining (Bean 1983; Rohlf 1989; Littell 1992). As Ehrlich and Ehrlich found, "The Endangered Species Act . . . helps set the United States on a path toward sustainability" (1996:123). An ESA controversy provides an excellent opportunity for policymakers to explain the dependence our grandchildren have on our ability to temper our consumption of resources. With each species listing, ESA hoists a red flag of economic growth run amok.

RECOMMENDATIONS FOR IMPROVING POLICY DESIGN THEORY

Policy design theory acknowledges the strengths and shortcomings of traditional models of public policy. It provides a framework for analyzing policy logic, incorporates the overlooked concept of social construction, recognizes the need for sound technical expertise, and acknowledges the importance of context. While it evades dogma by encouraging self-criticism, it adopts the norm that democracy should be served by all public policy. Perhaps more than any other aspect, it is this normative stance that distinguishes policy design theory from traditional models and perspectives. Pluralists tend to assume that democracy is served through the branches and levels of American government by constitutional fiat. They see public policy as a product of democracy, not vice versa. The policy sciences have evolved to focus on institutional arrangements for solving technical problems and take little interest in democracy, while policy specialists tend to favor technocracy. Public choice theorists serve the free market, an institution that to them is inextricable from democracy, even though socialist programs are part and parcel of democracy as well (Dunn 1987; Adler 1991). Critical theorists are concerned with democratic principles, especially equality, freedom of information, and public participation, but they tend to be critical of states attempting democracy, especially the most capitalistic ones (Hoy and McCarthy 1994). Their discourse is often utopian and alternatively anarchist or socialist to a greater extent than Western democracy would accommodate.

The ESA holds up well to the democratic analysis entailed by policy design theory (chapter 9). In fact, ESA gets a passing grade on all of the tests of policy design theory. Yet, despite its strongly supported goal, it is subject to the aforementioned inconsistency with its context. There are two possible explanations of this phenomenon. It may simply corroborate the aforementioned evidence that the context is the problematic element of the ESA/context paradox, but it may also indicate a shortcoming of policy design theory. The most accurate interpretation probably incorporates both explanations. We have discussed the former; here we are concerned with the latter.

While policy design theory recognizes that some institutions are so important as to merit service by all policy, it perceives of such institutions only in political terms and, therefore, embraces only one (democracy). That is perhaps a function of paradigm, because the authors of policy design theory are social scientists. From a natural science perspective, however, ecological concerns are even more important to the public interest than is democracy. Although democracy may be the most hopeful political form for maintaining ecosystem health (Hayward 1994), it is clear that without a healthy ecosystem, there can be no political form whatsoever. Natural science has been the missing link in public policy theories, except perhaps for the subset of policy specialism inhabited by conservation biology — which, unfortunately, is missing most of the remaining links.

Conservationists have been increasingly drawn to the social sciences out of practical necessity, but there has not been a reciprocal movement by advocates of democracy. Conservationists have recognized the inadequacy of natural science to solve conservation problems contextualized by socioeconomics, but political theorists have not recognized the inadequacy of the social sciences to solve democratic problems contextualized by nature. Perhaps they have to a limited extent, as evidenced by the growing discipline of political ecology (M'Gonigle 1999), but the extent has not been sufficient, as evidenced by a lack of ecological considerations in public policy theories.

The recommendation, then, is not to choke more democracy out of ESA but to breath into the young life of policy design theory a spirit of ecological integrity. Of course, this invokes the image of Pandora's box: Who will be next to stake a claim in the territory of policy design theory? The answer comprises a second recommendation: When policy design theory defines the omnibus roles of public policy (those roles in addition to solving a technical problem at hand), it should only recognize the greatest of humanity's needs: one each from the social and natural realms. Otherwise, policy design theory could deteriorate into a generic platform for "goodness," identifying the planks of which would constitute a crippling debate. Outside of the social and natural realms, there is little else to discuss. Spirituality may be as or more important, but the prudence of separating church and state is a history lesson without parallel. As John Adams warned, "Remember the *index expurgatorius*, the inquisition, the stake, the axe, the halter, and the guillotine" (1851:479). The prime candidate from the natural realm to complement democracy as an omnibus role of public policy is ecosystem health. Ecologists and philosophers from academia, government, and private organizations assembled at a 1990 workshop to develop this concept (Costanza et al. 1992). They agreed that an ecosystem is healthy if "it is stable and sustainable — that is, if it is active and maintains its organization and autonomy over time and is resilient to stress" (Haskell et al. 1992:9). Ecosystem health, therefore, is a concept that embodies the aspects of conservatism — and conservation — that virtually everyone would embrace, including stability, sustainability, and resiliency.

Like democracy, ecosystem health can be defined in a sentence or two, while a discussion of the definition may permeate the literature endlessly. For example, one of the criteria commonly proposed as a measure of ecosystem health is biodiversity (Karr 1992), yet one person's concept of biodiversity may be just as arguable as another person's concept of equality. Nonetheless, lack of definitional precision does not prevent Americans from valuing either democracy or ecosystem health. In fact, Americans value both concepts highly, and equally so (chapter 9). Democracy serves to capture the noblest principles of social life; ecosystem health serves to capture the most fundamental requirements of life itself. There is no need to specify that public policy should serve equality or public participation, for example; those principles constitute democracy. There is no need to specify that public policy should serve biodiversity or resiliency; those qualities constitute ecosystem health.

Perhaps the best argument for including ecosystem health as an omnibus role for public policy is the simplest: "Everything depends on reducing our impact on the natural environment" (Pollard 1994:261). This argument might as easily be stated, "Everything depends on maintaining ecosystem health." Whatever institution one venerates (unless it be oblivion), only the healthy ecosystem is a necessary condition for all others. If our founding fathers had written a constitution in today's environmental context, surely they would have had the wisdom to incorporate ecosystem health. It is not too late to start, and policy design theory may be thought of as a vehicle that is not too late to catch. Ecosystem health has to catch some vehicle that is heading into the policy arena, and not just for the areas where "environmental policy" is negotiated. Everything depends on it.

There remains the question, however, of how a policy design theory that serves democracy and ecosystem health would resolve the ESA/context paradox. It is hard to imagine a policy that serves ecosystem health more than ESA does. Yet, if a policy design analysis were conducted on ESA and included the standard of serving ecosystem health, ESA would remain inconsistent with its context. If, however, policy design theory, including the ecosystem health standard, were employed effectively for a long time hence, it would help to resolve the paradox by modifying the context. For instance, if it revealed the disaster of policies that would "at least double this $6 trillion or $7 trillion economy," it would help to defeat such policies. Progress would be made toward a steady state economy, a sustainable democracy, and the conservation of species. Until then, ESA will be trudging against the wind, with a weakening grip on the hand of posterity.

RECOMMENDATIONS OF SCALE

Extinction is a global phenomenon, and some observers think that the only legitimate strategy for solving the problem is a global approach. They may view analyses of U.S. domestic policy as myopic and unproductive. Ultimately, a global approach is required. However, there is the important question of what constitutes a global approach. We believe that to stem the tide of unnatural species extinctions, a strong, bellwether nation must achieve a steady state economy dependent only upon the value of the natural resources within its borders. That achievement would have positive psychological and practical implications globally.

Assume, for example, that the United States accomplished the feat. The psychological effect would be increased credibility for the United States in its international negotiations pertaining to economic growth and environmental policy. As it is instead, the North as a whole, and the United States in particular, are logically viewed by the South as hypocritical when they exhort developing nations to preserve and conserve.

The practical effect would be that U.S. resources could be devoted to global leadership in conservation. The dominant development theory has long been that economic growth to a threshold level was required to bring a nation into civilized, modernized security (Rostow and Kennedy 1990; Barro 1998). Because of distributional inequities and exploitation by foreign capital, however, that prospect is bleak for many or most undeveloped countries. By achieving a steady state economy, the United States would be "living on the interest" of natural capital, not on the principal. It could build a store of finances to assist other countries in reaching their security thresholds without annihilating their natural capital. Those countries could then follow the lead of the United States by establishing their own steady state economies. U.S. aid could, in fact, be predicated upon such establishment.

We also posit that the United States has the best chance to achieve a steady state economy and to help other nations do the same. Despite numerous red flags — in the form of endangered species, depleted aquifers, and eroded rangelands, among others — the United States retains a relatively high ratio of natural capital to population. Per capita consumption is too high, but lowering that is probably not as formidable as lowering population size (Czech 2000b). Perhaps most important, the United States has the diversity of natural capital required for self-sufficiency.

The window of opportunity is still open for the United States to achieve a steady state economy. That window is probably closed for many undeveloped countries, whose people are preoccupied with survival, and whose resources are destined for collapse, barring economic rescue. For the remaining countries, the window is somewhere in between. Western European countries, for example, may be closer to steady state economies than the United States, but they are not nearly as self-sufficient and do not harbor the resources to lead. There really is no other viable candidate, much less a democratic one.

Furthermore, there are moral grounds for placing the lead responsibility of a global steady state economy on the United States. We took the country from tribal people who had lived in relative harmony with the earth (Cronon 1983; Stannard 1992). Sanctioned by our government, our wealthier citizens exploit the natural resources of countries around the globe. Relative to almost all other countries, we are blessed with abundant health, happiness, and peace. If it is not our responsibility to lead, then it is no one's, and if it is no one's, then posterity's prospects are bleak indeed.

Clause-specific Assumptions of Endangered Species Act Authors

Assumptions are defined as implicit premises required to lead from the findings of Congress (Section 2(a)) to the accomplishment of ESA goals (Section 2(b)) or to validate an ESA clause. Blatantly incorrect or controversial assumptions are bold-faced, and questionable assumptions are italicized.

ESA Section	Abbreviated and Paraphrased Content	Assumption
2(b)	ESA purposes are to protect ecosystems of endangered species, to conserve endangered species, and to fulfill duties pursuant to treaties listed in Sec. 2(a)(4).	1. *A species may be endangered other than by threats to its ecosystem;* and 2. Treaties listed in Sec. 2(a)(4) are not sufficient to fulfill their stipulations without further legislation.
2(c)(2)	Federal agencies will work with state and local agencies to resolve water resource issues in concert with conservation of endangered species.	Water resource issues are especially problematic to endangered species conservation.
3(2)	"Commercial activity" involving species does not include museum exhibitions.	1. **The museum trade poses no threat to species;** or 2. The threat posed by museum trade is outweighed by the benefits to species of museum trade.

ESA Section	Abbreviated and Paraphrased Content	Assumption
3(5)(C)	"Critical habitat" does not include the entire geographic area that could be occupied by the species.	Habitat for a species can exist without being occupied by that species.
3(6)	Species of the class Insecta may not be classified as endangered if determined to be of "overwhelming and overriding risk to man."	1. *Only insects can pose such risk;* or 2. Insect species are less important to preserve than species of the other classes.
3(15)	"Distinct populations" qualify as "species" for the purpose of ESA, but only for vertebrates.	Vertebrates are more valuable or in some way more worthy of protection than invertebrates.
3(16) and 3(17)	"States" include the 50 states, D.C., Guam, etc. (and do not include Indian tribes).	*Tribes are exempt from ESA provisions pertaining to states.*
4(a)(1)	Natural and manmade factors should be considered in designating species as threatened or endangered.	*Species extinction is to be avoided, even if it appears to be a natural occurrence.*
4(a)(2)	The Secretary of the Interior has more authority over the listing process than the Secretary of Commerce, but cannot act on marine species listings without concurrence of the latter.	1. A firm hierarchy is desirable for effective implementation of ESA, and/or; 2. *Bureaucratic checks and balances are desirable for effective implementation of* ESA.
4(a)(3)(A)	Critical habitat shall be designated at the time of a species listing, but only "to the maximum extent prudent and determinable." Critical habitat designation may be extended by no more than one year (Sec. 4(b)(6)(C)(ii)).	*It is sometimes more prudent to delay the designation of critical habitat (up to one year) than to make the best estimation of it at the time of listing.*
4(b)(2)	The Secretary may decline to designate critical habitat if the economic or other benefits of declining outweigh the costs.	**A typical species can be conserved indefinitely in an endangered state.**
4(b)(3)(B)(iii)	The Secretary may find that a species should be listed, but	The federal bureaucracy (especially the FWS) is

ESA *Section*	*Abbreviated and Paraphrased Content*	*Assumption*
	may avoid listing the species if precluded by administrative limitations.	periodically or perpetually behind in its responsibilities due to high workload: personnel ratios.
4(b)(3)(C)(ii)	A decision by the Secretary not to list a petitioned species is subject to judicial review. When the Secretary lists a species, that decision is not subject to judicial review.	For listing decisions, it is better to err on the conservative (i.e., conservation) side.
4(b)(3)(C)(iii)	If the Secretary avoids listing a species due to administrative limitations, he must implement a monitoring system for that species.	*It is less expensive and/or time consuming to monitor a species than to formulate a listing regulation for the species.*
4(b)(6)(B)(ii)	If insufficient data exists for the petitioned listing of a species even after the six-month extension period provided in Sec. 4(b)(6)(B)(i), then the listing process is terminated.	**In cases of extended doubt, the costs of listing exceed the benefits of listing the (doubtfully) threatened or endangered species.**
4(b)(7)	Public participation rules may be sacrificed in emergencies.	1. **The Secretary will utilize the clause when emergencies arise.** 2. *The survival of a species is more important than public participation.*
4(d)	The Secretary may issue regulations for threatened or endangered species unless the state has entered into an agreement with the Secretary for such species' management, in which case the Secretary may not issue takings regulations for threatened, resident fish or wildlife species unless the state has corresponding regulations.	1. **A threatened species may recover with no protection; or** 2. **A state's position on a species is more important than species conservation unless the species has reached the point of becoming endangered, in which case species conservation becomes more important.**

ESA Section	Abbreviated and Paraphrased Content	Assumption
4(f)(1)	The Secretary will prepare recovery plans for listed species "unless he finds that such a plan will not promote the conservation of the species."	**Development of a recovery plan can fail to promote the conservation of a species, and can perhaps promote the further endangerment thereof.**
4(f)(1)(A)	In developing recovery plans, the Secretary shall give priority to species likely to benefit from such plans, and without regard to taxonomy.	FWS/NMFS budgets are insufficient to prepare plans for all species; and **1. Taxa are equally valuable; or 2. Relative values of taxa cannot be determined.**
4(f)(6)	Every federal agency shall consider the information presented during the public comment period following public notice of a recovery plan.	Allowing only those agencies that recognized their involvement with a recovery plan to consider public comment entails the risk that some agencies would fail to obviate conflict.
4(h)(3)	The Secretary must develop and publish a prioritization system for the listing of species.	FWS/NMFS does not have enough administrative resources to list all species that warrant listing in a timely manner.
5	The Secretary (and Secretary of Agriculture) shall acquire lands (including via purchase) for the purpose of species conservation.	*Land acquisition appropriations will be granted for the purposes of species conservation.*
6(c)(1)(D)	Before entering into a cooperative agreement with a state agency, the Secretary must determine that the agency is authorized to acquire "land or aquatic habitat."	1. Aquatic areas are distinguished from "land" in the vernacular and the acquisition of aquatic areas for the purposes of endangered species preservation could be challenged on grounds that only nonsubmersed land was to be acquired. 2. *"Habitat" is not species-specific.*

ESA Section	Abbreviated and Paraphrased Content	Assumption
6(c)(1) and 6(c)(2)	A state must meet several criteria to enter into a cooperative agreement with the Secretary for species conservation purposes. These criteria are more stringent for fish and wildlife than for plants. In particular, the state must have a program for acquiring habitat for fish and wildlife, but need not have such a program for plants.	1. *Plants are less valuable than fish and wildlife;* or 2. The political feasibility of plant habitat acquisition programs is low enough that requiring states to develop such programs would jeopardize cooperation with states.
6(d)(1)(D)	When the Secretary allocates funds to states for cooperative species conservation efforts, he must consider "the potential for restoring endangered species and threatened species within a State."	1. Appropriations will be inadequate for thorough species conservation, and; 2. In some states and with some species, ecological and political conditions render species recovery more likely than in others.
6(d)(2)(D)(ii)	The authorized federal share of funding for cooperative agreements (90%) is greater for agreements in which two or more states have collaborated than it is for an agreement with a single state (75%).	1. When species' ranges extend across state boundaries, cooperative conservation efforts are more likely to be successful, and; 2. A greater proportionate federal allocation will incite states to jointly cooperate with the Secretary.
6(e)	"Any action taken by the Secretary under this section shall be subject to his periodic review at no greater than annual intervals."	State programs may evolve over time to escape the intent or procedural requirements of Sec. 6.
6(i)	A "cooperative endangered species conservation fund" is established, into which 5% of Pittman-Robertson funds and Dingell-Johnson funds are annually deposited and authorized for expenditure on	1. *Five percent of the combined funds is enough to successfully administer endangered species cooperative programs with states;* and 2. *If five percent is an accurate gauge of the amount required,*

ESA Section	Abbreviated and Paraphrased Content	Assumption
	cooperative programs with states.	*Congress will annually appropriate the full 5%.*
7(a)(1)	All federal agencies shall administer species conservation programs.	**Lacking (in most cases) procedural specifications and sufficient appropriations, the agencies will actually develop and administer such programs.**
7(a)(4)	"Each Federal agency shall confer with the Secretary on any agency action which is likely to jeopardize [a species or its critical habitat]."	*Prior to conferring, an agency will have the ability to ascertain whether or not its action is likely to jeopardize a species or critical habitat.*
7(a)(3)	Federal agencies that license actions of others (including private citizens) shall consult with the Secretary on a licensed action when the licensee has reason to believe that an endangered species may be affected by the action.	1. Federal agencies may not be as aware of the impact of their licensed actions as licensees, if for no other reason than the licensee may be more familiar with the area involved; or 2. Federal agencies may not take the initiative to consult on licensing, even if they are aware of potential impacts.
7(b)(2)	"Consultation under subsection (a)(3) shall be concluded within such period as is agreeable to the Secretary, the Federal agency, and the applicant . . . "	*The three parties specified will be able to agree upon said period, without rules specifying how to reach that agreement.*
7(c)(1)	Biological assessments (of the likelihood of an agency action affecting an endangered species) may be made in partial fulfillment of the requirements of the National Environmental Policy Act (NEPA).	The survival and recovery of species contributes to the "quality of the human environment" (42 U.S.C. 4332, 1988) that NEPA is intended to protect.

ESA *Section*	*Abbreviated and Paraphrased Content*	*Assumption*
7(d) 7(g)(3)	During Section 7 consultation, the consulting agency or licensee shall make no irreversible or irretrievable commitments that could eliminate reasonable and prudent alternatives to the proposed action.	Commitments create political momentum for a project that make it difficult to stop, even if it must stop to adhere to ESA.
7(e)(3)	The Endangered Species Committee, established to consider ad hoc exemptions of Section 7 prohibitions, includes the Secretaries of Interior, Agriculture, and Army, the Chairman of the Council of Economic Advisors, the Administrators of the Environmental Protection Agency and National Oceanic and Atmospheric Administration, and a representative from each affected state as appointed by the President.	1. The agency heads specified would provide wisdom and prudence in dealing with the sober nature of their subject; and/or 2. Endangered species situations may entail conflicts of species conservation with agriculture, national defense, and the economy as a whole; and/or 3. The mixture of agency heads would provide a balanced approach to resolving difficult endangered species issues.
7(g)(1)	Exemption applicants may only include federal agencies, state governors, and federal action licensees, and exemptions are only considered for federally conducted or licensed projects.	1. Private sector projects are not concerned with the public welfare, as are governmental projects; or 2. Making the Endangered Species Committee accessible to private parties could create an extremely expensive burden in the upper echelon of the federal bureaucracy.
7(g)(2)(A)	Exemption applications may only be filed within 90 days of a determination that the project may not proceed as proposed by the action agency.	1. Administrative efficiency, especially for the Department of the Interior, is served by bringing prompt closure to a contested project issue; and/or 2. Given time, bureaucrats, license applicants, state

ESA Section	Abbreviated and Paraphrased Content	Assumption
		governors, and others could engage in political maneuvers that would affect the prudence of the Endangered Species Committee.
7(e)(3)	"The Committee shall be composed of seven members as follows . . . "	**Although subparagraph G goes on to state that the President "shall appoint one individual from each affected State . . . to be a member of the Committee," the President would in fact appoint only one such individual. (Six of the 7 members are specified in subparagraphs A–F.)**
7(h)(1)(A) (ii)	A Section 7 exemption may be granted if "the benefits of such action clearly outweigh the benefits of alternative courses of action consistent with conserving the species or its critical habitat, and such action is in the public interest."	*The conservation of a species may periodically be less beneficial to the public than the action that causes its extinction.*
7(h)(1)(A) (iv)	An exemption may not be granted if irreversible or irretrievable commitments were made in violation of Section 7(d).	Withholding the possibility of exemption from those that violate Section 7(d) will discourage a potential exemption applicant from trying to politically force a project through the ESA process.
7(i)	The Secretary of State may disable the exemption process if he finds that the exemption will violate a treaty.	*Maintaining the integrity of a treaty is more important than preventing an extinction.*
7(j)	The Secretary of Defense may impose a Section 7 exemption if necessary for national security.	*National security is more important than preventing an extinction.*

ESA Section	Abbreviated and Paraphrased Content	Assumption
7(p)	The President may grant Section 7 exemption for actions taken pursuant to the Disaster Relief Act.	*The saving of individual human lives is more important than preventing an extinction.*
8, 8A	The United States will assist other nations in developing programs to conserve species.	The worldwide survival of species, especially as it reflects global ecological integrity, is in the best interests of the United States.
9(a)(1) (D,F), 9(a)(2)(D)	It is unlawful to conduct interstate commerce in endangered species, but it is lawful to conduct intrastate commerce, as long as the specimens were not taken in violation of ESA.	*Interstate commerce provides a business opportunity lucrative enough to entice entrepreneurs into violating ESA, thus jeopardizing species; intrastate commerce does not.*
9(a)(1–2)	Endangered fish and wildlife species shall not be taken anywhere. Endangered plant species shall not be taken on federal lands.	*1. Plant species are not as valuable as fish and wildlife species;* and/or *2. A ban on the taking of endangered plants on private lands is unenforceable;* and/or *3. It is politically unfeasible to prevent citizens from taking endangered plants on private lands.*
9(b)(2)(A)	Taking prohibitions do not apply to raptors or their progeny that were held in captivity before ESA was signed into law, until such raptors or progeny are released into the wild.	Falconers and biologists held raptors in captivity and offered a potential means to re-establishing wild populations of raptors.
9(c)(2)	Importation of CITES Appendix II species is presumed lawful, but only if "such importation is not made in the course of a commercial activity."	Commercialism is a particularly potent incentive for violation of CITES (and ESA, which implements CITES).

ESA Section	Abbreviated and Paraphrased Content	Assumption
9(d)(1) (A-B)	Importers and exporters of fish and wildlife (including parts thereof) must obtain permission to engage in such business from the Secretary. Elephant ivory, raw and worked, is specified.	Dealers in ivory would have challenged the classification of worked ivory as "fish and wildlife."
9(f)	Imports and exports of fish and wildlife shall only occur at ports designated by the Secretary.	The Secretary would not have the resources to monitor international commerce unless such commerce were consolidated geographically.
10(a)(1)(A)	The Secretary may permit exceptions to Section 9 prohibitions "for scientific purposes or to enhance the propagation or survival of the affected species."	*Scientific purposes are unlikely to jeopardize the survival of a species, even if not likely to enhance the propagation or survival of the species.*
10(a)(1)(B)	The Secretary may permit takings prohibited by Section 9(a)(1)(B)(i.e., takings within the U.S. or the territorial sea of the U.S.) if such takings are incidental to an otherwise legal activity, but may not allow takings prohibited by Section 9(a)(1)(C) (i.e., takings on the high seas).	1. Harvesting on the high seas is entirely of whales and other species that are reasonably easy to target and thus entail no need for the incidental taking exception; and/or 2. There is no foolproof way to ensure that a taking is incidental, and *whales and other high seas species are more valuable than other species.*
10(d)	The Secretary may only grant a Section 9 exception if such exception "will not operate to the disadvantage of such endangered species."	**Incidental take will not operate to the disadvantage of an endangered species.**
10(e)(1)	Section 9 exemptions may be granted to Alaska natives "if such taking is primarily for subsistence purposes."	1. *It is possible to ascertain when a taking is made "primarily for subsistence purposes"; and*

ESA Section	Abbreviated and Paraphrased Content	Assumption
		2. That proportion of "primarily for subsistence" takings attributed to non-subsistence purposes would not be great enough to jeopardize the survival and recovery of a species.
10(e)(3)(i)	"The term 'subsistence' includes selling any edible portion of fish or wildlife in native villages and towns in Alaska for native consumption within native villages or towns."	1. The economy of Alaskan villages will not allow enough growth to jeopardize species through marketized "subsistence" takings; or 2. Alaskan village economies are more important than species survival; or 3. If marketized "subsistence" takings threaten a species' survival, the Secretary will apply further restrictions pursuant to Section 10(e)(4).
10(f)(2)	Owners of sperm whale oil and scrimshaw products held prior to ESA may be temporarily exempted from Section 9 prohibitions.	Large stocks of sperm whale oil and scrimshaw existed prior to ESA, and the prohibition of their sale would have created undue economic hardships.
10(f)(3)(C)	The Secretary may require documentation "to prove that any [sperm whale oil or scrimshaw product] claimed by the applicant to be a pre-Act endangered species part is in fact such a part."	1. Other products, some of which may be of as great or greater concern (e.g., elephant ivory) are difficult to distinguish from sperm whale oil or scrimshaw; and 2. It is difficult to ascertain the age of sperm whale oil or scrimshaw products.
10(f)(5)	No regulation prescribed by the Secretary to carry out the purposes of this subsection shall be subject to section 4(f)(2)(A)(i) of this Act.	ESA **contains a section 4(f)(2)(A)(i).**

ESA Section	Abbreviated and Paraphrased Content	Assumption
10(f)(6)(B)	"In the event that this paragraph is held invalid, the validity of the remainder of the Act, including the remainder of this subsection, shall not be affected."	The validity of Section 10(f)(6)(A) is questionable. (Section 10(f)(6)(A) makes an exception to the Section 9 prohibition of commerce in endangered species by allowing the General Services Administration to enter into contracts for the sale of sperm whale oil or scrimshaw.)
10(g)	If an action allegedly exempted from Section 9 is challenged, the exempted party shall have the burden of proof that the exemption was granted and valid.	1. The consequences of an invalid or fraudulent exemption are more dire than those of an inappropriate challenge to the exemption; and/or 2. There is a higher likelihood of fraud involving the procurement of Section 9 exemptions than there is of frivolous objections arising in response to valid Section 9 exemptions.
10(i)	The importation of fish or wildlife that would otherwise be in violation of ESA is not in violation, if legally exported from another country, and if exported to a country that allows its importation, and if the owner specified that the transport was not to pass through the United States.	Due to transportation emergencies or mistake, endangered species that were legally taken and exported may unforeseeably enter U.S. ports.
10(i)(5)	The transnational shipment exemption does not apply to shipments made in the course of a commercial activity.	The granting of importation exceptions for commercial operations involves more risk and enforcement challenges than can be tolerated.
10(j)(C)	Experimental populations of threatened or endangered species may be released by the	1. Threatened status allows the Secretary to be more lenient with prohibitions; and

ESA Section	Abbreviated and Paraphrased Content	Assumption
	Secretary, and "each member of an experimental population shall be treated as a [member of a] threatened species."	2. Leniency may be a political prerequisite for the reestablishment of certain species in certain areas.
11(a)(1), 11(b)(1)	"Any person who knowingly violates, and any person engaged in business as an importer or exporter of fish, wildlife, or plants who violates [certain clauses of ESA may be assessed a civil penalty (11(a)(1)) and convicted of a crime (11(b)(1))]."	1. Those engaged in foreign commerce in species, by the nature of their work, have no excuse for not realizing that they have committed the specified ESA clauses; and/or 2. Those engaged in foreign commerce must be held to a higher standard due to their potential for impact.
11(b)(2)	Persons convicted of criminal ESA violations may also lose federal licenses and permits related to livestock grazing, hunting, etc.	1. The fines associated with criminal violations may not deter the criminal from repeating the violation, and; 2. Withdrawal of certain federal permits makes it more difficult for the criminal to access the species.
11(b)(3)	It is legal to kill a specimen of an endangered species in self-defense.	A human life is more valuable than a live specimen of any other species.
11(g)(1)	The federal district courts "shall compel the Secretary to apply the prohibition sought if the court finds that the allegation that an emergency exists is supported by substantial evidence."	1. *In some instances, the court may have a better understanding of the threat to a species than the Secretary;* and/or 2. In some instances the Secretary, even knowing that an emergency exists, will not take action commensurate with saving the species.
11(g)(1) (B–C)	Citizens may file suit to compel the Secretary to apply "the prohibitions set forth in or authorized pursuant to section 4(d) and section 9(a)(1)(B) of this Act with	1. Takings prohibitions are more important to species conservation than other prohibitions; and **2. It would be judicially unwieldy to allow for citizen**

ESA Section	Abbreviated and Paraphrased Content	Assumption
	respect to [takings]," or "against the Secretary where there is alleged a failure of the Secretary to perform any act or duty under section 4 which is not discretionary with the Secretary."	**suits pertaining to more of than the specified ESA clauses, to an extent outweighing the contribution of such suits to conserving species.**
11(g)(3) (B)	"In any such suit under this subsection in which the United States is not a party . . . "	When a suit is filed to enjoin a party from violating an ESA provision, it may be filed directly against that party and not against the Secretary.
11(g)(5)	"The injunctive relief provided by this subsection shall not restrict any right which any person (or class of persons) may have under any statute or common law to seek enforcement of any standard or limitation or to seek any other relief (including relief against the Secretary or a State agency)."	It is possible that a federal court would grant standing to claimants filing suit for the enforcement of ESA provisions other than those specified by Section 11(g)(1), which simply specifies that citizens may file suit for the purposes specified therein.
12	The Smithsonian Institution will study threatened and endangered plants and methods for conserving them, and report to Congress within one year of ESA enactment.	The Smithsonian Institution has more botanical expertise and/or administrative capacity than the Department of the Interior.
15	Appropriations are authorized for the Departments of Interior, Commerce, and Agriculture, for the purposes of ESA implementation.	*1. The appropriations process (vs. mandatory funding) would suffice to meet the demands of ESA. (2) The amounts authorized would suffice to meet the demands of ESA. (3) Agencies not specified would receive authorization for adequate endangered species conservation budgets through other legislation.*

APPENDIX 2

Common and Latin Names of Species Mentioned in the Text

Common name	Latin name
Aleutian shield fern	*Polystichum aleuticum*
Amargosa niterwort	*Nitrophila mohavensis*
Audubon bighorn	*Ovis canadensis auduboni*
Axis deer	*Axis axis*
Bald eagle	*Haliaeetus leucocephalus*
Banded Trinity	*Thismia americana*
Beaver	*Castor canadensis*
Bison	*Bison bison*
Black bear	*Ursus americanus*
Black-capped vireo	*Vireo atricapillus*
Black-footed ferret	*Mustela nigripes*
Blunt-nosed leopard lizard	*Gambelia silus*
Bradshaw's lomatium	*Lomatium bradshawii*
Brown-headed cowbird	*Molothrus ater*
California condor	*Gymnogyps californianus*
Carolina parakeet	*Conuropsis carolinensis*
Cave crayfish	*Cambarus aculabrum*
Chapman's rhododendron	*Rhododendron chapmanii*
Coffin Cave mold beetle	*Batrisodes texanus*
Coyote	*Canis latrans*
Cui-ui	*Chasmistes cujus*
Darters	*Etheostoma spp.*
Dudley Bluffs bladderpod	*Lesquerella congesta*
Dwarf bear-poppy	*Arctomecon humilis*
Dwarf lake iris	*Iris lacustris*
Eastern gray wolf	*Canis lupus lycaon*

Common name	Latin name
Elephant	*Elephas maximus, Loxodonta africana*
Elfin tree fern	*Cyathea dryopteroides*
Elk	*Cervus elaphus*
Florida panther	*Puma concolor coryi*
Florida salt marsh vole	*Microtus pennsylvanicus dukecambelli*
Furbish lousewort	*Pedicularis furbishiae*
Giant panda	*Ailuropoda melanoleuca*
Glacier bear	*Ursus americanus*
Golden eagle	*Aquila chrysaetos*
Golden cheeked warbler	*Dendroica chrysoparia*
Gray bat	*Myotis grisescens*
Gray wolf	*Canis lupus*
Great auk	*Pinguinus impennis*
Green pitcher plant	*Sarracenia oreophila*
Grizzly bear	*Ursus arctos*
Harp seal	*Pagophilus groenlandicus*
Hawaiian monk seal	*Monachus schauinslandi*
Heath hen	*Tympanuchus cupido cupido*
Houston toad	*Bufo houstonensis*
Kangaroo rats	*Dipodomys spp.*
Kendall Warm Springs dace	*Rhinichthys osculus thermalis*
Labrador duck	*Camptorhynchus labradorius*
Lower Keys marsh rabbit	*Sylvilagus palustris hefneri*
Merriam elk	*Cervus elaphus merriami*
Mexican duck	*Anas diazi*
Mexican spotted owl	*Strix occidentalis lucida*
Minnesota trout-lily	*Erythronium propullans*
Mongooses	*Herpestes spp.*
Mosquitoes	*Culex spp.*
Mountain lion	*Puma concolor*
Mt. Graham red squirrel	*Tamiasciurus hudsonicus grahamensis*
Mud turtle	*Kinosternon subrubrum*
Mynas	*Gracula spp.*
Northern aplomado falcon	*Falco femoralis septentrionalis*
Northern spotted owl	*Strix occidentalis caurina*
Passenger pigeon	*Ectopistes migratorius*
Peregrine falcon	*Falco peregrinus*
Phibiscus snow scale	*Pinnaspis strachani*
Pitcher plant	*Sarracenia spp.*
Plains bison	*Bison bison bison*
Prairie dogs	*Cynomys spp.*
Raccoon	*Procyon lotor*

Common name	Latin name
Rats	*Rattus spp.*
Red-backed salamander	*Plethodon cinereus*
Red-cockaded woodpecker	*Picoides borealis*
Red wolf	*Canis rufus*
Rhinoceros	*Ceratotherium simum*
Salmon	*Onchorynchus spp.*
San Diego Mesa Mint	*Pogogyne abramsii*
San Joaquin kit fox	*Vulpes macrotis mutica*
Sea mink	*Mustela macrodon*
Sea turtles	*Chelonia, Caretta, Lepidochelys spp.*
Shenandoah salamander	*Plethedon shenandoah*
Silver rice rat	*Oryzomys palustris natator*
Smoky madtom	*Noturus baileyi*
Snail darter	*Percina tanasi*
Snake River chinook salmon	*Oncorhynchus tshawytscha*
Steamboat buckwheat	*Eriogonum ovalifolium var. williamsiae*
Steller's sea cow	*Hydrodamalis gigas*
Strawberry guava	*Psidium cattleyanum*
Thick billed parrot	*Rhynchopsitta pachyrhyncha*
Venus flytrap	*Dionaea muscipula*
Virginia round-leaf birch	*Betula uber*
Water hyacinth	*Eichhornia crassipes*
Whitetail deer	*Odocoileus virginianus*
Wood bison	*Bison bison athabascae*
Wood stork	*Mycteria americana*

APPENDIX 3

Legal Citations

STATUTES AS CODIFIED IN THE 1996 U.S. CODE

Bald Eagle Protection Act, 16 U.S.C. §668

Clean Air Act, 42 U.S.C. §§7401–7642

Clean Water Act, 33 U.S.C. §§1251–1387

Coastal Zone Management Act, 16 U.S.C. §§1451–64

Endangered Species Act, 16 U.S.C. §§1531–44

Family and Medical Leave Act, 29 U.S.C. §§2601–54

Federal Aid in Wildlife Restoration Act, 16 U.S.C. §669

Federal Environmental Pesticide Control Act, 7 U.S.C. §136

Federal Land Policy and Management Act, 43 U.S.C. §§1701–84

Fish and Wildlife Act, 16 U.S.C. §§742–54

Fish and Wildlife Coordination Act, 16 U.S.C. §§661–67

Fisherman's Protective Act, 22 U.S.C. §§1971–80 (including Pelly Amendment, §1978)

Fishery Conservation and Management Act, 16 U.S.C. §§1801–82 (including Packwood-Magnuson Amendment, §1821(e)(2))

Food Security Act of 1985, 16 U.S.C. §§3801–45

Lacey Act, 16 U.S.C. §§3371–3378 and 18 U.S.C. §42

Marine Mammal Protection Act, 16 U.S.C. §§1361–1407

Migratory Bird Conservation Act, 16 U.S.C. §715

Migratory Bird Treaty Act, 16 U.S.C. §§703–12

National Environmental Policy Act, 42 U.S.C. §§4331–70

Noise Control Act, 42 U.S.C. §§4901–18

Rivers and Harbors Act of 1899, 33 U.S.C. §§401–18, 502, 549, 686–87

Taylor Grazing Act, 43 U.S.C. §315

Whaling Convention Act, 16 U.S.C. §916

Yellowstone National Park Protection Act, 16 U.S.C. §§21–40

REPEALED STATUTES

Endangered Species Preservation Act, 80 Stat. 926
Endangered Species Conservation Act, 83 Stat. 275

INTERNATIONAL TREATIES

(Parties are noted in parentheses when numbering less than four as of 1 March 1997. Otherwise, the number of parties is noted.)

Convention Concerning the Conservation of Migratory Birds and Their Environ-ment, 19 November 1976 (United States and U.S.S.R.), 29 U.S.T. 4647, T.I.A.S. 9073

Convention for the Protection of Migratory Birds, 16 August 1916 (United States and Great Britain on behalf of Canada), 39 Stat. 1702, T. S. 628

Convention for the Protection of Migratory Birds and Birds in Danger of Extinc-tion, and Their Environment, 4 March 1972 (United States and Japan), 25 U.S.T. 3329, T.I.A.S. 7990

Convention for the Protection of Migratory Birds and Game Mammals, 7 February 1936 (United States and Mexico), 50 Stat. 1311, T.S. 913

Convention on International Trade in Endangered Species of Wild Fauna and Flora, 3 March 1973 (138 parties), 27 U.S.T. 1087, T.I.A.S. 8249

Convention on Nature Protection and Wildlife Preservation in the Western Hemi-sphere, 12 October 1940 (22 parties), 56 Stat. 1354, T.S. No. 981, U.N.T.S. No. 193

International Convention for the High Seas Fisheries of the North Pacific Ocean, 9 May 1952 (United States, Canada, and Japan), 4 U.S.T. 380, T.I.A.S. 2786

International Convention for the Regulation of Whaling, 2 December 1946 (49 parties), 62 Stat. 1716, T.I.A.S. 1849

SUPERSEDED TREATIES

International Convention for the Northwest Atlantic Fisheries, 8 February 1949, 1 U.S.T. 477, T.I.A.S. 2089

CASES

Bailey v. Holland, 126 F.2d 317 (1942)
Environmental Defense Fund, Inc. v. Ruckelshaus, 439 F.2d 584 (1971)
Florida Rock Industry v. United States I, 8 Cl. Ct. 160 (1985)
Florida Rock Industry v. United States II, 791 F.2d 903 (1987)
Florida Rock Industry v. United States III, 21 Cl. Ct. 161 (1990)
Florida Rock Industry v. United States IV, 18 F.3d 1560 (1994)
Hadacheck v. Sebastian, 239 U.S. 394 (1915)
Geer v. Connecticut, 161 U.S. 519 (1896)

Good v. United States, 39 Fed.Cl. 81 (1997)

Loretto v. Teleprompter Manhattan CATV, 458 U.S. 419 (1982)

Lucas v. South Carolina Coastal Council, 505 U.S. 1029

Martin v. Wadell, 41 U.S. 367 (1842)

Miller v. Schoene, 276 U.S. 272 (1928)

Missouri v. Holland, 252 U.S. 416 (1920)

Mugler v. Kansas, 123 U.S. 1 (1896)

Nollan v. California Coastal Commission, 485 U.S. 943 (1987)

Olson v. United States, 292 U.S. 246 (1934)

Pennsylvania Central Transportation Co. v. New York, 438 U.S. 124 (1978)

Pennsylvania Coal v. Mahon, 260 U.S. 272 (1922)

Ruckelshaus v. Monsanto Company, 467 U.S. 986 (1984)

Sweet Home v. Babbitt, 11 S.Ct. 714 (1995)

Tennessee Valley Authority v. Hill, 437 U.S. 174 (1978)

References

Adams, J. 1851. *Letters to John Taylor of Caroline, Virginia, in reply to his strictures on some parts of the defence of the American constitutions.* In C. F. Adams, ed., *The Works of John Adams,* vol. 6. Boston: Charles C. Little and James Brown, 443–522.

Adler, M. J. 1991. *Haves without Have-nots.* New York: Macmillan.

Allaby, M., ed. 1994. *The Concise Oxford Dictionary of Ecology.* Oxford: Oxford University Press.

Alvarez, K. 1994. The Florida panther recovery program: An organizational failure of the Endangered Species Act. In T. W. Clark, R. P. Reading, and A. L. Clarke, eds., *Endangered Species Recovery: Finding the Lessons, Improving the Process,* 205 26. Washington, D.C.: Island Press.

Anderson, S. H. 1995. Traditional approaches and tools in natural resources management. In R. L. Knight and S. F. Bates, eds., *A New Century for Natural Resources Management,* 61–74. Washington, D.C.: Island Press.

Arnold, F. 1998. It's not the economy. *Environmental Forum* 15(5):30–37.

Ayensu, E. S., and R. A. DeFilipps. 1978. *Endangered and Threatened Plants of the United States.* Washington, D.C.: Smithsonian Institution and World Wildlife Fund.

Ayers, R. 1998. *Turning Point: The End of the Growth Paradigm.* London: Earthscan.

Babbitt, B. 1995. *Federal and State Endangered Species Expenditures: Fiscal Year 1993.* Washington, D.C.: U.S. Fish and Wildlife Service.

Barker, R. 1993. *Saving All the Parts: Reconciling Economics and the Endangered Species Act.* Washington, D.C.: Island Press.

Barro, R. J. 1998. *Determinants of Economic Growth: A Cross-Country Empirical Study.* Cambridge: MIT Press.

Beacham, W. 1994. *The Official World Wildlife Fund Guide to Endangered Species of North America,* vol. 4: 1648–2319. Washington, D.C.: Walton Beacham.

References

Bean, M. J. 1983. *The Evolution of National Wildlife Law.* 2nd ed. Urbana, Ill.: Praeger.

Bender, M., ed. 1999. Box score: Listings and recovery plans as of August 31, 1999. *Endangered Species Bulletin* 24(4):32.

Benson, L. V. 1978. Fluctuations in the level of pluvial Lake Lahontan for the past 40,000 years. *Quaternary Research* 9:300–318.

Bergman, B. J. 1995. Leader of the pack. *Sierra* 8(6):50–55.

Bird, A. P. 1995. Gene number, noise reduction, and biological complexity. *Trends in Genetics* 11(3):94–100.

Boorstin, D. J. 1983. *The Discoverers.* New York: Random House.

Botkin, D. B. 1990. *Discordant Harmonies.* Oxford: Oxford University Press.

Bourland, T. R., and R. L. Stroup. 1996. Rent payments as incentives: Making endangered species welcome on private lands. *Journal of Forestry* 94(4):18–26.

Brewer, G. D., and P. deLeon. 1983. *The Foundations of Policy Analysis.* Chicago: Dorsey Press.

Brown, R. H. 1994. U.S. Department of Commerce Annual Report FY 1994. Washington, D.C.: U.S. Department of Commerce.

Brownlow, C. A. 1996. Molecular taxonomy and the conservation of the red wolf and other endangered carnivores. *Conservation Biology* 10(2):390–96.

Bryant, L. D., and C. Maser. 1982. Classification and distribution. In J. W. Thomas and D. E. Toweill, eds., *Elk of North America: Ecology and Management,* 1–60. Harrisburg, Pa.: Stackpole Books.

Buchanan, C. C., and M. E. Coleman. 1987. The cui-ui. In R. L. Di Silvestro, ed., *Audubon Wildlife Report,* 425–38. Orlando, Fla.: Academic Press.

Buck, S. J. 1991. *Understanding Environmental Administration and Law.* Washington, D.C.: Island Press.

Burling, J. S. 1992. Property rights, endangered species, wetlands, and other critters; Is it against nature to pay for taking? *Land and Water Law Review* 27:309–62.

Buultjens, R, ed. 1978. *The Decline of Democracy: Essays on an Endangered Political Species.* Maryknoll, N.Y.: Orbis Books.

Calder, W. A. 1984. *Size, Function, and Life History.* Cambridge: Harvard University Press.

Campbell, F. 1991. The appropriations history. In K. A. Kohm, ed., *Balancing on the Brink of Extinction: The Endangered Species Act and Lessons for the Future,* 134–46. Washington, D.C.: Island Press.

Carrier, W. D., and B. Czech. 1996. Threatened and endangered wildlife and livestock interactions. In P. R. Krausman, ed., *Rangeland Wildlife,* 39–50. Denver, Colo.: Society for Range Management.

Carroll, R., C. Augspurger, A. Dobson, J. Franklin, G. Orians, W. Reid, R. Tracy, D. Wilcove, and J. Wilson. 1996. Strengthening the use of science in achieving the goals of the Endangered Species Act: An assessment by the Ecological Society of America. *Ecological Applications* 6(1):1–11.

Carson, R. 1962. *Silent Spring.* Greenwich, Conn.: Fawcett.

Cheever, F. 1996. The road to recovery: A new way of thinking about the Endangered Species Act. *Ecology Law Quarterly* 23(1):1–78.

Christensen, C. 1938. On *Polystichum aleuticum* C. Chr., a new North American species. *American Fern Journal* 28:111–12.

Clark, T. W. 1997. *Averting Extinction: Reconstructing Endangered Species Recovery.* New Haven: Yale University Press.

Clark, T. W., R. P. Reading, and A. L. Clarke, eds. 1994. *Endangered Species Recovery: Finding the Lessons, Improving the Process.* Washington, D.C.: Island Press.

Clarke, J. N. 1996. *Roosevelt's Warrior: Harold L. Ickes and the New Deal.* Baltimore: Johns Hopkins University Press.

Clarke, J. N., and D.C. McCool. 1996. *Staking Out the Terrain: Power and Performance among Natural Resource Agencies.* 2nd ed. Albany: State University of New York Press.

Clinton, B., and A. Gore. 1992. *Putting People First: How We Can All Change America.* New York: Times Books.

Costanza, R., B. G. Norton, and B. D. Haskell, ed. 1992. *Ecosystem Health: New Goals for Environmental Management.* Washington, D.C.: Island Press.

Cowan, D., and T. J. Salant. 1999. *County Charter Government in the West.* Washington, D.C.: National Association of Counties.

Cracraft, J. 1989. Speciation and its ontology: The empirical consequences of alternative species concepts for understanding patterns and processes of differentiation. In D. Otte and J. A. Endler, eds., *Speciation and Its Consequences*, 28–59. Sunderland, Mass.: Sinauer Associates.

Cramer, G. L., and C. W. Jensen. 1994. *Agricultural Economics and Agribusiness.* 6th ed. New York: John Wiley and Sons.

Cronon, W. 1983. *Changes in the Land: Indians, Colonists, and the Ecology of New England.* New York: Hill and Wang.

Crozier, R. H., and R. M. Kusmierski. 1994. Genetic distances and the setting of conservation priorities. In V. Loeschcke, J. Tomiuk, and S. K. Jain, eds., *Conservation Genetics*, 227–37. Basel: Birkhauser Verlag.

Cubbage, F. W., J. O'Laughlin, and C. S. Bullock III. 1993. *Forest Resource Policy.* New York: John Wiley and Sons.

Czech, B. 1995a. Ecosystem management is no paradigm shift; let's try conservation. *Journal of Forestry* 93(12):17–23.

———. 1995b. American Indians and wildlife conservation. *Wildlife Society Bulletin* 23(4):568–73.

———. 1996a. *Ward v. Racehorse:* Supreme Court as obviator? *Journal of the West* 35(3):61–69.

———. 1996b. Challenges to establishing and implementing sound natural fire policy. *Renewable Resources Journal* 14(2):14–19.

———. 1997a. The Endangered Species Act, American democracy, and an omnibus role for public policy. Ph.D. diss., University of Arizona.

———. 1997b. Viewpoint: The importance of range science to federal grazing policy. *Journal of Range Management* 50:327–29.

———. 1999. Big game management on tribal lands. In S. Demarais and P. R. Krausman, eds., *Ecology and Management of Large Mammals in North America*, 277–89. Saddle River, N.J.: Prentice Hall.

———. 2000a. Economic growth as the limiting factor for wildlife conservation. *Wildlife Society Bulletin* 28(1): 4–14.

———. 2000b. *Shoveling Fuel For a Runaway Train: Errant Economists, Shameful Spenders, and a Plan to Stop Them All.* Berkeley: University of California Press.

Czech, B., and P. R. Krausman. 1997a. Implications of an ecosystem management literature review. *Wildlife Society Bulletin* 25(3):667–75.

———. 1997b. Distribution and causation of species endangerment in the United States. *Science* 277:1116–17.

Czech, B., P. R. Krausman, and R. Borkhataria. 1998. Social construction, political power, and the allocation of benefits to endangered species. *Conservation Biology* 12:1103–12.

Czech, B., P. R. Krausman, and P. K. Devers. 2000. Economic associations among causes of species endangerment in the United States. *BioScience* 50:593–601.

Daly, H. E. 1993. Introduction to essays toward a steady-state economy. In H. E. Daly and K. N. Townsend, eds., *Valuing the Earth: Economics, Ecology, Ethics*, 11–50. Cambridge: MIT Press.

Daly, H. E., and J. B. Cobb Jr. 1994. *For the Common Good: Redirecting the Economy Toward Community, the Environment, and a Sustainable Future*. Boston: Beacon Press.

Darwin, C. R. 1859. *On the Origin of Species by Means of Natural Selection.* London: John Murray.

Davidson, R. H., and W. J. Oleszek. 1994. *Congress and Its Members.* 4th ed. Washington, D.C.: Congressional Quarterly.

Deal, C. 1993. *The Greenpeace Guide to Anti-Environmental Organizations.* Berkeley: Odonian Press.

Devall, B., and G. Sessions. 1985. *Deep Ecology.* Salt Lake City, Utah: Peregrine Smith Books.

Devine, B. 1999. Clear-cut mission: Communities unite to free native landscapes from the grip of invasive species. *Nature Conservancy* 49(4):12–17.

DeVoto, B., ed. 1953. *The Journals of Lewis and Clark.* Boston: Houghton Mifflin.

Diamond, H. L., and P. F. Noonan. 1996. *Land Use in America.* Washington, D.C.: Island Press.

Dingell, J. D. 1989. Foreword to *The Endangered Species Act*, by D. J. Rohlf. Stanford, Calif.: Stanford Environmental Law Society.

DiSilvestro, R. L. 1989. *The Endangered Kingdom: The Struggle to Save America's Wildlife.* New York: John Wiley and Sons.

Dobson, A. P., J. P. Rodriquez, W. M. Roberts, and D. S. Wilcove. 1997. Geographic distribution of endangered species in the United States. *Science* 275:550–53.

Douthwaite, R. 1992. *The Growth Illusion: How Economic Growth Has Enriched the Few, Impoverished the Many, and Endangered the Planet.* Tulsa, Okla.: Council Oak Books.

Dryzek, J. S. 1990. *Discursive Democracy: Politics, Policy, and Political Science.* Cambridge, U.K.: Cambridge University Press.

Dubos, R. J. 1959. *Mirage of Health: Utopias, Progress, and Biological Change.* New York: Harper.

Dunlap, T. R. 1988. *Saving America's Wildlife.* Princeton: Princeton University Press.

Dunn, C. W. 1987. *Constitutional Democracy in America: A Reappraisal.* Glenview, Ill.: Scott, Foresman.

Dunn, E. S. Jr. 1983. *The Development of the U.S. Urban System,* vol. 2. Washington, D.C.: Resources for the Future.

Dwyer, L. E., D. D. Murphy, and P. R. Ehrlich. 1995. Property rights case law and the challenge to the Endangered Species Act. *Conservation Biology* 9(4):725–41.

Easter-Pilcher, A. 1996. Implementing the Endangered Species Act: Assessing the listing of species as endangered or threatened. *Bioscience* 46(5):355–63.

Echeverria, J. D., and R. B. Eby, eds. 1995. *Let the People Judge: Wise Use and the Private Property Rights Movement.* Washington, D.C.: Island Press.

Edmondson, B. 1991. Census reveals 33 new urban markets. *American Demographics* 13(11):8.

Ehrlich, P. R. 1994. Ecological economics and the carrying capacity of Earth. In A. M. Jansson, M. Hammer, C. Folke, and R. Costanza, eds., *Investing in Natural Capital: The Ecological Economics Approach to Sustainability,* 38–56. Washington, D.C.: Island Press.

Ehrlich, P. R., and A. H. Ehrlich. 1996. *Betrayal of Science and Reason: How Anti-Environmental Rhetoric Threatens Our Future.* Washington, D.C.: Island Press.

Eisner, T., J. Lubchenco, E. O. Wilson, D. S. Wilcove, and M. J. Bean. 1995. Building a scientifically sound policy for protecting endangered species. *Science* 268:1231–32.

Ekelund, R. B. Jr., and R. D. Tollison. 1988. *Macroeconomics.* 2nd ed. Glenview, Ill.: Scott, Foresman.

Ellickson, R. C., and C. M. Rose. 1995. Preface to *Perspectives on Property Law,* by R. C. Ellickson, C. M. Rose, and B. A. Ackerman, eds. 2nd ed. Boston: Little, Brown.

Epstein, R. A. 1995. Covenants and constitutions. *Cornell Law Review* 73:906–924.

Erickson, J. D. 2000. Endangering the economics of extinction. *Wildlife Society Bulletin* 28(1): 33–40.

Errington, P. L. 1946. Predation and vertebrate populations. *Quarterly Review of Biology* 21:145–77.

Faith, D. P. 1992. Systematics and conservation: On predicting the feature diversity of subsets of taxa. *Cladistics* 8:361–73.

Famighetti, R., ed. 1996. *The World Almanac and Book of Facts 1997*. Mahwah, N.J.: K-III Reference Corporation.

Ferejohn, J. A. 1974. *Pork Barrel Politics: Rivers and Harbors Legislation, 1947–1968*. Stanford: Stanford University Press.

Fischer, F. 1990. *Technocracy and the Politics of Expertise*. Newbury Park, Calif: Sage Publications.

Fleischner, T. L. 1994. Ecological costs of livestock grazing in western North America. *Conservation Biology* 8(3):629–44.

Fleming, D. 1972. Roots of the new conservation movement. *Perspectives in American History* 6:7–91.

Flick, W. A., R. A. Tufts, and D. Zhang. 1996. *Sweet Home* as forest policy. *Journal of Forestry* 94(4):4–8.

Folke, C., M. Hammer, R. Costanza, and A. M. Jansson. 1994. Investing in natural capital: Why, what, and how? In A. M. Jansson, M. Hammer, C. Folke, and R. Costanza, eds., *Investing in Natural Capital: The Ecological Economics Approach to Sustainability*, 1–20. Washington, D.C.: Island Press.

Folke, C., A. Jansson, J. Larsson, and R. Costanza. 1996. Ecosystem appropriation by cities. *Beijer Discussion Paper Series*, no. 86. Stockholm: Beijer International Institute of Ecological Economics.

Fox, S. R. 1981. *The American Conservation Movement: John Muir and His Legacy*. Madison: University of Wisconsin Press.

Frank, R. M. 1993. Regulating land and resources in the post-*Lucas* era: The impact of California's nuisance and real property law. *Land Use Forum* 2:44–50.

Frankham, R. 1995. Inbreeding and extinction: A threshold effect. *Conservation Biology* 9(4):792–99.

Franklin, B. H. 1992. *U.S. Department of Commerce Annual Report, FY 1992*. Washington, D.C.: U.S. Department of Commerce.

Friedman, M. 1962. *Capitalism and Freedom*. Chicago: University of Chicago Press.

Futuyma, D. J. 1983. *Coevolution*. Sunderland, Mass.: Sinauer Associates.

Galbraith, J. K. 1987. *Economics in Perspective*. Boston: Houghton Mifflin.

George, S. 1998. *State Endangered Species Acts: Past, Present and Future*. Washington, D.C.: Houghton Mifflin.

Gordon, R. E. 1996. *Conservation Directory*, 41st edition. Washington, D.C.: National Wildlife Federation.

Gore, A. 1995. *Common Sense Government*. New York: Random House.

Götmark, F. 1992. Naturalness as an evaluation criterion in nature conservation: A response to Anderson. *Conservation Biology* 6(3):455–58.

Gottlieb, R. 1993. *Forcing the Spring: The Transformation of the American Environmental Movement*. Washington, D.C.: Island Press.

Graves, G. 1995. Pursuing Excellence in Water Planning and Policy Analysis: A History of the Institute for Water Resources. Publication 405–210/57652. Washington, D.C.: U.S. Government Printing Office.

Green, D. P., and I. Shapiro. 1994. *Pathologies of Rational Choice Theory: A Critique of Applications in Political Science.* New Haven: Yale University Press.

Greider, W. 1992. *Who Will Tell the People?* New York: Simon and Schuster.

Grumbine, R. E. 1992. *Ghost Bears: Exploring the Biodiversity Crisis.* Washington, D.C.: Island Press.

Hamilton, A., J. Madison, J. Jay, and R. P. Fairfield. 1961. *Federalist: The Federalist papers; a Collection of Essays Written in Support of the Constitution of the United States.* Garden City, N.Y.: Anchor Books.

Hanley, T. A. 1982. The nutritional basis for food selection by ungulates. *Journal of Range Management* 35:146–51.

Hardin, G. 1968. The tragedy of the commons. *Science* 162:1243–48.

Haskell, B. D., B. G. Norton, and R. Costanza. 1992. What is ecosystem health and why should we worry about it? In R. Costanza, B. G. Norton, and B. D. Haskell, eds., *Ecosystem Health: New Goals for Environmental Management,* 3–20. Washington, D.C.: Island Press.

Hawkins, A. S., R. C. Hanson, H. K. Nelson, and H. M. Reeves, eds. 1984. *Flyways: Pioneering Waterfowl Management in North America.* Washington, D.C.: U.S. Fish and Wildlife Service.

Hayles, N. K. 1995. Searching for common ground. In M. E. Soulé and G. Lease, eds., *Reinventing Nature?: Responses to Postmodern Deconstruction,* 47–63. Washington, D.C.: Island Press.

Hayward, T. 1994. *Ecological Thought: An Introduction.* Cambridge, U.K.: Polity Press.

Hebert, A. 1997. Student songwriter Tad Johnson releases self-produced solo disc. *Campus Press* (University of Colorado at Boulder) September 11.

Heilbroner, R. L., and L. C. Thurow. 1987. *Economics Explained.* 2nd edition. New York: Simon and Schuster.

Heinen, J. T. 1995. Thoughts and theory on incentive-based endangered species conservation in the United States. *Wildlife Society Bulletin* 23(3):338–45.

Heintzelman, D. S. 1979. *Hawks and Owls of North America: A Complete Guide to North American Birds of Prey.* New York: Universe Books.

Heissenbuttel, J., and W. R. Murray. 1992. A troubled law in need of revision. *Journal of Forestry* 90:13–16.

Hirt, P. 1994. *A Conspiracy of Optimism: Management of the National Forests since World War II.* Lincoln: University of Nebraska Press.

Holling, C. S. 1994. New science and new investments for a sustainable biosphere. In A. M. Jansson, M. Hammer, C. Folke, and R. Costanza, eds., *Investing in Natural Capital: The Ecological Economics Approach to Sustainability,* 57–73. Washington, D.C.: Island Press.

Howard, P. K. 1994. *The Death of Common Sense.* New York: Random House.

Houck, O. A. 1995. Reflections on the Endangered Species Act. *Environmental Law* 25(3):689–702.

Hoy, D.C., and T. McCarthy. 1994. *Critical Theory.* Cambridge, Mass.: Blackwell.

Ingram, H., and S. R. Smith, eds. 1993. *Public Policy for Democracy*. Washington, D.C.: Brookings Institution.

Jaeger, R. G. 1970. Potential extinction through competition between two species of terrestrial salamanders. *Evolution* 24:632–42.

Jansson, A. M., M. Hammer, C. Folke, and R. Costanza, eds. 1994. *Investing in Natural Capital: The Ecological Economics Approach to Sustainability*. Washington, D.C.: Island Press.

Karr, J. R. 1992. Ecological integrity: Protecting Earth's life support systems. In R. Costanza, B. G. Norton, and B. D. Haskell, eds., *Ecosystem Health: New Goals for Environmental Management*, 223–38. Washington, D.C.: Island Press.

Kellert, S. R. 1980. *Knowledge, Affection and Basic Attitudes toward Animals in American Society*. Phase III results of grant # 14-16-0009-77-056. Washington, D.C.: U.S. Government Printing Office.

———. 1985. Social and perceptual factors in endangered species management. *Journal of Wildlife Management* 49(2):528–36.

———. 1993. Values and perceptions of invertebrates. *Conservation Biology* 7(4):845–55.

———. 1996. *The Value of Life*. Washington, D.C.: Island Press.

Kellert, S. R., and J. K. Berry. 1987. Attitudes, knowledge, and behaviors toward wildlife as affected by gender. *Wildlife Society Bulletin* 15:363–371.

Kempton, W., J. S. Boster, and J. A. Hartley. 1996. *Environmental Values in American Culture*. Cambridge, Mass.: MIT Press.

Kennedy, E. T., R. Costa, and W. M. Smathers, Jr. 1996. Economic incentives: New directions for red-cockaded woodpecker habitat conservation. *Journal of Forestry* 94(4):22–26.

Knight, R. L., and T. L. George. 1995. New approaches, new tools: Conservation biology. In R. L. Knight and S. F. Bates, eds., *A New Century for Natural Resources Management*, 279–96. Washington, D.C.: Island Press.

Kohm, K. A. 1991. The act's history and framework. In K. A. Kohm, ed., *Balancing on the Brink of Extinction: The Endangered Species Act and Lessons for the Future*, 10–22. Washington, D.C.: Island Press.

Krishnan, R., J. M. Harris, and N. R. Goodwin, eds. 1995. *A Survey of Ecological Economics*. Washington, D.C.: Island Press.

Lancaster, J. 1990. Lujan: Endangered Species Act "too tough," needs changes. *Washington Post*, May 12, sec. A1.

Landy, M. 1993. Public policy and citizenship. In H. Ingram and S. R. Smith, eds., *Public Policy for Democracy*, 19–44. Washington, D.C.: Brookings Institution.

Lasswell, H. D. 1958. *Politics: Who Gets What, When, and How?* New York: Meridian Books.

Lazarus, R. J. 1993. Shifting paradigms of tort and property in the transformation of natural resources law. In L. J. MacDonnell and S. F. Bates, eds., *Natural Resources Policy and Law: Trends and Directions*, 193–215. Washington, D.C.: Island Press.

Lease, G. 1995. Introduction: Nature under fire. In M. E. Soulé and G. Lease, eds., *Reinventing Nature?: Responses to Postmodern Deconstruction*, 3–15. Washington, D.C.: Island Press.

Lee, K. N. 1993. *Compass and Gyroscope: Integrating Science and Politics for the Environment*. Washington, D.C.: Island Press.

Leopold, A. 1933. *Game Management*. New York: Charles Scribner's Sons.

———. 1949. *A Sand County Almanac*. New York: Oxford University Press.

———. 1966. *A Sand County Almanac; With Essays on Conservation from Round River*. New York: Oxford University Press.

Levin, D. A., J. Franciso-Ortega, and R. K. Jansen. 1996. Hybridization and the extinction of rare plant species. *Conservation Biology* 10(1):10–16.

Lewis, T. A. 1995. Cloaked in a wise disguise. In J. D. Echeverria and R. B. Eby, eds., *Let the People Judge: Wise Use and the Private Property Rights Movement*, 13–20. Washington, D.C.: Island Press.

Li, W. H., and D. Graur. 1991. *Fundamentals of Molecular Evolution*. Sunderland, Mass.: Sinauer Associates.

Lin, A. C. 1996. Participants' experiences with habitat conservation plans and suggestions for streamlining the process. *Ecology Law Quarterly* 23:369–446.

Lineberry, R. L. 1980. *Government in America: People, Politics, and Policy*. Boston: Little, Brown.

Littell, R. 1992. *Endangered and Other Protected Species*. Washington, D.C.: U.S. Bureau of National Affairs.

Lowe, D. W., J. R. Matthews, and C. J. Moseley. 1990. *The Official World Wildlife Fund Guide to Endangered Species of North America*, vols. 1–2. Washington, D.C.: Walton Beacham.

Lund, T. A. 1980. *American Wildlife Law*. Berkeley: University of California Press.

Lydeard, C., and R. L. Mayden. 1995. A diverse and endangered aquatic ecosystem of the southeast United States. *Conservation Biology* 9(4):800–805.

Maehr, D. S., and G. B. Caddick. 1995. Demographics and genetic introgression in the Florida panther. *Conservation Biology* 9(5):1295–98.

Mankiw, N. G. 1992. *Macroeconomics*. New York: Worth Publishers.

Mann, C. C., and M. L. Plummer. 1995. *Noah's Choice: The Future of Endangered Species*. New York: Alfred A. Knopf.

Martin, A. P., and S. R. Palumbi. 1993. Body size, metabolic rate, generation time, and the molecular clock. *Proceedings of the National Academy of Sciences of the United States of America* 90:4087–91.

Martin, P. S., and C. R. Szuter. 1999. War zones and game sinks in Lewis and Clark's West. *Conservation Biology* 13(1):36–45.

Mattson, D. J., and J. J. Craighead. 1994. The Yellowstone grizzly bear recovery program: uncertain information, uncertain policy. In T. W. Clark, R. P. Reading, and A. L. Clarke, eds., *Endangered Species Recovery: Finding the Lessons, Improving the Process*, 101–30. Washington, D.C.: Island Press.

McCool, D. C., ed. 1995. *Public Policy Theories, Models, and Concepts: An Anthology.* Englewood Cliffs, N.J.: Prentice-Hall.

McHugh, T. 1972. *The Time of the Buffalo.* New York: Alfred A. Knopf.

Meffe, G. K., and C. R. Carroll, eds. 1994. *Principles of Conservation Biology.* Sunderland, Mass.: Sinauer Associates.

Meltz, R. 1994. Where the wild things are: the Endangered Species Act and private property. *Environmental Law* 24:369–417.

M'Gonigle, R. M. 1999. Ecological economics and political ecology: Towards a necessary synthesis. *Ecological Economics* 28:11–26.

Miller, G. 1996. Ecosystem management: Improving the Endangered Species Act. *Ecological Applications* 6(3):715–17.

Moe, T. M. 1990. The politics of structural choice: Toward a theory of public bureaucracy. In O. Williamson, ed., *Organization Theory*, 116–53. Oxford: Oxford University Press.

Mohlenbrock, R. H. 1983. *Where Have All the Wildflowers Gone?* New York: Macmillan.

Monkkonen, E. H. 1988. *America Becomes Urban: The Development of U.S. Cities and Towns, 1780–1980.* Berkeley: University of California Press.

Montgomery, C. A., and R. A. Pollock. 1996. Economics and biodiversity: Weighing the benefits and costs of conservation. *Journal of Forestry* 94(2):34–38.

Moseley, C. J. 1992. *The Official World Wildlife Fund Guide to Endangered Species of North America*, vol. 3:1181–647. Washington, D.C.: Walton Beacham.

Murphy, D. D. 1991. Invertebrate conservation. In K. A. Kohm, ed., *Balancing on the Brink of Extinction: The Endangered Species Act and Lessons for the Future*, 181–98. Washington, D.C.: Island Press.

Murphy, D. D., D. Wilcove, R. Noss, J. Harte, C. Safina, J. Lubchenco, T. Root, V. Sher, L. Kaufman, M. Bean, and S. Pimm. 1994. Editorial: On reauthorization of the Endangered Species Act. *Conservation Biology* 8(1):1–3.

Myers, R. L. 1985. Fire and the dynamic relationship between Florida sandhill and sand pine scrub vegetation. *Bulletin of the Torrey Botanical Club* 112:241–52.

———. 1990. Scrub and high pine. In R. L. Myers and J. J. Ewel, eds., *Ecosystems of Florida*, 150–93. Orlando: University of Central Florida Press.

National Research Council. 1994. *Rangeland Health.* Washington, D.C.: National Academy Press.

———. 1995. *Science and the Endangered Species Act.* Washington, D.C.: National Academy Press.

Noss, R. F. 1991. From endangered species to biodiversity. In K. A. Kohm, ed., *Balancing on the Brink of Extinction: The Endangered Species Act and Lessons for the Future*, 227–46. Washington, D.C.: Island Press.

Noss, R. F., and B. Csuti. 1994. Habitat fragmentation. In G. K. Meffe and C. R. Carroll, eds., *Principles of Conservation Biology*, 237–64. Sunderland, Mass.: Sinauer Associates.

Novacek, M. J. 1992. The meaning of systematics and the biodiversity crisis. In

N. Eldredge, ed., *Systematics, Ecology, and the Biodiversity Crisis*, 101–8. New York: Columbia University Press.

Nowak, R. M. 1991. *Walker's Mammals of the World*. 5th ed. 2 vols. Baltimore: Johns Hopkins University Press.

O'Brien, D. M. 1993. *Storm Center: The Supreme Court in American Politics*. New York: Norton.

Odum, E. P. 1989. *Ecology and Our Endangered Life-Support Systems*. Sunderland, Mass: Sinauer Associates.

Oelschlaeger, M. 1994. *Caring for Creation*. New Haven: Yale University Press.

Opler, P. A. 1976. The parade of passing species: A survey of extinctions in the United States. *The Science Teacher* 43(11):30–34.

Orwell, G. 1987. *Animal Farm: A Fairy Story*. Vol. 8 of *The Complete Works of George Orwell*. London: Secker and Warburg.

O'Toole, R., ed. 1996. *Different Drummer* 3(1):1–63.

Page, T. 1992. Environmental existentialism. In R. Costanza, B. G. Norton, and B. D. Haskell, eds., *Ecosystem Health: New Goals for Environmental Management*, 97–123. Washington, D.C.: Island Press.

Palmer, J. D. 1990. Contrasting modes and tempos of genome evolution in land plant organelles. *Trends in Genetics* 6(4):115–20.

Patlis, J. M. 1994. Biodiversity, ecosystems and species: Where does the Endangered Species Act fit in? *Tulane Environmental Law Journal* 8(1):33–76.

Pennock, D. S., and W. W. Dimmick. 1997. Critique of the evolutionarily significant unit as a definition for "distinct population segments" under the U.S. Endangered Species Act. *Conservation Biology* 11:611–19.

Pianka, E. R. 1974. *Evolutionary Ecology*. New York: Harper and Row.

Pitt, R. 1996. *Groundwater Contamination from Stormwater Infiltration*. Chelsea, Mich.: Ann Arbor Press.

Platt, R. H. 1996. *Land Use and Society: Geography, Law, and Public Policy*. Washington, D.C.: Island Press.

Pollard, I. 1994. *A Guide to Reproduction: Social Issues and Human Concerns*. Cambridge, U.K.: Cambridge University Press.

Pope, C. 1996. Corporate citizens. *Sierra* 81(6):14.

Popper, K. R. 1994. *In Search of a Better World*. New York: Routledge.

Radin, M. J. 1995. Property and personhood. In R. C. Ellickson, C. M. Rose, and B. A. Ackerman, eds., *Perspectives on Property Law*, 8–18. 2nd edition. Boston: Little, Brown.

Rauber, P. 1996. An end to evolution. *Sierra* 81(1):28–33.

Raven, P. H. 1990. The politics of preserving biodiversity. *Bioscience* 40(10): 769–74.

Reading, R. P., and B. J. Miller. 1994. The black-footed ferret recovery program: Unmasking professional and organizational weaknesses. In T. W. Clark, R. P. Reading, and A. L. Clarke, eds., *Endangered Species Recovery: Finding the Lessons, Improving the Process*, 73–100. Washington, D.C.: Island Press.

Rees, W. E. 1992. Ecological footprints and appropriated carrying capacity: What urban economics leaves out. *Environment and Urbanization* 4:121–30.

Rees, W. E., and M. Wackernagel. 1994. Ecological footprints and appropriated carrying capacity: Measuring the natural capital requirements of the human economy. In A. M. Jansson, M. Hammer, C. Folke, and R. Costanza, eds., *Investing in Natural Capital: The Ecological Economics Approach to Sustainability*, 362–91. Washington, D. C.: Island Press.

Reeves, H. M. 1984. Wells H. Cooke. In A. S. Hawkins, R. C. Hanson, H. K. Nelson, and H. M. Reeves, eds., *Flyways: Pioneering Waterfowl Management in North America*, 87–89. Washington, D.C.: U.S. Fish and Wildlife Service.

Reffalt, W. 1991. The endangered species lists: Chronicles of extinction? In K. A. Kohm, ed., *Balancing on the Brink of Extinction: The Endangered Species Act and Lessons for the Future*, 77–85. Washington, D.C.: Island Press.

Reidel, C. 1988. Natural resources and the environment: The challenge of economic and social development. *Population and Environment* 10(1):48–58.

Richards, C., and P. L. Leberg. 1996. Temporal changes in allele frequencies and a population's history of severe bottlenecks. *Conservation Biology* 10(3):832–39.

Robinson, J. G. 1993. The limits to caring: Sustainable living and the loss of biodiversity. *Conservation Biology* 7(1):20–28.

Roelke, M. E., J. S. Martenson, and S. J. O'Brien. 1993. The consequences of demographic reduction and genetic depletion in the endangered Florida panther. *Current Biology* 3:340–50.

Rohlf, D. J. 1989. *The Endangered Species Act*. Stanford, Calif.: Stanford Environmental Law Society.

Rolston III, H. 1991. Life in jeopardy on private property. In K. A. Kohm, ed., *Balancing on the Brink of Extinction: The Endangered Species Act and Lessons for the Future*, 43–61. Washington, D.C.: Island Press.

Romesburg, C. H. 1981. Wildlife science: Gaining reliable knowledge. *Journal of Wildlife Management* 45:293–313.

Rostow, W. W., and M. Kennedy. 1990. *Theorists of Economic Growth from David Hume to the Present: With a Perspective on the Next Century*. New York: Oxford University Press.

Roush, J. 1995. What we can learn from the Wise Use Movement. In J. D. Echeverria and R. B. Eby, eds., *Let the People Judge: Wise Use and the Private Property Rights Movement*, 1–10. Washington, D.C.: Island Press.

Rumburg, C. B. 1996. Foreword to *Rangeland Wildlife*, by P. R. Krausman, ed. Denver: Society for Range Management.

Salant, P., and D. A. Dillman. 1994. *How to Conduct Your Own Survey*. New York: John Wiley and Sons.

Salwasser, H. 1991. In search of an ecosystem approach to endangered species conservation. In K. A. Kohm, ed., *Balancing on the Brink of Extinction: The Endangered Species Act and Lessons for the Future*, 247–65. Washington, D.C.: Island Press.

Saunders, D. A., R. J. Hobbs, and C. R. Margules. 1991. Biological consequences of ecosystem fragmentation: A review. *Conservation Biology* 5(1):18–32.

Savory, A. 1988. *Holistic Resource Management*. Washington, D.C.: Island Press.

Sax, J. L. 1993. Property rights and the economy of nature: Understanding *Lucas v. South Carolina Coastal Council. Stanford Law Review* 45:1433–55.

Schelling, T. C. 1995. Prices as regulatory instruments. In R. C. Ellickson, C. M. Rose, and B. A. Ackerman, eds., *Perspectives on Property Law*, 532–45. 2nd ed., Boston: Little, Brown and Company.

Schneider, A. L., and H. Ingram. 1993. Social construction of target populations: implications for politics and policy. *American Political Science Review* 87(2):334–47.

———. 1997. *Policy Design for Democracy*. Lawrence: University Press of Kansas.

Schumpeter, J. A. 1976. *Capitalism, Socialism and Democracy*, 5th ed. London: George Allen and Unwin.

Scott, J. M., T. H. Tear, and L. Scott Mills. 1995. Socioeconomics and the recovery of endangered species: Biological assessment in a political world. *Conservation Biology* 9(1):214–16.

Shepard, P. 1995. Virtually hunting reality in the forests of simulacra. In M. E. Soule and G. Lease, eds., *Reinventing Nature?: Responses to Postmodern Deconstruction*, 17–29. Washington, D.C.: Island Press.

Simmons, R. T., and C. E. Kay. 1997. Politics, bureaucracy and the Endangered Species Act. Working paper. Utah State University, Logan.

Simon, J. L., and A. Wildavsky. 1993. Facts, not species, are periled. *New York Times* May 13.

Smith, A. A., M. A. Moote, and C. R. Schwalbe. 1993. The Endangered Species Act at twenty: An analytical survey of federal endangered species protection. *Natural Resources Journal* 33(4):1027–76.

Smith, G. W., and R. E. Reynolds. 1992. Hunting and mallard survival, 1979–1988. *Journal of Wildlife Management* 56(2):306–15.

Soulé, M. E. 1983. What do we really know about extinction? In C. M. Schonewald-Cox, S. M. Chambers, B. MacBryde, and W. L. Thomas, eds., *Genetics and Conservation: A Reference for Managing Wild Animal and Plant Populations*, 111–24. London: Benjamin/Cummings.

———. 1995. The social siege of nature. In *Reinventing Nature?: Responses to Postmodern Deconstruction*, 137–70. Washington, D.C.: Island Press.

Soulé, M. E., and G. Lease. 1995. *Reinventing Nature?: Responses to Postmodern Deconstruction*. Washington, D.C.: Island Press.

Stanley, H. W., and R. G. Niemi. 1995. *Vital Statistics on American Politics*. Washington, D.C.: Congressional Quarterly Press.

Stannard, D. E. 1992. *American Holocaust: The Conquest of the New World*. New York: Oxford University Press.

Studds, G. E. 1991. Preserving biodiversity. *Bioscience* 41(9):602.

Sunstein, C. R. 1993. On property and constitutionalism. *Cardozo Law Review* 14:907–22.

Switzer, J. V. 1994. *Environmental Politics: Domestic and Global Dimensions.* New York: St. Martin's Press.

Tear, T. H., J. M. Scott, P. H. Hayward, and B. Griffith. 1995. Recovery plans and the Endangered Species Act: Are criticisms supported by data? *Conservation Biology* 9(1):182–95.

Trefethen, J. B. 1975. *An American Crusade for Wildlife.* New York: Winchester Press, Boone and Crockett Club.

Trotsky, L. 1974. *The History of the Russian Revolution,* vol. 3. Ann Arbor: University of Michigan Press.

Tuttle, M. D. 1979. Status, causes of decline, and management of endangered gray bats. *Journal of Wildlife Management* 43:1–17.

Udall, S. L. 1988. *The Quiet Crisis and the Next Generation.* Salt Lake City, Utah: Peregrine Smith.

U.S. Fish and Wildlife Service. 1995. Facts about the Endangered Species Act. Washington, D.C.: U.S. Fish and Wildlife Service Public Affairs Office.

Vane-Wright, R. I., C. J. Humphries, and P. H. Williams. 1991. What to protect?: Systematics and the agony of choice. *Biological Conservation* 55:235–54.

Vileisis, A. 1997. *Discovering the Unknown Landscape: A History of America's Wetlands.* Washington, D.C.: Island Press.

Viterito, A. 1991. Future warming for U.S. cities. *Population and Environment* 13(2):101–11.

Waples, R. S. 1998. Evolutionarily significant units, distinct population segments, and the Endangered Species Act: Reply to Pennock and Dimmick. *Conservation Biology* 12(3):718–21.

Washington Post. 1996. Campaign '96: Transcript of the vice presidential debate. *Washington Post,* October 10, sec. A25-A28.

Willers, B. 1994. Sustainable development: A new world deception. *Conservation Biology* 8(4):1146–48.

Williams, F. 1995. Sagebrush rebellion II. In J. D. Echeverria and R. B. Eby, eds., *Let the People Judge: Wise Use and the Private Property Rights Movement,* 130–35. Washington, D.C.: Island Press.

Williams, P. H., C. J. Humphries, and R. I. Vane-Wright. 1991. Measuring biodiversity: Taxonomic relatedness for conservation priorities. *Australian Systematic Botany* 4:665–79.

Williams, T. 1996. Defense of the realm. *Sierra* 81(1):34–39.

Wilson, E. O. 1984. *Biophilia, the Human Bond with Other Species.* Cambridge, Mass.: Harvard University Press.

Wilson, J. Q. 1989. *Bureaucracy: What Government Agencies Do and Why They Do It.* New York: Basic Books.

Wilson, W. 1901. Democracy and efficiency. *Atlantic Monthly* 87(3):289–99.

Windsor, D. A. 1995. Editorial: Equal rights for parasites. *Conservation Biology* 9(1):1–2.

Witting, L., M. A. McCarthy, and V. Loeschcke. 1994. Multi-species risk analysis, species evaluation and biodiversity conservation. In V. Loeschcke, J. Tomiuk, and S. K. Jain, eds., *Conservation Genetics,* 239–49. Basel: Birkhauser Verlag.

Woodwell, G. M. 1989. On causes of biotic impoverishment. *Ecology* 70:14–15.

Worster, D. 1995. Nature and the disorder of history. In M. E. Soulé and G. Lease, eds., *Reinventing Nature?: Responses to Postmodern Deconstruction,* 65–85. Washington, D.C.: Island Press.

Yaffee, S. L. 1982. *Prohibitive Policy: Implementing the Federal Endangered Species Act.* Cambridge: MIT Press.

———. 1994a. *The Wisdom of the Spotted Owl: Policy Lessons for a New Century.* Washington, D.C.: Island Press.

———. 1994b. The northern spotted owl: An indicator of the importance of socio-political context. In T. W. Clark, R. P. Reading, and A. L. Clarke, eds., *Endangered Species Recovery: Finding the Lessons, Improving the Process,* 47–72. Washington, D.C.: Island Press.

Yagerman, K. S. 1990. Protecting critical habitat under the federal Endangered Species Act. *Environmental Law* 20:811–56.

Yeates, M. 1980. *North American Urban Patterns.* New York: John Wiley and Sons.

Zhang, D. 1996. State property rights laws: What, where, and how? *Journal of Forestry* 94(4):10–17.

Zinn, J., and C. Copeland. 1996. *Agricultural Wetlands: Current Programs and Legislative Proposals.* Report No. 96–35 ENR. Washington, D.C.: Congressional Research Service.

Zuckerkandl, E., and L. Pauling. 1965. Evolutionary divergence and convergence in proteins. In V. Bryson and H. J. Vogel, eds., *Evolving Genes and Proteins,* 97–166. New York: Academic Press.

Index

About the Authors

Brian Czech is a conservation biologist in the national office of the U.S. Fish and Wildlife Service. He was born and raised in Wisconsin and spent most of his adult life in the West. He completed a bachelor's degree in wildlife ecology from the University of Wisconsin, Madison, a master's degree in wildlife science at the University of Washington, and a Ph.D. in renewable natural resources with a minor in political science from the University of Arizona. Specializing in policy development for the National Wildlife Refuge System, he won a Fish and Wildlife Service Star Award in 1999 for outstanding service. He is the author of *Shoveling Fuel for a Runaway Train: Errant Economists, Shameful Spenders, and a Plan to Stop Them All.*

Paul R. Krausman is a professor of Wildlife and Fisheries Science at the University of Arizona and Associate Director of the Arizona Agricultural Experiment Station. He was born in Washington, D.C., and raised in North Africa while his father was a diplomat with the State Department. He has a bachelor's degree in zoology from Ohio State University, a master's degree in wildlife management from New Mexico State University, and a Ph.D. in wildlife science from the University of Idaho. He has received numerous teaching and research awards, including the 1999 O. C. Wallmo Award for excellence in mule deer research. He is the editor of *Rangeland Wildlife* and a co-editor of *Ecology and Management of Large Mammals in North America, Mountain Sheep of North America,* and the *First International Wildlife Management Congress.* He was Editor-in-Chief of the *Journal of Wildlife Management* from 1988 to 1989, and currently serves as an associate editor for 6 wildlife science journals.